# Same Sex in the City
### (So Your Prince Charming Is Really a Cinderella)

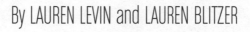

## By LAUREN LEVIN and LAUREN BLITZER

 SIMON SPOTLIGHT ENTERTAINMENT
New York London Toronto Sydney

To the friends and family who've stood by and supported me
—Lauren Levin

To all the girls I've loved before . . .
—Lauren Blitzer

Some names and identifying characteristics have been changed.

SISE

SIMON SPOTLIGHT ENTERTAINMENT
An imprint of Simon & Schuster
1230 Avenue of the Americas, New York, New York 10020
Text copyright © 2006 by Lauren Blitzer and Lauren Levin
All rights reserved, including the right of reproduction in whole or in part in any form.
SIMON SPOTLIGHT ENTERTAINMENT and related logo are trademarks of Simon
& Schuster, Inc.
Manufactured in the United States of America
First Edition 10  9  8  7  6  5  4  3  2  1
Library of Congress Control Number 2006004567
ISBN-13: 978-1-4169-1632-1

# contents

# lauren levin acknowledgements

Much love to my family for joining me on this thrilling roller coaster of a ride they call your early twenties. Sorry, the price of admission was so high. Through the ups and downs you oohed and ahhed, shared in my joys and triumphs, and held on tight through every bendy twist in direction. Thanks for your unconditional love, zest for life, contagious work ethic, and excessive phone calls. Drew my kid brother, my hero. Mom (and Alan) thanks for your strength, sacrifice, and calming chats. Dad, my best man (and Mimi) may we always share a love for the simple things in life (apple orchards, piles of leaves, etc.). The MN grandparents, for expanding my world— our walks around the lakes and Sunday Mall of America/dinner excursions are some of my best times. The FL Grandparents, for making a young-hearted old soul out of me . . . many hugs for the R & R from the freeze, golf-cart rides, literary leanings, and soup. Steve, Marie, Ivan, and Rebecca Burickson. Aunt Margee, Carol, Alan, Scott, Mark, Stacy Shapiro, Dani and Danny.

To the many friends who've kept me laughing, kept in touch, and give the best advice free of charge. Near and far, you've taught me how to find my way in the big city and grow to be a better person. My J's: Jessica Sheena, Jill Greenberg, and Jen Kaminsky, I don't know where I'd be without you three. Amanda Bartfeld, Jodi Rachlin, Liz Urqhardt, Ryan Langer, Rachel Brav, Ronni Gershowitz, Dayna Feurerstein, Linda H, Lara Crystal, Bret Gutstein, Jamie Beilen, and the rest of the 'Nell Crew. Mary Baier, Kelly Day, Jenna Christensen, Kari Hayden, Dan Beer, Jimmy Foster, and the rest of the Edina guys and girls, Sarah, Lyss, Nat, Reagan, Donny, Jules, Caren M, Jess G, Erika Waxman, and Mike Rothman . . . peace in the Lower East.

And finally, (whew), my smart and savvy mentors, thanks for that open-door/open-mind policy. Prof. Ritch-Savin Williams, Prof. Ellis Hanson, Prof. Sue Shapiro, Karen Robinovitz, and a few good women who took a chance on me.

# lauren blitzer acknowledgements

First off, I want to say thank you to my parents and my family, especially Auntie Lol, Auntie Debbie, and Aunt Jane. It wasn't an easy time, but knowing I had your unconditional love from the start made it that much easier. Thank you!

A few people have been by my side since I've met them. The first I had the pleasure of meeting during my very first few minutes of life: Julie, you are, have been, and always will be the sister, best friend, and person I trust most in this world. You've made my life easier and much more enjoyable, and I'm so grateful to have someone so beautiful in my life, forever.

A friend once said to me, at a desperate time, "Something huge is about to happen. I can just feel it." Well, Amy, or Fairy Gay Mother, as I like to call you, you were right and have been right about most everything for the past five years. Your unconditional, unselfish, and undying love for everything I love and hate about myself has helped me grow up to be the woman you knew I would be. I thank you and love you, A-train.

To the ladies of the house, thank you both for your ongoing support and many, many nights of lounging on the couch snuggled with three laptops and crappy television. Emily, you have been my best friend for seventeen years and I'm not sure what I would do without you, literally. Crystal, you are a rock to me, always have been. I appreciate it more than I express.

To Cookie L., thanks for the good times, the shoulder to cry on, the ferocious golf swing, and your availability at anytime. You always have my best interest in mind and I'm thankful to have someone so genuine in my life.

Lastly, Winkle, Sperry, Sperrywinkle, Poops, P-Ditty, LP, Loopie, all the names I call you because Lauren is just too common these days. I wasn't expecting to make a new best friend at twenty-three years old, but you had me at "love love." Although we are like night and day, you light up my life and face every time I see or think or hear about you. Thank you for just being you and loving me!

# the lauren's acknowledgements

So many people, so little room! Firstly, Marjorie Jaffe—none of this would be possible without you. Our powerhouse agent, Denise Marcil, you are a superstar! You kept us laughing and smiling, and your kicks under the table always kept us in line. We adore your smiling face and your silly hats! You just "got us" and our idea from the get-go, truly remarkable.

Next, our extraordinary editor, Tricia Boczkowski. You are a god-send, woman! Your funky accessories and old school bicycle brightened our days. Somehow you managed to capture our voice, indulge our fantasies, pump us up, and put your boyfriend to the side on our behalf. Those ridiculous food combinations helped us stay fueled. The next time we eat a veggie hot dog and an egg wrapped in a tortilla, we'll think of you!

Our wonder woman publisher, Jen Bergstrom. You can gab, gossip, and promote with the best of them. Your support and interest in our project was truly unique. They don't get much hipper than you.

Our publicists, Jen Robinson and Paul Crichton. All press is good press!

The Laurens would also like to thank: the outstanding women we interviewed, Jamie Beilen, Sandra Makani (styling credits), John Digarbo (photo credits), each other (big ups), and all the women who blazed this trail for us. Hugs and kisses galore to everyone else who stood behind us and helped us through this endeavor.

# preface

If there's a book you really want to read but it hasn't been written yet, then you must write it.

—Toni Morrison

Girlfriends, hear us out! As adolescents we roamed through bookstores, surreptitiously searching the shelves for a book to help guide us through a perplexing time. All we wanted was someone or something we could relate to, a book to make our questions and desires feel less foreign. Where, among these countless tomes, were all the books on same sex relationships hiding? We found plenty of erotica, written mostly by women in their forties, but none of these books gave us the road map we desperately needed—a guide to living life as out-and-proud femme lesbians.

So we decided to write our own kind of "chick lit." And in the process of writing this book—the one we wished we had when we were younger, the one we need in our dating lives now, the one we hope to turn to when we're older—we have witnessed the gay community become more and more recognized by mainstream media. Whether on television, in newspapers, in film, or even on the radio, being gay is no longer something we must hide or keep secret. In fact, it seems to be somewhat trendy these days. Who would have thought that an alternative lifestyle that was once so looked down upon is now becoming accepted and even *en vogue*.

We're not Dr. Phil. We don't claim to be relationship experts and we're certainly not here to tell you how to feel or what to do. But we have learned a lot about ourselves and the lesbian community in researching this book. We have taken a snapshot of a particular point in time through the oral histories we've collected from women of diverse backgrounds and perspectives. And although we each come at this book from different angles—Lauren L. came out less than a year ago and Lauren B. has been out for five years—the goal is to celebrate our shared experience. Hopefully, reading about our successes and vulnerabilities will help you navigate your own.

It's a great time to be gay, ladies! It is our hope that the words on the following pages offer you comfort, make you proud, give you guidance, turn you on, and help you find the happiness you deserve. The Beastie Boys had it right, "Girls, Girls, Girls! Come on . . ."

CHAPTER ONE:

# lesbian, the label

Labels are for filing. Labels are for
clothing. Labels are not for people.
—Martina Navratilova

You dress to the nines and enjoy an occasional manicure and pedicure. Wear flannels and tapered jeans everyday? No way. Sure, you find women hot . . . but doesn't everybody?

You don't look gay. You don't own any power tools. Guys check you out. Nobody would ever guess you've fantasized about your friends . . . or even fallen in love with them. Sure, you've had feelings for guys. Yet, you wonder what it would feel like to kiss a woman.

We've been there.

For years, we stood by our gold Prada stilettos, Citizen blue jeans, little black dresses, and pink Polo shirts . . . in the closet. We'll be the first to tell you, there's a hell of a lot more room in your closet once you come out of it. Being gay comes from within. It's not the stereotypical cropped haircut that makes someone gay. Just because we enjoy a weekly blowout and rocking little miniskirts doesn't mean we crave men. Our Prince Charming is, rather, a Cinderella.

In our pre-introspective teen years, we would have cringed if you told us we were gay. Us, gay? Hardly. Lesbians? No way, no how.

Something about that label made it sound like we'd contracted some horrible disease. Sure, at the tender age of fifteen, we fell in love with our camp counselors . . . but, what girl hasn't fallen for her camp counselor? Women flirt with women. Girls develop girl crushes. It's only natural.

Yet, as we grew older, these lezzie crushes were more intense, and more frequent. Neither of us ever had super-serious boyfriends, but we have had sex with men. We've slept with men and women for the same reasons: because of desire, because we wanted to try it. And don't get us wrong, we enjoyed sex with men. But not like we do with women. Take it from lesbian comedian Lea Delaria: "It's not that I don't like penises, I just don't like them on men!"

Society leads us to believe that all women fall into one of three boxes: straight, bisexual, or gay. Yet, no one talks about the fact that many of the girls who say they fall into the straight box have chowed box. Just look at Marissa's bi-curious experimentation on *The O.C.* Or turn on MTV and watch any season of *The Real World.* Girls who experiment with their sexuality are all over the place, it's natural and it's normal. Girls kissing girls is no longer taboo. It's hot.

Research has shown, time and again, that women's sexuality is remarkably fluid. And there is a gray area, where many women choose to live and love. You may not look as "dykey" as, say, Chastity Bono or k.d. lang, but that doesn't mean you love women any less than they do. Some of your friends may have never been with men, some have never fantasized about women, and plenty are probably right in between.

Nowadays, people are even coming out of the closet as "asexual." Oftentimes, they first associate as gay, or at least people think they are gay for their lack of getting any. Soon enough, however, asexuals throw their hands up and admit that they are happy alone and don't crave physical intimacy with either men *or* women.

Despite our general aversion to labels, when push comes to shove, labels can actually be a good thing. It's nice to be able to identify and socialize with others whose desires are similar to your own. If labels didn't exist, there would be no "gay pride." In the end, labels are just a matter of preference. Our friend Sloane prefers to be called "queer." She feels the word queer implies that there is some discrepancy in her desires. She's not straight, but she's not gay, either. She's just a little "off," and thus identifies as queer.

## Gaynglish

Entering a gay bar can make you feel as though you need a dictionary to weed through all the diverse labels. You'll hear terms like "boi," "lug," or "dink" tossed around carelessly. When we were both rookies on the lesbo scene, we had no idea what any of these words meant. So here's a quick primer:

A **boi** is a girl who looks like a boy. She may even look so much like a boy, you'd mistake this boi for an actual boyžžžžand that is exactly her intention.

**Lugs**, on the other hand, are a rare breed found mostly in small women's colleges in the Northeast. These girls are "Lesbians Until Graduation," who take advantage of the spirit of experimentation and self-discovery that four years of higher education affords.

**Dinks** are a breed of homosexuals who are "Dual Income, No Kids." Dinks can be men or women and are usually rather wealthy. With no kids to support, they have money to spend on things like real estate and, say, Marc Jacobs.

Whichever way you chose to live your life, be sure that your happiness is the first priority. The rest will just fall into place.

# lauren levin

● ● ● ● ● ● ● ● ● ● ● ● ● ● ● ● ● ● ● ● ● ● ● ● ● ● ● ● ● ● ● ● ● ● ● ● ● ● ● ● ● ● ● ●

For six years, I lived as a closeted bisexual. I believed I possessed the profound ability to fall in love with a person, regardless of gender. I fell for people's souls, not their bodies.

Yet, I never revealed my bisexuality to anyone. I thought being bisexual was cheesy. It was so "Girls Gone Wild." I didn't want to associate myself with drunken girls who take off their tops and make out with chicks in bars in Cancún. Not to say, I never participated in this kind of lewd behavior. And dammit, I enjoyed it. However, that was a once-in-a-spring-break experience. It was certainly never the norm.

You could've put me on layaway; I was bi now, gay later. When I finally realized I preferred women over men, I came out of the closet (which was already more cramped and stifling than my tiny East Village studio apartment). It took a while, but, thank God, I finally did. The process of coming out is a confusing period in anyone's life. I feared people's reactions, particularly the responses of those who might try to tell me that girls were just a phase. But, in actuality, few people told me this. Yet those who did sounded so incredibly condescending. The way they carelessly brushed aside the biggest decision I'd ever made in my life felt belittling. In fact, their assumptions made me doubt my sexuality as well. Was I ready to label myself a lesbian? Was I truly gay?

As silly as it sounds, this fueled me to act out the insecurities of my loved ones. I became "Super Gay Woman," Superwoman's sapphic-twin nemesis. The first few months after I came out, I felt as though I had something to prove. You say I'm not a lesbian, well, I'll show you who's gay. I morphed into a ragingly hormonal, rabid gay superhero.

In retrospect, my behavior was more of a performance piece. It was hard to go five minutes without mentioning I was gay. The more people told me, "You're not a lesbian," the gayer I became. My libido was on par with an acne-prone teenage boy's. Every straight girl I met was a "conversion" waiting to happen. Every gay girl I met, I believed, wanted a piece of fresh gay meat. My friends noticed the immense changes going on inside of me but seemed to bite their tongues.

Months after my debut as Super Gay Woman, the excitement of coming out began to wear off. Sure, it was great to reveal something I'd kept hidden for the better part of my adult life. However, the reality of being gay began to set in. I started to lose my gay pride and to embrace a kind of gay burnout instead.

Thankfully, it didn't take long for me to find a happy medium. Sure, it's still an ongoing battle inside of me. Yet, for the first time in my life, I don't feel I have something to prove. Branding oneself as anything is hard to do, especially if it's not mainstream. Change is a part of human nature. And a year after coming out, my pride in who I am gets stronger by the day. Having the confidence to label myself built character, but having the courage not to let that label restrict me took wisdom and insight. Loved ones may think you've chosen a harder life by being gay. But, really, associating with a label can make your life more fulfilling if you don't take it too seriously; remember, a label is just a label, nothing more.

It took years for me to imagine committing myself to a label. Everyone assumed I was straight, and I hid behind a facade of hetero normalcy. Growing up, we're surrounded by images of girls and boys holding hands with each other. Even nursery rhymes are straight. It's always "Jack and Jill." But, what if Jill's more into Jackie? Could they still get up the hill? It's a hurdle I had to overcome.

Oddly enough, what always makes me feel better about being gay is hanging out with my straight friends. They consider me cool and unique and are genuinely interested in talking about my life and what it's like to date women. They are fascinated by the whole thing, and it makes me feel as though I've got the key to some secret store of knowledge. So I may not look like their idea of a lesbian, but in the eyes of my straight friends, I've got a whole other world of experience under my belt.

I am who I am. Take me or leave me. Love me or hate me. 'Cause I am learning to love myself, and my relationship with myself is the most rewarding relationship in which I'll ever be involved.

# lauren blitzer

I am a proud femme lesbian and a JAP-WASP mixed breed. Like most girls, I dress in a way that makes me feel comfortable and attractive. In my case, I just so happen to dress like a lot of the straight girls I work with.

Shopping has always been one of my favorite hobbies. When I receive my paycheck, I have to try hard not spend it all on shoes. I fit in with the rest of the young NYC man-hungry women on the prowl, except that while those women search for a rich Jewish husband, I search for a nice Jewish wife.

At first glance, I am not what I appear to be. The discrepancy became more apparent than ever my first day on the job at a fashionable women's magazine. The moment I set foot in the Condé Nast cafeteria, I heard the shuffle of Manolo Blahniks and Jimmy Choos. As foreign as the cafeteria was, at least I was familiar with the clickety-clack of expensive heels. Come on, now, I grew up on the Upper East Side of Manhattan. I know my shoes.

I felt nervous in the enormous cafeteria. In fact, nervous is an understatement. I was petrified. I looked like all of the women I had seen walking in and out of the Condé Nast building, but there was something different about me. I felt intimidated, scared, and painfully gay.

The buzz of "Omigod" and "You look sooo cute" filled the perfume-laced air. Blondes of all shades and brunettes alike swarmed the fresh fruit display, home to healthy low-fat yogurt and granola. My eyes widened and wandered as I got lost in this sea of Theory pants and YSL shirts. Each woman, more beautiful than the next, walked by me. They shot dirty looks at other women who either weren't dressed to par or looked better than them. The cafeteria literally reeked of criticism, jealousy, and the latest designer fragrances.

I walked through the cafeteria in a daze, as eye candy raced by me. Damn, these women were beautiful. But, as gorgeous as these fashionistas were, not one really appealed to me. What was lacking in most cases was depth. I don't like petty women. As my thoughts turned romantic, I alerted myself that, hello, these women are all straight! There were the obvious straight girls who sported gigantic engagement rings, and then there were the girls I assumed were straight because of how they dressed. These girls literally woke up at four a.m. just to straighten their hair more perfectly than Frederic Fekkai could do himself.

However, as I stared at a particular blond bombshell, I realized I was making the same assumptions that I don't like people to make about me. Maybe not every woman who works for Condé Nast is straight. I sure as hell am not, even though I look it.

The majority of the women at work never even thought to question my sexuality. Boys like me, so therefore I like boys.

They figure everyone is straight unless they don't look straight. Thankfully, I can offer these people some enlightenment. I hope women can look at me and see that it's okay to like women and be in touch with your sexuality. It's okay to take care of yourself and want to look fabulous. Sexuality dictates whom you love, not how you look.

## susie

. . . . . . . . . . . . . . . . . . . . . . . . . . . . . . . . . . . . . . . . . . . . . .

When I went to college, I was straight. Well, as straight as any eighteen-year-old, open-minded, sexually charged female could be. I attended the University of Vermont, and my freshman year was miserable. I smoked too much pot and involved myself with way too many lame eighteen-year-old boys who didn't appreciate who I was. They wanted more than I was willing to give and, in general, were one big snooze fest. Before my first spring break, I began looking for a new place to call my own.

Growing up, I'd kissed girls. Mostly for the pleasure of sixteen-year-old boys, who got hard at the mere sight of two legs and a skirt. I was the go-to girl for girls who'd never kissed girls. There was a night in my parents' basement when three cliques of girls were hanging out. A couple of the girls had never kissed another girl before. I was nominated to initiate them in to the girl-kissing world, and I was fine with that. I loved kissing, for God's sake! And other than passing thoughts, I'd only had one sex dream, about a girl I hardly spoke to in high school. But, it was a really hot dream. To this day, thinking about it makes me blush. I had no inkling that I'd ever date or fall in love with a woman. I dated baseball and football players!

Anyway, I left Vermont for a small women's college in northern California. This school was the answer to my prayers. Mills was a liberal haven, with a small campus and no boys to annoy me, for at least another three years. I was free! I started playing basketball almost right away. I played on a team with seven other women for one season. We didn't score a lot of baskets, but we had a good time, and it was a great way for me to meet people. Interestingly enough, the basketball season included a few different couplings. First, the forward was dating the point guard. They'd been dating since high school and came to Mills together. They broke up, and the forward found solace with the shooting guard. Six years later, the forward and the shooting guard are still girlfriends, living together in Portland, Oregon. Fittingly, I was a swing player.

About three weeks into the season there was a dance, the Fetish Ball. A woman named Flynn invited me to go with her.

She came up to me in a tea shop, sat down, and said, "Do you want to go to the Fetish Ball with me?"

I looked perplexed. "What about your girlfriend?"

"She's out of town," Flynn said

I assured Flynn I was flattered, but straight. I was also completely put off by Flynn's response about her girlfriend being out of town. "What a bitch," I thought. "Her girlfriend goes out of town and she's out here hitting on the first straight girl she sees."

We were in classes together; we talked. It turned out Flynn was cool. She was fun, smart, and, for a butch dyke, quite attractive. I learned that she and her girlfriend were in a "polyamorous" relationship, a relationship where they were each other's primary partners but still dated and slept with other people. This was the first time I'd heard of this as a formal "type" of relationship. It allowed me to see Flynn as less of an asshole, and just as a lesbian who was attracted to me. Flynn started taking stats for the basketball team. She hung around me quite a bit. One day, about two months into her role as statistician, we got pizza after a game. Everyone left the restaurant, but Flynn and I were just getting into the politics of the impending war in Afghanistan, so we stuck around. She made me smile. I soon became aware of why she was really doing stats for our crappy basketball team.

From that conversation, we decided to organize students to resist the war and Bush. We worked together, organizing for six months. One night, the co-op I lived in threw a party. Midway through the night, I saw Flynn leaving. I ran after her, and from about twenty feet away called out, "Be sure to come back!" I had fallen for her. I didn't even know I could fall for a woman.

Flynn came back to the party, and we ended up talking about what it would mean for me to date her. Then we kissed, and the chemistry was almost unbearably overwhelming. It went on like that. We dated, had some of the most incredible sex of my life, and had an incredible amount of fun. We dealt with her polyamorous relationship, which ended about six months into our being together, due to the fact that she and I spent "too much" time together. That was probably true.

I was deeply attracted to Flynn's intense masculinity. She made me feel like a woman. I started wearing skirts, heels, and jewelry. Her masculinity complemented my femininity in a very pronounced way. I'd never been that girly before, and haven't been since. When I played basketball, I wore bows in my hair because I knew it turned her on. Turning Flynn on turned me on to no end. I'd give anything, today, for the chemistry she and I had back then.

The whole time, I knew I wasn't gay. I didn't know what I was, but I knew that I wasn't strictly attracted to women. Partially, because Flynn wasn't exactly a woman. She had one of the most intense male energies I'd ever been around. She was a perfect balance of masculine and feminine traits. Flynn was protective, thoughtful, loving, caring, strong, stable, and sensitive. She was also intent on pleasing me, with just the right amount of machismo. She was, and remains, in a word, *hot*.

A couple weeks into dating me, Flynn recommended a few books for me to read, since I wasn't fitting in to the standard "bi" definition. I wanted to know what the hell was up with me. She lent me *Stone Butch Blues* and *The Ethical Slut*. But the one I read and identified with most was *Pomosexuals*, edited by Carol Queen and Lawrence Schimel. These people spoke my language.

*Pomosexuals* contained stories of people and couples who were simply not defined, or who defined themselves outside the "normal" structure of sexuality we've carried on and developed through time. I didn't fit into the structure I'd been bequeathed: lesbian, bisexual, straight, gay man trapped in a femme's body. None of it described me. I am a postmodern sexual: I am sexual with the people I choose to be with for reasons independent of who I "should" be doing; and, perhaps most of all, my sexuality is not a defining characteristic of who I intrinsically am.

I'm not a lesbian. I'm not straight. I'm not bi. I'm just me; I'm a lover. Pomosexuality defines the undefined, I suppose. It's not that I don't have a type; it's just that there's not a word for someone who likes masculine people, regardless of their sex. And I don't want a label. As a favorite quote of mine states, "There is only one church, and membership is your bellybutton." We are all sexual beings; we all belong here; we are all fine and good just the way we are.

# liza

## I Got Hammered and Made Out with My Friend for $30 in Front of 12 Guys. . . . Am I a Lesbian?

Maybe I had been watching too much *Real World*. Maybe I was bored. Perhaps I wasn't living up to the hot sorority girl image I had worked so hard to achieve. Or maybe it was the six shots of Absolut Kurant and twelve guys chanting my name in a dingy second-floor apartment above Johnny's Big Red Bar & Grille that made me do it. I don't know. I don't remember. I'm lying; I do remember—thanks to the Internet photos that surfaced a few days later.

We were hanging out at Steve and JP's apartment. Being that it was winter in Ithaca, New York, we had been drinking heavily for a few months. I had reached a fashion crossroads where the only clothes that still fit me were drawstring sweatpants and hoop earrings. There was a stack of sparkly tube tops in the closet that, sadly, never saw the strobe light of the bar again. I was going out every night, vomiting alone in alleys, and waking up on stained beanbag chairs.

There were ten other guys who lived in that apartment, so most of them were hanging out, along with a few random dudes, my friend Camilla, and the girl on the couch the guys fondly called "Crack Whore." Some of the guys were tossing around options for the rest of the night; somewhere between "go to another bar" and "stay here and play quarters," someone at the table slurred, "Watch Liza and Camilla make out!"

Oh, God, I am not that kind of girl. I laughed. Camilla laughed. We weren't even paying attention. I was talking about something else as doe-eyed young men excitedly slid shots down the table. One guy was running to the fridge to get another bottle of Absolut. There was an electric buzz in the room, and dudes who hadn't even been sitting at the table emerged from doorways with concealed cameras.

The intensity was building. I was starting to feel weird. These guys knew me. They hung out with me in my sweat-pants and hoop earrings all the time. They usually didn't even try to make out with me, unless they were blackout drunk. But here they were, hovering, like middle-aged women spotting the sale rack at an Ann Taylor outlet. Even Crack Whore had gotten off the couch and was sidling over. Someone must have sensed my apprehension and mistaken it for coquettish curios-ity. Likely, it was the same individual who instigated the "Make Out! Make Out!" chants.

Amidst a frat-tastic sea of rowdy Internet-porn subscribers, Camilla and I locked eyes. We laughed. We were good friends; would it really be that big a deal? Of course not; if nothing else, it would be a fabulous story the next morning. She was probably thinking how her boyfriend (who was loudly chant-ing next to her) would think it was hot. I was picturing my next game of "I never," and how I would feel like less of a loser if I could drink to "I've never made out with a girl" along with the rest of my girlfriends. I was supposed to be doing crazy things that I could never do again. I mean, come on; doesn't every-one have a lesbian story from college?

My thoughts of college experimentation were quickly interrupted, as someone had started a betting pool. Crinkled bills littered the beer-stained tabletop. Now, in addition to becoming a momentary lesbian, I was about to become a whore. A whore! Someone who accepts money for sexual favors! I was out; no way. This was something I could never be okay with, no matter how drunk I was. I looked again.

There was a sizable amount of cash on the table.

By this point, Camilla and I were looking anywhere but at each other. We were also staggering quite a bit. "Oh, fuck it," she said. "I'll do it." She laughed, took a shot, and looked at me. I couldn't back down. I looked at the cash again. No way was I taking it, even if we did make out. The guys were all screaming now, straining to get a better look. God, I wished I didn't like attention so much; this was really embarrassing.

I inched toward Camilla; if we were going to do this, I would at least try to make it look hot. We touched each other awkwardly, and the boys jeered even louder. I closed my eyes and wondered if I would like it. Our lips touched and the counting began: "one Mississippi, two Mississippi . . ."

Our tongues were touching; it was a real kiss. Would things be awkward in the morning? Would she call me? Would we IM? Would we tell anyone about this? Would we joke about it at our sorority chapter meeting? And Camilla's pretty hot—does that mean I'm the butch one? Oh, my God, I'm wearing sweatpants. . . . Of course, I'm the butch one!

We started to touch—not quite second base, but we definitely got into it. A camera flashed. I pulled away. We had made it to "ten Mississippi," and I felt like I was going to pass out. We looked at each other, at the money on the table, at the guys screaming, at the empty shot glasses, and I felt so college. I spanked Camilla's ass. It was cool.

We ran into Steve's room and plotted how to best conceal the sordid events of the past four minutes.

"I can't believe we did that!" she said.

"Was I good?" I asked.

"Yeah, you were," Camilla assured me.

Surprisingly, that meant a lot to me. She was a notorious bitch, and I knew she wouldn't lie. I wanted it in writing: *Although Liza is only moderately sexually active, has zero rela-*

*tionship experience and no cool stories about doing it in crazy places, she is, in fact, a very good kisser. She also makes out with chicks.* Well, I didn't get it in writing. But I did get a naughty picture on the Internet, and the satisfaction of knowing I was "sexually experimental."

## one more thing...

Whether you are queer, straight, bi, questioning, or have the libido of a leaf, remember that you don't have to label yourself to appreciate the tales of women who do. And, by all means, you don't have to justify yourself or your desires to anyone. Just be you.

# path to self-realization

2

For a long time I thought I wanted to be a nun. Then I realized that what I really wanted to be was a lesbian.
—Mabel Maney

The road to realizing and, consequently, accepting one's sexual identity is a difficult one. Thankfully, as society begins to get a clue, the road is becoming less bumpy. More and more, teenagers view sexual attraction as fluid and not limited to an opposite-sex partner. Teens are getting sexually flexible messages from the media, as well as from their parents. These "sex flex" messages basically state: Same-sex sexuality is not such a big deal. Children who become aware of their homosexual attractions no longer need to endure the painful combination of loneliness and longing that characterized the childhoods of so many gay adults. On television, they can watch fictional and real teens who are out, on shows like *Desperate Housewives*, *Next* on MTV, and, our personal favorite, *Degrassi Junior High*.

For those of you who may be struggling with your self-realization as a lesbian, we have compiled some simple tips to help you reconcile your feelings.

## Free your mind and the gay will follow

Try not to be afraid of your desires. The earlier you figure out your sexuality, the better. If you can come to terms with who you are and be comfortable in your own skin at a young age, you'll be better off, and you'll have more time to stress about a career and money. According to more than a dozen studies reviewed by Ritch Savin-Williams, author of *The New Gay Teenager*, the average age for self-realization has dropped to twelve for lesbians. 1

## Don't isolate, communicate

Bisexual, gay, queer, or whichever label you choose or choose not to take, we want you to talk about it. We want to hear your story. It's nice to feel comfortable confiding in your friends about questioning your sexuality. However, if you're not comfortable doing so, you can turn to someone more detached from you—an anonymous online pal, or a psychologist. The crucial thing to note is that your road to self real ization is an important one, and it's your own.

## Hello, I'll be your tour guide: the older, wiser lesbian

For any woman who is questioning her sexuality, finding a mentor is a really good way to help advance her personal development. You may want to find your own older, more experienced lesbian to confide in and learn the ropes from until you graduate and become one yourself! More often than not, they have the answers you are looking for, which is a relief during a time of introspection. In other words, YOU ARE NOT ALONE.

## SIEA (Struggle, Identity, Empathy, and Awareness)

People who thoughtfully question themselves have a tendency to be more enlightened than those who never had to think twice about who they are. You might struggle with how to integrate your homo-sexual identity into the larger world. Most gay people grow up feeling "different," and that affliction helps them empathize with individuals. This automatically raises your level of consciousness and, in most cases, increases your sensitivity to others.

## Pride, not prejudice

Reaching the point of self-realization is great. Self-acceptance is even better, and having "gay pride" is wonderful. Pride is meaningful. Being proud of who you are, and not what you are, is an essential element to being happy with your identity. But not everyone is able to do this right away. Gay pride serves a function, especially for young teens or people just coming out of the closet. It's a necessity of any oppressed minority. Consider Black pride, girl power, or even the Puerto Rican Day Parade. They all take something that is traditionally denigrated and turn it into something powerful. If being gay is something to be proud of, versus something to be ashamed of, self-acceptance comes naturally.

$$1(\text{piece of the } \pi) + 2\,(\text{gay}) = \text{you}$$

Being gay doesn't define you as a person. It's merely a part of the sum total. "Straight kids don't define themselves by sexuality, even though sexuality is a huge part of who they are," says Savin-Williams of gay teenagers. "Of course, they want to have sex, but they don't say, 'It is what I am.'" He believes young 'mos are moving toward a "postgay" identity. Being gay doesn't mean you have to march in a parade. Part of it is political and part is personal, developmental. You have to accept one part of yourself, the gay part, before you can become a whole person.

Like Dorothy on her journey to Oz, we all have our own yellow brick road to follow to realize our sexuality. Some might experience obstacles and setbacks, but ultimately, if you have a heart, a brain, and courage, you'll find your way.

# lauren levin

· · · · · · · · · · · · · · · · · · · · · · · · · · · · · · · · · · · · · · ·

Some people look at porn to figure out their sexuality, but, at seventeen, I looked at poetry. I stumbled across a website that made me acknowledge my aching for the female touch. The site was hosted by Bryce, a college girl who wrote sarcastic movie reviews and exquisite journal entries. Her picture was on the site as well. And damn, Bryce was hot!

By reading her journal, I could tell Bryce was in aching pain over someone named "T." She spoke so passionately about her pain, about being childish and in love, about the battle of maintaining a platonic friendship with someone she loved so deeply. Bryce piqued my curiosity. Was she talking about (gasp) a GIRL?

Hastily, I e-mailed her to find out. Bryce wrote me back and explained that she believed "sexual preferences" were stupid. She didn't confine herself or anything like that. But, basically, she had been in love with a woman before. She just didn't choose to label herself as being lesbian or bisexual.

Whoa, this chick was cool! I totally agreed with what she'd said. I didn't know any feminine girl who had made out with another girl, let alone fallen in love with one. From then on, Bryce and I were tight. Well, as tight as you can be with someone over the Internet. We engaged in constant e-mail banter for nearly six years. Whenever I fell head over heels in love, Bryce was there for me talk to. All through college, Bryce helped me stay sane. She never once jumped to conclusions; she never once told me I was gay. She was just there for me; there was nobody else. She had open ears and an open mind. She taught me 'most everything I know to be true. Still, I don't even know her last name.

We've never met. To this day, I've never met Bryce. The

intrigue and curiosity we felt about each other was mutual, and of course, I desperately want to meet one of the most influential people in my life. I used to dream about just kissing her all the time, but we lived far apart and Bryce usually had a girlfriend. Regardless, she remains one of the most positive influences in my life.

Though I had Bryce to confide in, I didn't take much action about my sexuality. I watched the braver ones. I remember every cutesy lesbian couple I ever saw. There was that hippie couple in Ithaca rolling around in the grass, the two gorgeous women I saw kissing and holding hands one Sunday afternoon on the Lower East Side, and countless others. I wanted a girlfriend before I even knew I was gay.

Soon, there were more and more "hers," less and less "hims." I kept telling myself that next time I'd fall for a him. Knowing in my heart I was different than the rest of the population was hard. Yet, I didn't realize I was gay . . . just different. I lived in an incredible amount of pain. However, I didn't even realize I was in pain. I believed I was loving life, living like a rock star.

And yet, I saw no future for myself. I looked at other people's lives and they weren't like mine. I didn't want what my friends wanted. I didn't know what I wanted. All I knew was what I didn't want. And for a girl who has always known exactly what she wanted, and never stopped until she got it, not being able to map out a future for myself was the single hardest thing I've ever had to face.

I never disclosed to anyone this anxiety about my future. I went with the flow, and, like my friends, I scanned the city for Mr. Right. On my way to discovering it was, in fact, Miss Right I was searching for, I did a lot of partying. I blew cocaine. I was bursting with self-loathing. I morphed into my own worst enemy and was truly killing myself. I knew what I was doing, but I didn't care.

I wish I'd known I wasn't a freak, just a lesbian. Knowing I was gay would've been easier to accept. But, I never wanted to admit what, to some degree, I'd always known. I wanted to mask those dubious feelings with drugs. There were so many nights I blacked out. I couldn't even begin to count them all.

I hope you don't ever have to wish away the things I did. I hope you can come to accept yourself for who you are.

I almost lost everyone I cared about . . . my friends, my family. There were mornings I woke up shocked that I was still alive. Getting out of bed wasn't remotely an option. Every time this happened, I swore to my friends and to myself that it wouldn't happen again. I would change. I never wanted to feel this awful again.

No doubt about it, I was incredibly depressed. Hating my job, hating New York, and hating myself were all taking a toll on me. To top it off, I was dating women on the side, but telling no one. The medication the doctors prescribed didn't help. Every morning I dreaded taking the Wellbutrin. Popping those mood-enhancing pills was a constant reminder of my depression. Taking the drugs told me something wasn't right with me. Funny, I never felt the same way anytime someone put a key of coke in front of my nose. I didn't see my drug use as a sign of pain in my life.

After months of therapy and a successful new job at Google, I again became the person I always was. Still, I didn't know what was wrong with me. Why on earth did I not see any future for myself? Here I was, a cute, Ivy League–educated, relatively wealthy, popular girl who saw nothing but dimness in her future. I'd even scored a new boyfriend, a Jewish doctor. My grandmother in Boca's wet dream! What was wrong with me? What did everyone else see that I did not?

The clincher to my self-realization all began on a boring Wednesday night watching *Entertainment Tonight*. On the screen was a gorgeous photographer, Anna. Instantly, Anna caught my attention. This girl had an edge, and I liked it—a lot.

The next day at work, I Googled Anna. I found her website and on a whim decided to e-mail her. It was a quickie. I told her she'd like my style and that I had a crush on her. To my surprise, I received a response from Anna in my in-box fifteen minutes later, and we exchanged witty e-mails for a good half hour. When I received an e-mail from Anna asking what time I got off work, my jaw dropped; and when I received her next e-mail, asking me to join her at her house in the Poconos for the night, my jaw hit the ground.

I was floored. This woman had never even met me. I could be an Amish midget with a severe case of Tourette's syndrome for all she knew. I ducked out of work early and literally ran home.

An hour later, Anna pulled up in front of my apartment. When she stepped out of the car, I almost turned around and walked away. Anna was, no question about it, the hottest girl I'd ever laid eyes on. We began to talk, and we didn't stop for at least the next fifteen hours.

Anna was thirty-seven years old, and indeed gay, but head over heels in love with her girlfriend. They had just bought their place in the Poconos together and were thinking of adopting a baby. Of course, she didn't tell her girlfriend she was taking me there, but, much to my dismay, she explained that tonight was to be completely platonic. She told me she was always busy, and the whole celebrity thing made it hard for her to make friends. Friends or lovers, it didn't matter. When I was with Anna, being gay felt like being left-handed: no big deal. It was normal and totally acceptable.

I was infatuated with this woman. When we got to her house we cracked open a bottle of wine and chatted away. I saw a picture of her fifty-five-year-old girlfriend and was less than impressed. But they were practically married. Anna made it clear that, although she was attracted to me, she could never live with herself if she cheated on Deirdre. I told her I'd never been with a woman before; couldn't she be my first? She said it would happen for me one day but that it couldn't be with her. Disappointed, I sauntered up to the guest room.

The next day, Anna and I took her dog up the mountains. It was undoubtedly one of the happiest days of my life. It was the day I found the missing puzzle piece. I found my future. Happiness was indeed possible. I wanted what Anna and Deirdre had. I wanted to spend the rest of my life with the woman of my dreams. I wanted to have children with my best friend, my lover. Never before did I know a normal life was possible as a gay woman. I realized that everything I didn't think I wanted, I actually longed for. The only difference was that I wanted to share this life with a woman, and not a man.

On the ride home, I swore I'd find my own Anna. Even if I had to go out alone, I would hit up the gay bars. Anna encouraged me to do so, and gave me some pointers on sending out open vibes to women.

The next morning, I began to cry hysterically. I was gay. I was gay and I knew it. But being gay didn't feel natural anymore, like it had the day before. It felt cold and lonely. What on earth was I going to do?

I called my friend from high school, Heidi. Heidi had recently come out of the closet and was very much in love with her girlfriend. The minute she picked up the phone, I blurted through my tears, "I'm gay, Heidi. I'm gay." I'll never forget the moment I finally admitted to myself what I'd known all along: I was gay.

Dealing with being gay didn't make the other problems in my life disappear. I continued to use cocaine; I didn't know how to behave any other way. Finally, I admitted to my younger brother that I was using drugs. Drew hopped on a plane to New York a couple days later. He arrived at my apartment and began to cry. Watching Drew cry was incredibly painful. I love my little brother more than anything in the world. He used to look up to me, but on that day Drew told me he didn't know me anymore. He said he didn't want to speak to me again unless I changed. So I did. I changed. I began outpatient therapy and stopped using coke.

Waking up with a clear head is amazing. I used to live in such a blurry world. When I go out at night, I come home when it's still dark out. That, in and of itself, was a step in the right direction. I'm not one to take advice from Paris Hilton, but she's right: "There's no one worth meeting past two a.m."

From the time I realized I liked women at age seventeen up until the moment that I admitted to myself that I *prefer* women wasn't an easy road. It took years to love being gay! I find women so much more dynamic, challenging, and exciting. . . . I just wouldn't have it any other way.

# lauren blitzer

Seeing two beautiful, deceivingly straight-looking women holding hands on the street turns about as many heads as a ghetto thug drinking a *venti* Strawberries & Crème Frappucino with whip. Bling or no bling, the sight causes an uproar amongst women and men alike. To be asked by random men on the street if you and your girlfriend are into threesomes more than five times a day starts to get a little repetitive, and more irritating than the stink of chicken kebob on every third street corner. But, hey, it's New York City. I would expect nothing less.

Life was simple growing up. I had no worries, no real hardships. I led a privileged life and was grateful for it. But for the first time in my somewhat sheltered life, nothing could protect me from the confusing emotions I was about to go through, nor lighten the anxiety I was feeling.

It all came to a head, more or less, when I was sixteen. Sixteen was Diesel jeans, Petite Bateau, and a casual meal that consisted of grabbing a bite at a nice restaurant on a credit card I never saw the bill for. My exclusive private school was directly across from Central Park, on the Upper West Side of Manhattan. Like every other girl there, I was dropped off each morning by my father in his nice car. We all knew how to have fun and went as far as our fake IDs would carry us.

Strangely enough, my fake ID opened the door to discovering my own sexuality. The bar was called Venue, which is now Mod, and it was something else prior to that. That's the beauty of life in this city—everything is ever-changing. I returned weekend after weekend with a sorry excuse for a fake ID, the kind made from a MetroCard and the print-out of a scanned New York driver's license. Every time I handed it over to the bouncer, I nearly wet myself for fear of getting caught and the humiliation that always followed. But it worked, night after night.

Like clockwork, each and every time I walked into the bar I would get a feeling in the pit of my stomach. I wasn't sure if it was excitement or a twenty-four-hour stomach virus. My heart would beat faster and faster with each step I took into the dark, maroon-covered room. I became so painfully aware of my environment, my presence, and my insecurities. With every step, I felt more naked and exposed than I ever had in my life.

Looking back, there was only one reason for my anxiety. Her name was Rachel. Rachel was a bartender, and she made everything I thought I knew a mystery. She confirmed that everything I didn't want to be true was just that: true. Why didn't I have a boyfriend? Why didn't I care? What was wrong with me?

For months I would just stare at her—secretly, of course, making sure that none of my friends suspected anything, and that she didn't catch me looking. All the while, only wanting her to look straight into my eyes and help me make sense of it all.

I had no idea why I felt like my heart was coming out of my mouth every time I caught a glimpse of her. Her dark hair and dark eyes reeked of mystery and sex. Her tight body and perfect smile made my heart melt. Just the way she picked up the bottles of alcohol with her strong hands made my mouth dry and my knees collapse.

I imagined her being close to me and wondered how it would feel. What if I was that bottle of Ketel One she so carefully pulled out from the rest? Would she handle me that gently, with her obvious experience? My imagination ran rampant.

At the time, I had no idea why I was so drawn to this woman. Looking back, nothing could be more obvious. Yet, back then, I was numb to my own emotions. I was so wrapped up in how exhilarating this woman made me feel that I couldn't see anything else. It took months for me to put myself in a position that would require her to talk to me. I got up the courage to actually grab her arm one night and ask her for a drink.

I didn't really drink at the time, but I felt it was the only way for us to have any kind of interaction. She responded to me immediately. Not just by getting me what I ordered, but by meeting my eyes with equal curiosity. Rachel saw something in me that I wouldn't see with full clarity for at least another three years. Her almost intrusive eyes penetrated my heart and soul faster than the rum-and-Coke I ordered could hit my lips. The way she just got me was so incredibly scary. After that night, my face was as stained in her mind as hers was in mine. She knew my name and I knew hers. This fantasy I had created in my head was becoming a reality, and it shook me to the core.

After our first interaction, I thought about her day and night. Monday would roll around, and I would spend the rest of the week obsessing over going back to Venue the next weekend. I would always suggest it as our bar of choice, but when I caught myself seeming desperate about going there, I would champion some other bar instead to throw my friends off the scent. I didn't want them to assume anything. I knew I was being strangely defensive and protective about my relationship with this venue, Venue.

Each little interaction with Rachel was better than the next. I would be at the bar until three in the morning, sometimes even after my friends left. Rachel was my drug of choice. Being around her was the best high I've ever felt. When the week came along, filled with fake high school boyfriends and classes, I began to crave her like a wanton crackhead.

Alone and struggling with my feelings, I became less and less aware of what was going on. I became more defensive about my relationship with her. My friends would tease me because they knew something I didn't know . . . that she was GAY . . . a LESBIAN.

Every day at school I felt like I was wearing a huge rainbow *L* on my chest, like a flamingly gay Hester Prynne. I wanted it gone. I didn't want to feel this way, ashamed and embarrassed. Suppressing my desires was painful and unsatisfying, too. I would use my alone time at home to think about Rachel. I would sit for hours on end staring into space and creating fantasies about her in my head. It was scary as hell because it felt so right, so exciting.

But it was wrong. I didn't want to be gay. It just couldn't be. I convinced myself that every other girl was going through this in some capacity and just didn't share it with one another. There had to be other girls out there having strange crushes on woman they barely knew. Maybe they thought about a particular female teacher too much, or just a pretty face that walked by. Maybe it was a friend's mother, or the woman who works at the trendy jean shop on Lexington. I couldn't be alone.

One fateful Saturday night, we all went to Venue and ended up staying very late. We started drinking with the staff, and as Rachel got drunk, we took two seats in a somewhat secluded corner. Rachel leaned over the table and grabbed the small candle, our only source of light. I sat uncomfortably in my chair, trembling inside and out. She was talking to me in a low, sexy voice, and to this day I have no idea what she was saying. All I could hear were the tones of her voice in my head as I watched her dip her fingers into the hot wax and reach out to rub it on the inside of my forearm. It hurt and felt amazing all at once. She watched my reaction as I bit my lip to try and hide how excited I really was. I wanted to grab Rachel's face in my hands and kiss her harder and more passionately than I ever thought possible. Yet, I just sat and let her pour the wax on my arm. Every part of me ached for Rachel, for more of her.

We sat very close to each other, and that's when she told me she thought I was gay. Immediately, I got defensive. It was because I knew she was right. Yet, at sixteen, or at any age for that matter, you don't want anyone to tell you who you are. You want to figure it out on your own, however long it takes you. I knew I would eventually get there, but I wasn't ready to hear it. Nor was I ready to face the truth.

We talked for a while about my confusion. I was open and honest. Rachel was very attentive. She moved closer to my face and almost cornered me. She knew it wasn't right, but I know she wanted to kiss me more than ever. My mouth was dry. My palms were sweaty. I wanted nothing more, though I knew if she were to kiss me my world would be turned upside down.

I wasn't ready to know myself at sixteen. To feel and think that nothing could be more amazing than this woman's lips against mine. I left that night obsessing about whether or not I had made a mistake. I wondered if I should turn the cab around and feel what I was so scared to feel. But I never did.

That night with Bartender Rachel changed my life. It was the bridge between coming to terms with the idea of being gay and actually coming to the realization that I am a lesbian. It took many years after that part of my life for me to accept myself.

# sarabeth

●●●●●●●●●●●●●●●●●●●●●●●●●●●●●●●●●●●●●●●●●●●●●●●●

When I was in the sixth grade, my teacher called my parents into school for a parent-teacher conference. She was concerned, she said, not about my stellar academic performance, my well-adjusted behavior, or even my plethora of friends. What worried her was quite straightforward: If my parents didn't do something soon, I might turn out as, well, "a lesbian."

Sorry, Ms. Stein, but it was already too late. I think I first knew I was gay when I was nine years old. I say "I think," because I didn't really know what a lesbian was. I'd never met one, and we never learned about lesbians in school. The only real education I'd had was from what I'd heard on the playground. Basically, my classmates broke it down for me like this: Lesbians were girls who liked girls, and lesbians were something no one should ever become.

Every lesbian goes through their own personal denial before they accept and, hopefully, embrace who they are. Most people I know struggled with this during high school or college. But, for me, it was right around puberty. Or perhaps I should say, just before puberty (I was still completely flat-chested, scrawny, and without any hair "down there").

In sixth grade, a few months before the infamous parent-teacher conference, a new girl entered our class. In elementary school, it's always tough to be the new girl. You are immediately checked out by every student, as they look for signs of weakness.

But all I could see were breasts. These were the first breasts I had seen on a person my age in my entire life. No one in my class had boobs yet, which immediately made her very popular with the boys. I'd hear them talking about her, about "them," in the halls, after school, on the playground. I didn't understand what those expressions meant, but I knew I didn't like them. I wanted them to stop talking about her. I wanted her all to myself. If I got her, I had no idea what I would actually do with her, but I wanted her all the same.

Every day, on the way to school, I would say a little prayer in my head that today they would look different. Today, I would see her breasts and feel nothing. Little bumps under her sweater, no biggie. Or maybe they would be gone. Her nipples had popped out so abruptly, why couldn't they retract just as quickly? Or maybe she'd move again. I'd imagine her dad was in the army, and he was being sent to Virginia or, better yet, Siberia. Then I would never have to worry about getting caught stealing a glimpse of those beautiful bouncing breasts from across the cafeteria table again. So every day I prayed, but, much to my relief, none of my wishes ever came true.

She was always still there with her red sweaters, long black hair, and, of course, her breasts. They would always be there, she would always be there. Over time, my prayers became few and far between. I finally came to accept that this girl who crept into my dreams, whom I just wanted so badly to hold my hand, was never going to leave. I accepted her, and her breasts, as a permanent fixture in my daily life. I realized that, despite my wishes to the contrary, tits were here to stay. But my emotions, my longings—what I was—that would take at least another decade to accept.

# fury

In the midst of picking up, yet again, a strewn-about pair of size eight sneakers (not mine), wifebeaters, and hair clasps, I stopped to ask myself, "Who are you? And how did you get here?" When did I trade in the man in boxers I adored, for a girlfriend who looks damned good in boxers?

For most of my thirty-nine years, I lived my life in one definitive way. I worked hard and paid my taxes on time (some years); I loved my parents, sisters, and adoring daughter. Like any model, I partied, occasionally very hard, with the beautiful people. I dated Europeans—men. Yet, today I look around and can't help but notice that "he" is definitely a "she."

Now, don't get me wrong; throughout my travels, I have always been *that* girl. No one ever knew what to expect from me. I was always full of surprises. Hence, under the guise of being the "hot" one that "got the party started," I kissed quite a few damsels; always, though, under the very watchful and interested eye of a beautiful, macho, European man.

So how does a grown woman who never before thought to question her sexuality move from Park Avenue to the East Village, with a girlfriend and a dog no less? She falls in love, and she falls hard.

A little over a year and a half ago, Amy walked into the lounge I managed. She was looking for a bartending job. Her confidence struck me, and immediately I put her to the test. Amy was, and is to this day, the best damn bartender I have ever seen.

Let me preface this by saying, our story will be a little difficult to explain. 'Cause, trust me, we would differ on some salient points, but since I'm the one who got "touched"—or "converted," as Amy likes to say—my version is the one you'll hear.

Soon after Amy started working, I found myself conducting a lot of business behind the bar. I'd never been the type for a caffeine boost, but suddenly, I was drinking lots of coffee. There was something about the way she handled the espresso machine and steamed the milk, just for me, that piqued my interest in this woman. Soon, I was getting to work earlier, with added enthusiasm that stemmed more from the bartender making my coffee than from the coffee itself. At the time, I just thought Amy was interesting, and she made me laugh. Now, looking back, *that* makes me laugh!

Slowly but surely, Amy was seducing me, and I was letting it happen. She was absolute poetry behind my bar. Watching her work (and I did a lot of that), was like hearing musical chords come to life. I yearned to be her instrument, the strings she could pluck. Foolishly, I thought I had control over what was happening between us. I thought I had a say; and probably I did. But, unbeknownst to me, I'd already said yes.

The dance began. She was the lesbian, and I, the "straight" girl. Over and over, I told Amy I was straight. But she saw through my flaming heterosexuality. Before even I realized it, Amy knew I was screaming "straight" only because I was trying to convince myself of it. She certainly paid no attention to it.

Amy listened and listened and listened. Now, as any woman out there knows, the one thing we wish our boyfriends would do is, simply, listen. Amy got me talking so much, I became an open book for her to read. Clearly, she was an avid reader, because I soon found that she was gently giving me all I ever wanted. Then, she'd leave. And, naturally, I'd follow.

In the meantime, I spent a lot of time questioning myself

and my sexuality. I was trying to figure out what, exactly, was happening. Subtly, I'd ask my closest friends what they thought of "girl on girl" action. I was surprised to learn that most had tried it, and those who hadn't, wanted to.

Finally, one morning, I found my questions had been answered. I awoke and realized that God had sent me exactly the person I had been praying for. Apparently, I'd forgot to tell him, "A MAN!" But who am I to mess with fate?

That's when I knew it was time. It was time to be honest with myself and with Amy. It was time to have the real conversations with the people in my life who matter most. I called in my lawyer; her name is Roxx, and she is my youngest sister and my best friend. Roxx is also the most fabulous lesbian I know.

Roxx came out when she turned sixteen. My sisters and I knew what was up with her, but my mom hadn't the faintest idea. Sadly, the moment Roxx revealed her sexuality to my mother, she was kicked out of our house. My mother is a traditional Trinidadian woman, and our little island was a conservative one. Roxx left our home devastated, and moved in with her girlfriend.

Being that Roxx knows the joys of "the sisterhood," you would think this to be an easy conversation for me to have. Wrong! My sister cautioned me "not to do this." Her advice was as much for Amy's sake as it was for mine, maybe even more so. She understood the problems that would arise if her sister, whom she always considered "straight," decided to entertain a relationship with a lesbian. To Roxx, giving in to Amy would just be a dalliance for me; but for Amy, this was her life.

I considered carefully what Roxx had said, but I realized that Amy was someone I had to explore. There was no going back. My desire for Amy was a force to be reckoned with, and the desire to explore what was budding in me was too great to ignore. There was a thread that kept pulling me toward this unknown; but, at the same time, it felt so familiar. When I was with Amy, it felt like home.

Then, "D day" came. All of us know that day, the one that starts out like any other, until something inexplicable shifts, and you just know that it's time. I had no idea that I'd soon be exploring the intangible web of feelings that Amy and I had threaded; the two of us just felt it . . . together.

So, I succumbed to Amy's seductions. Before I knew it, we were in a full-blown, beautiful relationship. Now, don't forget that I speak solely for myself; she may have had this evening planned. However, I like my romantic version better; and also, it allows me to believe I had some say in the matter. I'd be lying if I said that I can tell you who touched whom first. I would be embellishing if I said I remembered every detail, and not even for the sake of good copy would I do that.

Truthfully, all I remember are the feelings. I think back to that night and visualize the release. I close my eyes and taste her touch. I smile when I remember the fear I had in not measuring up to her experience. I was the student with a serious crush on her teacher. I was the teacher's pet who got *straight* As. I learned and learned and learned. For the first time in my life, I voluntarily signed up for extra tutoring. I didn't mind detention, so long as it meant more lessons. I felt like a flower that had been repotted, basking in the sunlight and blooming with each passing day. I smile when I remember the fear I had in not measuring up to her experience. Years later, I pat myself on the back, knowing that the student has become the teacher.

I will never discount the wonderful memories I have of the very special men in my life. Without my ex-boyfriend, I'd never have had my wonderful daughter, Monique. To this day, I thank them for the love they bestowed on me. I am the woman I am today because of them. I am able to be the partner and lover that I am because of them.

But, in Amy's arms I realized that very few things compare to being caressed by your lover as gently as one would hold the petal of a flower. To be overtaken by such joy, passion, and emotion that your only objective is to drink it all in and taste her nectar. You give your soul to your lover, risking pain in order to connect your life and your body with hers.

Of course, there were times when I thought, *What am I doing?* But for all my doubts, there were the times when I knew that this was perfectly okay. Remember, I was *that* girl. My friends accepted my new girlfriend, and never even stopped to ask if I thought I was gay. The way they just allowed me to be whoever and whatever I pleased made me happy. After all, with a name like Fury, what could possibly be off-limits?

Systematically, I came out to everyone I loved. Some I told, and others just saw. I got mixed reviews, but absolute acceptance. I have a sister who told me, "This is so disgusting," but loves me anyway. My aunt, the "grande dame" of our family, whom I've always looked up to, gave me my favorite piece of advice. "Fury," she told me. "It is heart-warming that you care for others' opinions, but do any of these people know when you get your period? How much you pay for rent? What you've eaten today? If the answer is no to any of these, then what does it matter what anyone thinks, as long as you are happy?"

My aunt was right. Amy was the only person who could've answered yes to all of those questions. She played the biggest part in my life, and I wouldn't have had it any other way.

Then, of course, there was my daughter, Monique. My daughter is eighteen years old, very beautiful, kind-hearted, loving, and somewhat naive. Even though she lives in Trinidad, we are beyond close. She's always said that she has the coolest mother, ever. I'm an even bigger fan of Monique. Revealing my relationship with Amy to my daughter was my biggest fear. Sure, she had already met Amy, when she came to visit for Mother's Day, but I did not reveal our relationship to her; they just "met" each other. I was scared that my daughter would not accept me anymore, and that a love I once believed to be unconditional would turn out to be just the opposite: conditional.

Months into living with Amy, Monique and I went on vacation to Jamaica. This week would be the perfect opportunity to tell her who Amy really was in my life. Sitting poolside, drinking some beers, I knew it was time. After working myself up to it, talking around the issue—and, quite frankly, almost apologizing for what I was about to share with her—I came out and told her.

"There is something I want to tell you," I said, taking a deep breath. "Monique, I'm in love." I smiled.

"That's great, Mom. Who is he?" she asked with sincerity.

"Remember my friend, Amy? She's my girlfriend. We're living together," I replied. I could barely contain myself, anticipating her response

When Monique finally spoke, I truly understood what it was like to have someone love you, in spite of yourself. I fell in love with my child, this incredible young woman, all over again!

"Mummy, I love you. Who is to say what's 'normal'? I just love you." Monique hugged me. She then escaped my arms and looked at me. "I like Amy. She's mushy, but I like her." We both laughed.

And at that very moment, all the fears that had surrounded me—about not being accepted, not being good enough to be loved, not measuring up; about being abnormal; about needing to define who I was—all those fears receded. I let them go and abandoned them. To this day, I do not think that my daughter, my precious child, even knows how much she did for her mother.

Since that night, a lot has happened. Aim and I live together; we have a dog. We didn't rent a U-Haul on our second date or anything, but when we were both ready, we found a cute little apartment in the East Village, where we live and love. Together, we've spent many wonderful times with both our families. Our first Christmas with my family stands out. Remember my mother, who kicked Roxx out at age sixteen for being gay? Well, both she and my sister who thinks being with a woman is "soooooo disgusting" pestered me constantly to help them with ideas for a Christmas present for Amy. After meeting my girl-friend (and drinking one of her apple martinis), my mother told me, "I think we'll keep her." I think I will too.

I periodically reevaluate where I am in life. I constantly think about the changes that have occurred since Amy—since us. I sometimes wonder if the supposed equality that happens when you share your life with someone of the same sex is something that I can sustain forever. You see, I very much like the natural differences that occur in a heterosexual relation-ship. I am quite old-fashioned, and I appreciate the defined roles that we all have in this world.

So, yes, at times I wonder. But then I imagine my life with-out Amy at the center of it. I think about the "sisterhood" I feel when we are together—you know, getting manicures and pedi-cures, shopping (although she hates it, but loves to see me smile), never having to explain "that time of the month," cook-ing (although I hate it, but love to see her smile.) You get the idea? There is something so natural about women sharing a life together. I mean, on some level, we've been doing it for centuries. Women, by nature, have been conducting "love affairs" with one another forever, no matter what you choose to define them as.

I look at Amy and know there is no way I could miss out on this chapter in my life. I am wise enough to appreciate the love, intimacy, respect, and passion in our relationship. At the same time, I've learned that life can take some very unexpected turns, and I am equally prepared for those. I used to agonize over defining myself in this love affair. Finally, I've decided labeling myself is not necessary. I am in love with a woman who I think is very special. Isn't that enough?

There are mornings that I wake with Amy next to me, and reach over as my body gravitates to the heat of hers. I settle my head on her chest and place my mouth around her nipple; and in that moment, just before I lose all conscious thought (and my sanity), I thank God for the very first lesbian who took a chance and made this a life we can all be proud of. I hope that you get to experience your heart, without fear, at least once in your life. Good luck.

# maggie
......................................................

From a very young age, I knew I was different. My family always sensed something unusual about me. I always dreamed of being rich and famous. I'd fantasize about Ed McMahon showing up at my door, holding an oversize check from the Publishers Clearing House, addressed to me. But in my small town in rural Maine, that $3,000,000 doorbell never rang. Ed must have lost our address.

Our town chose to ignore that the word "gay" existed. It just wasn't part of the local vocabulary. I don't think it was because they deemed it wrong or sinful; it's because they just never had to deal with it before. People aren't gay here; they just aren't. I was definitely in the wrong town, in the wrong skin. Why did I have to look like a boy—why? When I was younger, it was cute. When I got older, it was weird.

I was barely six years old when I would ride my bicycle down the long, bumpy road to her house. My bike was pink. The handlebar's tassels used to slap my wrists as I rode in the cool autumn weather; it was as though my bike knew I was doing something wrong. I'd make it there in record time, leaving my house, my toys, and my family behind. As always, Mary would wait on the front porch of her house for me. Her house was small and green. She smelled like strawberry shortcake and looked like a perfect Cabbage Patch Kid. I loved her, and she let me. Youth was so innocent.

But time passed, and soon I went from two wheels to four. My family bought me a small, crappy, used truck for my sixteenth birthday. I was ecstatic. Now I could drive to her house, but I didn't go in anymore. She looked like a girl and I looked like a boy. I'd wait in my truck late at night. We were too different, but my love for her never dwindled. I wore my dark hair cropped and messy. I kept my breasts hidden under flannel shirts, which I tucked into my jeans. Mary had long blond hair and she sometimes wore skirts to school. I drove fast, past her green house, and when her lights were on, I knew she could see me. It became a ritual, an obsession. All day long I dreamt about her face. And sometimes when I drove by her house, she'd just let me stare at her. Mary stared back, but we never said a word. Occasionally, she'd get a glimpse of me in the hallways at school, where I seemed to be as transparent as the glass that divided us each night on my drive to nowhere.

I graduated from high school, feeling alone and asexual. To think about being with a man made me sick, and the thought of being with a woman made me feel like a man, which I wasn't. It didn't make sense to me that I could feel this way for another woman, without actually being a man. Like I said, my town didn't take too kindly to anything beyond what their eyes could see. Beyond anything black or white, they couldn't comprehend. And I was a very drab gray.

I attended college at the University of Maine and began a

new life. I was a girl who looked like a boy, and that had to be okay outside of my town. Since I had never really had any sexual encounters with anyone, I was totally and utterly repressed. Much like my voice, my life was monotone. I had the vision of a dog.

But then I met Laurie, and I stopped missing that drive past that old green house. Laurie was twelve years older than me; she, too, looked more like a man than a woman. She carried in herself a confidence I didn't know women who looked like us could have. She was who I so badly wanted to be. I watched her, but I wasn't going to watch from afar anymore.

Laurie worked at the local Eastern Mountain Sports school in my college town. She was a climbing instructor. I figured the only way to get in touch with my outdoorsy side was to try to get Laurie to teach me to climb. But, when I walked into the store, I spotted a HELP WANTED sign. Laurie asked if she could help me find anything. I told her I wanted a job. I seemed to fit the mold in terms of their employees. Sure, I hadn't climbed before, but I knew how to camp. I had no problem getting a job. Laurie trained me at the store. She talked to me every morning and asked me how my night had been. Laurie asked me to go climbing. Everything felt like it was happening naturally. For the first time in my life, I didn't feel invisible.

One fateful day I took Laurie up on that climbing trip she offered. I was so nervous; I was always nervous around her. The most profound words I could ever seem to spit out were, "Good," "Totally," and "How was yours?" But I had a two-day climbing trip ahead of me, and I was not going to slip up and let my past get the best of me.

We started to make our way up the hill. I walked behind her, watching her every move. We didn't talk all that much, but the beauty and silence of nature kept both of us entertained for the long hike up. Hours ticked by like minutes, and the next thing I knew, we were setting up camp on the top of a small peak. She knew what to do, and I did as I was told. I was so in awe of her and her instruction. I felt like a prisoner trapped beneath my insecurities. I was awkward, intimidated, and self-conscious. Laurie was everything I wasn't.

Later that evening, around a campfire we built together, we drank beers and roasted a couple of hotdogs. Snuggled next to each other in our sleeping bags, something happened that I never thought would. Laurie moved very close to me, putting my two shaking legs in between hers and kissed me. The night was so dark and the stars were perfectly aligned. I'd never tasted anything better than this woman's lips on mine, as the cool air calmed my hot, red face. My body was alive, my blood was hot and flowing, and my pulse beat through me like crazy.

That night, I made love to Laurie. We never spoke about being gay. Innately, we just behaved like lesbians. I let everything go—my inhibitions, my insecurities. Laurie knew what she was doing; it didn't take much to bring me to orgasm. I was ready eight years ago; I just couldn't seem to get past the driveway of that green house. But here I was, in a tent built for one, making love to the woman who brought me to life. I didn't really know what I was doing. My body led the way, my mind following close behind. I knew I was doing something right when I heard Laurie cry out in ecstasy.

That night in the woods was all it took for me to know who I was. I was not asexual. Far from it: I was gay. Very gay. Finally, I had acquired my own identity. I went from being lost my whole life to becoming whole. Laurie was my Ed McMahon. I was home. After we made love, Laurie went on to show me so much more than the pleasures of being with another woman. She showed me I could be who I wanted to become. I could feel comfortable in my own skin, I could dress and act the way I wanted. I could ignore the stares and the "Wrong bathroom, fella!" shouts I heard on a daily basis. Better yet, I could possess the confidence and swagger that makes anyone attractive.

Although I felt deeply for Laurie, it was more admiration and envy than love and longing. She was the most influential person in my life. She got me reading gay literature, and told me one day we'd go to Boston together for the Pride Parade. She was my best friend, and she still is. Laurie colored in my gray life. Now I see the vivid colors. But as I grew into my own skin, I knew Laurie was not the woman for me. I liked girls, beautiful girls.

Even though I look "gay," it was hard for me to realize I was gay. Sure, people called me a dyke, but how could I have been a dyke when I'd never even been with a girl? One night in the woods with Laurie changed my life forever. I am out. I am proud. And I've got myself a banging girlfriend.

# tabitha

My history as a lesbian began at the age of five. I could sit and stare at women for hours on end. The scent of a woman drove me mad and made me feel funny in strange ways. I wanted to be around girls at all times. My favorite place was on their laps, playing with their hair, smelling their sweet perfume, and loving every gentle smile they wore. My purpose in life was to torment any woman I had a crush on—and I had many (still do). The laundry list of women I tormented started with family members, friends of the family, and all of my teachers. Men were never thrown into the mix. I wasn't crazy about their beards, guttural laughs, and pot bellies, or their pungent odors, for that matter.

By age eight, my same-sex desires had become more evident. My cousin and I would play husband and wife. And as the older one, I always played the man. By the time we were ten, my role as a husband had gone from a little game to the sole purpose in my life. I loved the idea of being a "bread-winner" and the "protector of our home." As the leader, I was naturally the instigator of any and all passion to be had. We were almost too old for our actions, and, much to my surprise, not everyone was this sexual at the gentle age of eight.

When I turned twelve, I had a boyfriend who I occasionally enjoyed playing with. But it was never as much fun as playing with my girlfriends. To tell you the truth, back then I didn't even know what a lesbian was. I never heard the word until I was seventeen and met one. She was a hot twenty-six-year-old, and I had to have her.

My early teenage years were difficult for my mom and me. Growing up in the seventies, and coming from a Spanish/Catholic background, there was neither communication nor understanding. I lived in a cramped apartment in Hell's Kitchen in Manhattan. Even though I shared a three-bedroom apartment with eight other people, I had no one to share my secrets with. I became angry, destructive, and, evidently, more confused. Why was I different? Why did I desire every girl I saw?

As a fearless, driven, and impatient person, it blows my mind that I was so patient in coming out. I don't know how I managed to endure the wrong relationships as long as I did. It's a wonder I didn't consider suicide or, worse yet, pack on an extra four hundred pounds from my combined depression and Ben & Jerry's addiction.

I feared my family's reaction to the true Tabitha, and lied behind a fake smile. My stepfather always said I was the pretti-est girl with the saddest eyes. From my viewpoint it was simple: One of us had to go, my sanity or my family. I chose the latter.

And being a dreamer and a doer, I decided to head out in search of the real Tabitha. I was just sixteen years old when I left home. I never looked back. I was eager for the life that awaited me, and grateful for the many sleepovers I had before I left!

I convinced a few friends to join me in a cross-country tour via Greyhound.

We left New York and headed out West. Although I felt different, I followed in the footsteps of my friends and dated many guys. Thousands of miles away from New York just wasn't far enough for me to comfortably date girls. Truth be told, my family held me in a stronger grip than I cared to admit. I still wonder what would have been if I'd just had the courage to tell them I was gay.

By the time we reached sunny California, I was in heaven. I found a job as a receptionist and made friends quickly. One in particular comes to mind. Her name was Tina, and Tina was the one who introduced me to Tracy. And Tracy was a lesbian!

In California, I soon found out that being from New York was considered way cool. All eyes were on me, and I milked my tough New York image and accent for all it was worth. Thankfully, this New York teenager captured Tracy's attention. And I wanted to be around her constantly. I finally knew what being gay meant, and I wanted her in every way. I made it clear to her friends that I was *more* than interested. They thought my crush was cute and sweet, since I was only seventeen and Tracy was twenty-six. From time to time they teased her about my obsession. But it didn't matter to me.

Lusting after her the way I did made me sick. It's not like me to walk away from something or somebody I want. It *is* like me to fantasize, however, but not when there is nothing holding me back from turning that fantasy into reality.

One night we were all hanging out at a bar and I just got up, walked over to where Tracy sat, rested my knee on hers, and looked into her eyes. I kissed her gently and whispered into her ear. From that moment forth, I had a twenty-six-year-old girl-friend. WOW! She had more money than anyone I knew, a tight body, and a face you couldn't help but love. My girlfriend was the entire package.

Every day, for two straight months, we were together. We went out to clubs (VIP-style), fiddled around, held hands, and fell in love. We slept together every night, but never went all the way. Tracy made me work hard for what I wanted—that being sex, of course.

While dating Tracy, I met Tim, a corrections officer who wanted me in the worst of ways. Toward the end of my two months with Tracy, I started to get scared. LA was a great place to be free and gay, but something was distracting me. I hadn't once talked with my family for the two months I'd been dating Tracy. I was scared they would know I was a lesbian, just from my tone of voice. When I was fourteen, my mother caught me with a girl. She told me she didn't want to know what I was up to. But what I heard was, *If I find out you're gay, I'll disown you.*

Memories, fear, and the loss of communication with my mom consumed me. Around that time, Tim, my corrections officer friend, came over and had a long talk with me. He told me he loved me. Under a shadow of doubt and misery, I told Tim I wanted to be with him. Under one condition: I would keep my plans with Tracy that night. And he actually waited for me at my apartment.

I was sick to my stomach with grief; I was going to leave my first girlfriend. I hated Tim, my family, and myself all evening long. Tracy and I got pretty hammered. We went back to her place, and, wouldn't you know it, she wanted me that night. Out of all the nights we were together, she wanted this one to have no boundaries. I was drunk, tired, hungry, and sad. Despite this, for my first time making love to a woman, it was incredible!

At two in the morning, I got up with no explanation, dressed, and kissed Tracy good-bye. With tears in my eyes, I left. All I heard was her calling out my name, again and again. I'll never forgive myself for that. But at that moment I panicked. I had a man waiting for me in my apartment and a mom haunting my mind (while having sex—ouch). I was afraid. I couldn't stand up to anyone, not yet. I didn't feel I was strong enough. I went home crying, saw Tim there staring at me, and sobbed harder. I cried in his arms without saying a word.

I took my crazy, passionate anger out on Tim until the wee hours of the night. And then I was done. Done with him, and done with desiring women. I wasn't ready to face my family or who I was.

I vowed to overcome my fears, have a plan, and execute it. I became goal-oriented and driven. I sacrificed my happiness for the happiness of others. I married the first man I was mildly smitten with. My goal at that moment was to forget everything and win my family over, by being with a man. He was quirky like me and we rode motorcycles together. When I delivered my daughter, Alexis, in August 1992, I took one look in her eyes and knew I once again had to fly the coop. At twenty-six, I freed myself from my husband, but not from the grip of my family.

So, then I married Man Number Two, a friend in need of a green card. We had a perfect union. We traveled the world, wore expensive clothing, and it was with him that I made my first million. Everything was fine and dandy until September 11, 2001, when I lost my dearest family member, my godmother, my aunt Lydia Bravo. Her death sent me to a place I now know as a bottomless pit called Hell, which I am only now coming out of. Nothing is as bad as losing a loved one to pure evil.

After 9/11, I found myself flying home to New York monthly.

I did this for almost two years. I ran away from my life with a mission in mind. I promised myself I'd leave my husband, raise my daughter, and come out of the closet. As if these goals weren't lofty enough, I decided to open my own business.

It took me one year to leave Man Number Two. Before I did, I spent months reading women's journals (first embraces) and watching gay TV. Soon enough, my husband caught on. After a late return from New York, he asked if I was gay. It took all I had inside of me to hold back my tears of joy. With as straight a face as I could muster, I told my husband I was, in fact, gay. I'd finally said it out loud. I divorced him immediately. What I needed to face next was my family.

Most of the lesbians I know first came out to their friends. Leave it to me to first come out to my husband, and then my daughter. Alexis and I have one of the closest mother/daughter relationships I've ever seen. She was ten years old when I told her I was gay. I hoped she'd learn from my mistakes, and always accept herself for the beautiful person she is. I told Alexis my story, what being gay meant, and asked for her forgiveness. My daughter had gone through ten years of having a mom who was miserable, with her not knowing why. It blows my mind that, at such a young age, Alexis possessed an extraordinary amount of courage and independence. After learning I was gay, she said, "Mom, what took you so long?" as she cried for all the hell I'd put myself through.

Months later, while visiting my second girlfriend in New York, I met my mom for an all-day walk-a-thon in Central Park. My mother wasn't two minutes off the train when I blurted out, "I'm here visiting a woman!" As I expected, my mom wasn't ready for this news. I didn't know if she'd ever be. I prepared to walk away from our mother/daughter duties for life, and I believe my mom knew it. She called me up a week later and told me everything was all right. She just wanted my daughter and me to be happy. I assured her we were.

Years later, I feel I am one of the luckiest women alive. I could have waited until I was sixty years old to come out. Or, even worse, lived my entire life as a lie. Today, Alexis and I live with my amazing girlfriend, Lauren. I've waited all my life for this feeling, and now I have it. Finally, I set myself free.

## one more thing . . .

It seems that no matter how old you are when you figure out your sexuality, the road is never as straight as you planned. But when you finally reach the right place at the right time, clarity is yours. Some experience panic, others an overwhelming sense of completion and closure. Whatever the reaction is, the truth surfaces, and many of the questions that challenged us for so long are finally answered.

CHAPTER THREE:
# the first time

I love doing lesbian love scenes. Before I did my lesbian scenes in *Gia*, I talked to actresses who said love scenes are easier with another woman than a man. *Bound*'s Gina Gershon and Jennifer Tilly said they'd lie there and discuss the sale at Barney's between takes.

—Angelina Jolie

If you haven't gotten drunk and made out with one of your girlfriends yet . . . what are you waiting for? It's how most of us begin, and, chances are, your friends will be into it. Remember, everybody likes to experiment. Why do you think Mr. Wizard was so popular?

Vacation is a perfect time to do this. Guys will cheer you on because they think it's hot. And you can always play the "drunken amnesia" or "what happens in Acapulco stays in Acapulco" card. If you are scared to initiate the kiss, consider asking your guy friends to dare you to French your friend. They will happily oblige. However, know that the drunken make-out session is not the end all be all. Sure, it's a great place to start, but we thought we would know if we were gay after our first lesbian kiss. Not true at all.

Our first same-sex encounters happened at a relatively older age. A

Penn State study of three hundred and fifty women found that the mean age at which lesbians first have sexual contact with other girls is sixteen. Perhaps people are experimenting with their sexuality at a younger age due to the increasing presence of homosexuality in high schools. In 1997 there were approximately one hundred gay-straight alliances (GSAs) on U.S. high school campuses. Today, there are at least three thousand. According to the Gay, Lesbian & Straight Education Network, nearly one in ten high schools has one, and in the 2004–05 academic year, GSAs were established in U.S. schools at the rate of three per day.

The meaning behind everyone's first time varies. For some, there's no turning back to boys, and for others, it's just one step on the path to self-actualization. (For Lauren B. it was the former, and for Lauren L. it was the latter.)

All right, so now you've made out with one of your friends. That was quick. Congratulations! You've just rounded first base, rookie. Now comes the fun stuff: hooking up with chicks. This step is remarkably harder to accomplish.

There's a lot wrapped up in your first lesbian sexual experience. Whether it's your first time having sex at all, or your first time having sex with another woman, being nervous is normal. There's so much hype surrounding your "first time" and "losing your virginity." Here are some tips to make that first lesbian sexual experience as special and incredible as possible.

## Don't let the bottle get the best of you

Our advice to you is to be dead sober. What's that you're saying? Hook up sober? No way, no how. We believe the first time you make love to a woman is so importantžžžžyou are going to want to remember it. Alcohol or drugs may lower your inhibitions and make the first move easier. Just the same, you're more likely to do or say something you'll regret.

## When I think about you I . . .

Before you can even think about turning someone else on, you've got to know what excites you. We're talking about masturbation, flicking the bean, clicking your mouse—whatever the kids call it these days. Spend some time one-on-one with yourself. As you touch yourself and find out what feels good, you'll know how and where to touch *her*. Better yet, you'll be able to tell her what turns you on.

## Dream a little dream of her

If you want to sleep with another woman, chances are, you've thought about girl-on-girl sex. How does it go in your wildest dreams? Does an innocent massage between friends turn sexy and passionate? Does a more experienced lover push you up against a wall and have her way with you?

## Raise your hand, and speak up

Communication is the key to any good sexual relationship. If she's doing something you like, moan or breathe heavily to let her know how good it feels. Let her know where you want to be touched. Ask your lover if what you're doing feels good; ask her what she wants from you. Use that suggestion box!

## Ditch the hardware

Your first time should be pure, ole-fashioned lesbian lovemaking. Have fun in the flesh! Don't get us wrong: We love our girl toys just as much as the next lesbo. But we never whip 'em out on the first date.

## Be the tortoise, not the hare

You've got all night to make love. Tease her with your touch. Undress her slowly. Appreciate each inch of her soft skin. Kiss her stomach. Take in her scent. Fondle her breasts. Kiss her neck. Caress her inner thighs. Take in her smell. Massage her ass. You want her desperate for your touch, to feel her shiver. Lay your naked body on top of hers. Foreplay with girls is incredible. There's a whole lot of fun to be had before you ever even touch her down there. When she reaches her breaking point, and just can't seem to handle it anymoreżžžžžgo for the gold!

## It's not all about the "O"hhhhh

Orgasm may or may not happen the first time. Keep in mind, like losing your virginity to a man, punching your V-card with a girl could be less than perfect. That's okay. The point is to get physical, get close, and express your feelings of love or desire.

Girls, just remember to relax! We know there's a lot on your mind. But, at least when you're with a woman, size is never an issue.

# lauren levin

• • • • • • • • • • • • • • • • • • • • • • • • • • • • • • • • • • • • • • • • • •

The first time I had sex with a woman was an amazing experience, but it wasn't the mind-blowing, passionate affair I'd imagined it would be—that came later. I was twenty-four, and away with my family on a cruise that my great-aunt had signed us up for. At this point, I knew I was gay and had come out to my friends. This was the week I'd planned on coming out to my family. I hadn't really planned on cumming.

The second night of the cruise, I came out to my entire family. Yet, I still felt an emptiness inside of me. I'd taken the biggest step in a gay person's life, but I had never slept with a woman. I ached for physical justification of my new lifestyle.

The night after I came out, my cousins and I went to the nightclub on board, Nightwalkers. When we first entered the club, I thought we must have been in the wrong place.

Everyone inside looked years younger than me—we're talking braces and acne. I thought we'd walked into the teen club. It was like anyone with a note from their mom could get into this place.

We headed to the bar and ordered our first round of drinks. 50 Cent was blaring out of the speakers and the dance floor was packed. One girl, dressed in a tight pink miniskirt and matching pink crop-top, caught my eye. Not because she was my type or anything; in fact, she looked kind of slutty. She was the kind of girl people look at with a mix of intrigue, awe, and disdain. She was dancing with a woman. The girl she was dancing with immediately captured my attention.

She looked a few years younger than me; she was cute and had shoulder-length blond hair. There was something about this girl that screamed "gay." Maybe it was the piercing beneath her lip, or her low-riding jeans and wifebeater, or just the way she moved. I wanted to know her.

As I chatted and drank with my cousins, my eyes kept wandering to the mysterious girl. Soon enough, it was time for her to hit the bar and get another drink. I moved away from where I'd been standing, creating a void I hoped the blonde would soon fill. Much to my delight, she did.

Her name was Krissy. She introduced me to her friend Tiffani and we sat down and got to talking. I discovered Krissy was twenty-two and a student at the University of Colorado. One of the guys to our left bought us a round of shots. I'm never one for Jagermeister, but I didn't want to be the girl who turns down a free shot. I downed it and felt as though I was going to vomit. Apparently, it showed.

"So, Jager's not your thing, huh?" Krissy laughed.

"Yeah, not one bit. I'm more of a tequila girl," I explained, trying to sound mildly hardcore.

"Yeah, same here. We'll have to do Petron next time." Krissy smiled.

"Oh, my God, I love this song," I said, as Ciara's "One, Two Step" came on. "Let's dance."

Krissy grabbed Tiffani and we all busted a move on the dance floor. By the time Ciara was done rapping, Tiffani was being groped by some dude with gelled hair and a gold chain, and Krissy and I were left to our own devices.

We began dancing closer and closer together. Her hands were on my hips, and I was gettin' low and quite seductive.

Krissy eyed me curiously. "Do you date women?" she asked.

"Yeah," I lied with confidence. So what if I'd never *really* dated one. I just came out for Christ's sake. "Do you?"

Again, Krissy laughed. "Yep. Wow, I can't believe it. I just wouldn't have guessed that right off the bat. That's so cool. Did you know I was gay?"

"I had a feeling. Some girls just send a vibe, ya know?" Krissy nodded as I feigned experience.

"Yeah, I came out when I was in high school," she told me. "It was cool. Everyone just figured I was a dyke anyway."

"That's awesome," I told her. I didn't want to tell her I'd come out the night before. "What about Tiffani?" I inquired.

"She told me she's bi, but . . . you know." She shrugged her shoulders.

"Yeah, I could see that." My suddenly acquired database of lesbian knowledge impressed me.

"Do you want to get out of here?" Krissy asked.

I nodded my head and Krissy grabbed my hand, pulling me out of the club.

She knew her way around the ship much better than I did. She swung open some heavy door and soon we were standing on a deserted deck. I wanted her badly. I needed this.

I pushed Krissy up against the wall and started kissing her. She seemed to be taken aback by my aggressiveness and softened up our kisses a bit. *So this is what it's like with a lesbian,* I thought. *Lesbians rock!*

I was drunk on vodka, Jager, and Krissy. I wanted more of her.

"Here, let's lay these on the ground." I grabbed a couple cushions from one of the chairs and laid them on the ground.

Krissy got on top of me. I was nervous, excited, and anxious. There were so many emotions stirring up inside of me, I thought I was going to explode. She kissed my lips, my ears, and my neck. In no time, she was pulling off my shirt. I took off her wifebeater, and unclasped a bra other than my own for the first time.

She kissed my breasts, gripping them softly and gently. I was incredibly turned on. I wanted to stay out there under the stars with her forever. Suddenly, a door slammed.

"Krissy? Krissy? Are you out here?" Tiffani shouted. We threw our shirts back on immediately. Krissy stood up and pulled me off the ground.

Tiffani didn't ask questions. She just told us Krissy's brother had been looking for her. We all walked back to Nightwalkers. Krissy and I, obviously frustrated, hugged and parted ways. We searched for our respective family members. As much as I wished we could've stayed together, it comforted me to know we had the rest of the week to kiss and touch and hold.

I fell asleep in my cabin, rocking on the waters, peaceful and calm. I'd gone further than I'd ever gone before with a woman. I enjoyed my time with this stranger more than I had with any guy I'd spent many a night with. That quick little hookup with Krissy was the proof in the pudding. I liked women . . . a lot. Thank God, there was no need to pretend I didn't any longer.

The next day's shining sun filled me with anticipation. I didn't want to seem desperate by seeking Krissy out, so instead, I laid out by the pool with my cousins and kept my eyes peeled. Unfortunately, the girl I couldn't stop thinking about was nowhere in sight. Finally, nighttime rolled around and we went to the club, where immediately I spotted Krissy. She looked me up and down and smiled.

Neither of us planned on drinking: we were still too hung over from the night before. After beating around the bush (so to speak) for a while, Krissy pulled me outside. She said she'd found a more private spot, one where we wouldn't get caught.

Again, we spread out some cushions and Krissy lay down on top of me. She stroked my hair and my cheekbones. She kissed me with grace and passion. I was more in the moment than ever before. I couldn't remember the last time I'd hooked up sober. I wanted to feel everything about being with Krissy. I never wanted to forget this night.

The night was Velveeta-cheesy. There we were on a cruise ship, under the stars, gazing into each other's eyes, knowing what the evening had in store.

Krissy stopped the kissing and caressing. I was shaking. "Is this your first time with a woman, Lauren?" She'd sensed my clumsy eagerness. Women detect these things a mile away.

"Ahhh, yeah, it is," I admitted. "I mean, I've hooked up a little with girls before, but nothing like this."

Krissy explained that she'd dealt with first-timers before. She thought it was cool that I had come out before even sleeping with a woman. She was incredibly sweet and sensitive to my nervousness. She felt my body twitch as she kissed my stomach.

"Have you ever even come with another person before?" She glanced up from my stomach.

"No," I told her.

Krissy looked me straight in the eye, "Well, I'm going to change that."

She knew my body well and continued to kiss me all over. I could tell she was experienced, and it turned me on. I was so wet and drunk with my own desire. We rolled around, kissing, talking, and teasing. I never wanted this to end. I'd died and gone to heaven.

There was no turning back. I could've stayed up there under the stars with Krissy forever. Unfortunately, all good things must come to an end, and, six hours later, they finally did. I thanked her; we did a little dance, then returned to our separate cabins.

The next morning, I couldn't stop thinking about the night before. I needed it to happen again. My imagination ran rampant, and I developed all sorts of different scenarios—when I would see her again, what I would wear the next time she dropped by my room, how we would make love in the ocean. Clearly, I had fallen for this chick.

When I finally saw Krissy the next day, she seemed less than pleased. Something in her had changed. She shied away from all my gestures.

Krissy pulled me away from the rest of the group. "Lauren, look, I don't really know how to say this, but what happened last night can't happen again. I have a girlfriend back in Colorado. . . ." She continued to speak as I held back tears.

The night before had been so incredibly good, all I wanted was to do it again. I didn't have any strings attached, but it seemed like every lesbian I met already had a girlfriend. Their urge to merge was killing me.

The rest of the week was painful. I didn't hook up with Krissy again. But I did make out with a bunch of bi-curious girls! Who knew that my great-aunt had signed us up for a lesbian love boat?

Although she hurt me, I didn't regret sleeping with Krissy. I flew back to New York, excited about what lay ahead. My vacation was a productive one. My night with Krissy was beautiful—and I was sober. You never forget your first.

# lauren blitzer

It was not until I made love to a woman that I truly accepted and embraced being gay. The first time I slept with a woman played an integral part in my becoming who I am today. I only wish everyone's first experience with sex could be this wonderful.

When I was in college, the feelings I had toward women grew stronger and stronger with each man that walked in and out my life. I developed certain infatuations with girls in my classes, girls who lived in my dorm, and girls I saw frequently enough to recognize in a school filled with thousands.

Then, during the summer following my sophomore year of college, that whole idea of meeting someone when you least expect it couldn't have proven more true.

Through NYU, I had enrolled in a summer study-abroad program in London—Art History and English Lit. I was never one to crave adventure outside the tristate area. I would have anxiety when leaving my family and comfort zone. But something told me the fear of leaving wasn't a good enough reason to stay. Getting outside my somewhat insulated sphere, with no crutches and nothing to lean on but myself, would be the only way I would ever really know myself. I secretly challenged myself. It was like having a bat mitzvah all over again; I was becoming a woman! I wanted to be the person I knew I had brewing inside, the cool, confident, and, dare I say, sexy Lauren.

And then one Wednesday evening in June my life as I knew it was forever changed. I discovered a lesbian bar with a cabaret license around the corner from my apartment that was open until two a.m., and suggested it to my friends as an alternative to the eleven p.m. "last call" at the pub. I was beyond excited, nervous, and so happy we were in a different country.

My anonymity in London made walking into a lesbian bar seem not so threatening. No one would recognize me, and I didn't care about anyone's opinion of me there. After all, I had taken the spring-break pledge: Whatever happens in London stays in London. But, for whatever reason, I had a very weird feeling that something or someone was about to take my breath away. And not one part of me considered the consequences of it, maybe because I was completely and totally available and open to the experience.

*Oh, well,* I thought, *it's not like I'm gay or anything. Maybe my fantasy of meeting someone will just remain a fantasy.*

The night went on, and after about an hour, my friend Kari nudged me in the side and told me there was a girl staring at me.

I looked over and saw a dark-haired woman looking in my direction. She was just my type, or at least that's what I said to myself. She looked like any girl I might see at a straight bar and admire for both her style and looks. To Kari I said, "What are you talking about? She's so *not* checking me out."

During the evening, I caught her staring more and more. She caught me curiously looking back. I managed to get the girls to sit down, conveniently, near her. We needed a rest, as we'd just finished our karaoke rendition of "Eternal Flame" up on stage. Yet, as I turned to subtly check her out, it so happened that she was right behind me, ready to ask if I wanted a drink. I totally lost my cool. Of course, I couldn't understand her accent over the loud music. I said, "What?" and she smiled shyly and asked me again if I wanted a drink. I thanked her kindly as she got me one.

We proceeded to talk for the rest of the night. I asked her so many times to repeat herself. I just wasn't used to the accent yet—terribly embarrassing. Hard-core flirting was taking place, as we both played with our hair, looked away during an awkward silence, and smiled at each other.

This British woman captivated me from the start. Her deep, dark-brown eyes shot through me and her cute body was just waiting to be touched. She made me feel like I never wanted to leave. But last call came around, and as we left the bar she wrote her number on a napkin. After saying good-bye, I realized we hadn't even gotten each other's names.

I took five steps, opened the napkin, and came to a complete standstill. I looked down and read her name . . . Rachel. Rachel, the most beautiful name in the world. Her name was so clearly a sign that this woman was destined to change my life.

I'd walked away from one Rachel before, and I refused to do it again. A few days went by, and I, of course, obsessed about whether or not she was going to call. Finally, she did, and we made plans to meet for drinks the next night.

I had a surge of energy the day leading up to seeing her that even ten Red Bulls couldn't provide. The night of the date my heart was beating a mile a minute. I felt so awkward. I wanted to be exactly where I was, but I didn't know how to be the girl in this girl-on-girl date. I sat at the bar trying to do, and say, everything right.

Rachel sensed I was uncomfortable. However, being the shy, proper girl she is, she tried her best to make me feel safe and welcome. We shared our histories and got to know each other. I enjoyed every second of it, and, again, I never wanted to leave her. We sat a few inches from each other and occasionally in a bout of laughter she would lean in a grab my leg, or touch my arm. Suddenly, I became so conscious of my whole body. Each part of me she touched came to life. Blood rushed to my leg, to my arm, and to my hand as hers unassumingly grazed mine. We'd had so much fun talking that we couldn't stop as we drove closer and closer to my apartment. But I knew that moment was coming. The moment when I would have to exit the car and kiss or not kiss her. It wasn't that I didn't want to, but I wasn't sure if I was ready to. I really liked this girl and I didn't want to mess it up.

She pulled the car up to the curb and we just sat for a while. I felt horribly awkward, and as each second crawled by, I felt the sweat develop more and more on my brow. Finally, I opened the door and said good night quickly, almost abruptly. I told her I'd had a really good time and thanked her for everything. I practically ran out of her car. Looking back, I was so uncomfortably nervous, I kind of want to cry about it. I was finally breaking out of that mold I had been living in for so many years. But it was definitely a process. I was coming closer and closer to emerging as the person I so craved to be — myself.

I couldn't make it up the stairs fast enough, as I tried to sweat off the embarrassment I felt. My cell phone began to vibrate with a text message. I knew it was her. I looked down at the little envelope that appeared on the view screen. I didn't want to open it, but I couldn't help myself.

The message read, "Is that how you say good night in NYC?" I laughed out loud. At that point, I was sure she didn't want to deal with an amateur like me. Praise the Lord, I was oh-so-very wrong.

I replied with, "I'm so sorry I ran out of the car. This is all so new to me." She wrote me back. She told me not to worry and that she was around the block if I wanted to give her a proper good-bye. I told her next time. As I wrote that, I promised myself that I meant it.

The next day, Rachel texted me with the name and address of a bar. I was with my friends, and they made it their job to get me to that bar, no matter how nervous and hesitant I was. They both wanted to have their own lesbian experiences but settled on living vicariously through me. See, straight girls really rock sometimes!

I walked into the bar looking like a twelve-year-old in my golf shirt, rolled-up jeans, and flip-flops. My friends were in similar attire. And then I caught a glimpse of her in her suit and thick-rimmed glasses and took a moment to admire her undetected. She was wearing one of those I-mean-business-in-a-hot-hot-way suits.

Soon enough, we were all in her convertible going to another bar in Greenwich, right outside central London. I began to feel a bit more comfortable with her. I touched her arm whenever I could. I touched her back when it was appropriate, like when I was following her through a doorway or guiding her to the bar.

At one point, everyone left the room and it was just us. I knew what I wanted to do, but I was still too scared. We stood very close; she giggled and so did I. I didn't know what else to do. I had to turn my head because I felt like she could actually see through me; I was just that open. The night went on like that. My friends got more and more drunk, as did Rachel.

We were having such an amazing time, we didn't realize it was almost five o'clock in the morning. We needed to leave, and I was the only sober one of the bunch. I had to drive in London. The steering wheel was on the wrong side of the car and the car on the wrong side of the road, and it took me twenty minutes to go one mile. But, finally, knuckles white, we got to Rachel's apartment, alive and well.

My friends passed out in the living room, and I sat down in a chair. Rachel was in the guest room. She called to me; she wanted to show me something. I walked into the room and my whole body trembled and my knees grew weak. I had absolutely no saliva left in my mouth. Rachel stood in front of me. I felt a magnetic pull toward her body as she inched closer to mine.

I looked into her eyes as she placed her lovely hands on my hips. Our eyes met and we kissed. It was warm and beautiful. My body tingled. I pressed my hands on her, pulling her close to me. We stopped for a second, and I snuggled my face in that space between her shoulder and her neck. It fit perfectly. I stayed there for a while. She wrapped her arms around me and we stood there enjoying the feel of each other.

And then her door buzzer went off. She was going to Spain for a few days with her family and there was a cab waiting to take her to the airport. The timing couldn't have been worse. After that kiss, I would've done anything to make that cabbie go away, to make the world go away. But I managed to wake my friends, and as Rachel and I followed them out of the apartment, she grabbed me for one last kiss. Her sweet lips were hot and wanting more. She kissed me with everything she had in her. This was the kiss that would send me back home as an entirely new person. Or maybe I always was that person, and I'd finally accepted myself for who I truly am.

I was completely and utterly blinded by Rachel. I could think about nothing else. I didn't care about all the fears and uncertainties that came along with knowing I was gay. Nothing mattered except the absolute completeness that I felt within myself. I was finally confident. I knew what I wanted, and I was getting it!

If this was what love and happiness were about, then gay I was. It was amazing how smooth the transition was. I had moved into another way of living, and nothing could have felt more right. To think I had denied this since I was sixteen felt like an incredible waste of time.

Fortunately, Rachel returned a week later, and called as soon as she got off the plane. We made plans to spend the next two weeks together at her house. I barely knew this woman, but something told me to extend my ticket and stay. You only live once, and if I didn't jump on this opportunity I would probably regret it forever. It was the first time in my life I wasn't afraid.

The day she picked me up was very awkward and intense. We both tried to remain normal, all the while feeling like we were going to explode. We drove with her friends to Brighton, a seaside town outside of London, and I sat in the backseat, taking every opportunity to stare at her via the rearview mirror. I was obsessed with her face; there was still something about her that drove me crazy. I was strangely calm, and for once I wasn't thinking about the next day, the next hour, or anything else, only about her and me, and each passing moment.

Apparently, Brighton had quite the gay scene, so we had several places to go that night. As we walked down a narrow cobblestoned street I felt her hand reach out and grab mine. I was holding hands with a woman, and it felt so incredibly natural. Her hand was warm and small and fit perfectly in mine. I took a deep breath of the ocean air and vowed to remember the feeling for the rest of my life.

When we were alone, both of us were still extremely uncomfortable with how intense things were between us. Every glance we shot at each other was loaded with sexual longing and exploration. We got a drink to loosen up. As we stood at the bar, she put her hand on my waist, and my whole body changed. I craved her nearness. She was so close to me, I could feel the heat radiating from her body. It felt like a second skin.

We walked onto the crowded dance floor and I closed my eyes. She grabbed me close. I felt like if I opened my eyes, the fantasy I was actually living would end up being just a dream.

As our bodies swayed together, Kylie Minogue's "I Can't Get You Out of My Head" came on, and I laughed at how appropriate it all was.

Since the night we'd met, this woman had been in my head, on my mind, in my fantasies. Now I felt her breath on my lips as she grazed my cheek with hers. I craved her mouth, and she was making me crazy for her. Finally, her lips landed on mine, slowly slipping them apart. Our mouths felt like they had been made for each other as our tongues intertwined. Eyes closed and dizzy with lust, my face red, I felt like my body was burning up. I couldn't stop kissing her; it felt as natural as breathing. I pushed her into a corner, an aggressive move for a first-timer, and we kissed until the lights came on and it was time to go home.

I was going to have my first sexual experience with a woman. I was too excited to be nervous. I felt so incredibly safe with Rachel that I knew this night would be one I wouldn't forget. We stumbled back to her friend's flat, stopping practically every second to kiss as if we needed each other's lips like oxygen.

Nothing was talked about, nothing discussed. We both knew what was about to happen. The night was a blur of tangled bodies and sheets. I was closer to Rachel than I had ever been to anyone. Sure, I had slept with men, but it was nothing compared to this. Every touch was better than the next, which just confirmed to me that I was exactly where I should be, in bed with a hot British woman. Her hands were gentle to the touch, her lips explored my body, and her soft skin felt like it belonged on mine. I never wanted it to end. And when it did end, I wanted to do it over and over again. If this is what it meant to be gay, then sign me up!

I woke up the next morning with her arms around me and her naked skin on mine. I spent the next hour watching her, enjoying every second of her sleeping presence. Rachel had shown me what it was like to make love. I finally understood how amazing it all could be. I turned to her sleepy face and knew that I loved her. I felt free. I could finally relate to all those times my friends would obsess and cry over boys. I understood what love was all about. I, Lauren Blitzer, was indeed gay.

# daniela

••••••••••••••••••••••••••••••••••••••••••••

Looking back on my first sexual experiences with girls is not an easy thing for me to do. It certainly wasn't a transformation that took place overnight. But, thankfully, I've come a long way since then.

About a year ago, I took a trip to Mancora, Peru, to visit friends and stay with my ex-boyfriend, Wawa. I knew this would be a good time to try and figure out a few things. Liking girls more than guys was consuming me, and I figured a different environment and a new perspective would surely help. Really, I was traveling to South America with the hopes of realizing I was straight. I wanted to fall in love with Wawa.

Well, I definitely did rid myself of doubts. And I most certainly fell in love. But it wasn't with Wawa. I remember the first time I saw her. She was walking along the beach. She carried a surfboard under one arm, and a half-smoked cigarette in her other hand. It wasn't the long brown hair, or the tan skin, or the cut abs that drew me to her. I mean, sure, that helped. But, really, it was her confidence and her independence. This girl had an edge and a mystery to her that almost immediately held me captive. It was my first encounter with a girl who made my head spin, and my deepest desire was just to know her. Or so I told myself.

But I was preoccupied at the time. I was living with Wawa. An amazing man—a perfect ten, if you will. Wawa is successful, intelligent, funny, caring, and respectful. He's also drop-dead gorgeous. His sandy blond hair, sky-blue eyes, tan skin, and chiseled body would make anyone look twice. If I was ever going to truly love a man, it would be this one. How perfect, how disgustingly appealing . . . for a straight girl, that is, or a confused girl, or maybe just a girl living in denial. To some extent, though, I think I always knew that *something* was indeed missing. It all began to make sense once that beautiful girl on the beach strutted her way into my life.

Mery Jo.

Upon arrival in Mancora, Mery Jo and I happened to make almost the same name for ourselves on the surf scene: Hot Brunette Longboarder with a Little Bit of Attitude and a Whole Lot of Skill. We were just about the same height, with a similar build and long brown hair. We rode mini-longboards, both custom-made. Mine was red and white and Mery Jo's was pink and white. We both had a knack for making our presence known when we entered the water, as we were almost always the only girls at the break point. We were told that our moves—my extraordinary drop and her flawless cutback—were virtually the only things that set us apart when we rode waves. Simply put, we were fierce.

It was intimidating to stumble across someone who was so incredibly like me, especially in circumstances where competition is only natural. Suspense was mounting as we spent our days catching each other's glances and exchanging subtle grins. We were undoubtedly fascinated with one another: *Something* drew us together.

It wasn't an instant connection, but we were intrigued and attracted from the get-go. When an opportunity to finally break the ice came around, I was so anxious, I could barely contain myself. I was lying on the beach, enjoying the sun, when suddenly I heard the sweetest-sounding voice:

"Hey, good wave out there yesterday."

I knew it was her before I even opened my eyes. The day before, Mery Jo and I had ridden the same wave together, during an intense late-afternoon surf session. I knew which wave she was talking about. I remembered screaming something along the lines of, "Hey, bitch, get off my wave!" But I had no idea that it was her who had cut in front of me. Nevertheless, I vainly tried to remain calm and collected.

"Really? You were watching me?" I asked.

"No, I was with you," she replied.

Oh, God, she *was* that girl. I couldn't have possibly felt more suicidal. I prayed for spontaneous combustion. But, instead, I unexpectedly regurgitated the most ridiculous words: "Hey, I need to get wasted. How 'bout some drinks?"

Normally, this would have been a perfectly fine idea, except for the fact that it happened to be ten a.m. on a Tuesday.

As it turned out, Mery Jo was a very laid-back girl. She giggled and expressed slight confusion, then agreed. The six-minute walk to the bar was probably the longest six minutes of my life. I tried to carry on a conversation as my thoughts raced: *God, she looks incredible. Am I honestly going to a bar at ten in the morning? Did she honestly just say yes? I don't even feel like drinking. Do I even know her name?*

We arrived at a cute dive bar, known for its beachfront location and cheap whiskey drinks. I ordered two, on the rocks. I noticed a hint of apprehension in her eyes, and soon realized that she was intimidated and intrigued by me, too. At the same time, there was a definite authenticity and kindness about her that comforted me. Before we knew it, conversation rolled in smoothly, like the whiskey down our throats and the waves on the beach.

Like most women destined to fall in love, we quickly became acquainted through telepathy. We read each other's minds and completed each other's sentences. It all happened so fast, so nonchalantly. That dividing line between best friends and lovers turned from fine to nonexistent almost instantly. Ironically, we both claimed to be straight. Looking back, the only thing straight about us was our hair. And we both went to great lengths to get even that straight. We were two girls, blindfolded, feeling our way through a place we'd only dreamed of, but somehow knew so well.

A few days after we'd met, we were already having intimate late-night chats. On this particular night, I have no recollection of what we were discussing. All I remember is being suddenly whacked on the back of the head by an epiphany: *Oh, my God, I am starving for her kiss.*

Never before had I felt such a strong urge to kiss someone. I had come to grips with the fact that I had an incredibly strong attraction to this girl. I drowned myself in my desire for days, without realizing I was sinking. There was no turning back. I'd held out until I could no longer control myself. As words flowed out of her mouth, I gently placed my hand on top of hers and leaned in closely. Mery Jo paused and met my glance. I helplessly went in for her lips. I gave her a soft, slow peck. As I began to pull away, my eyes still shut, I felt her hand graze my neck and her warm breath touch my lips. Fireworks exploded. The world stopped moving. Her mouth was all I knew. We were flying, in ecstasy.

The following months were nothing short of heaven. For the first time, a woman and I openly admitted that we were attracted to each other. We were obsessed, in love, and inseparable.

So, what about Wawa, the most perfect man alive? Well, I did what any normal, sexually confused, twenty-something girl would do: I invited Mery Jo to join us in a threesome. Wawa was fanatical about the idea of not one, but two beautiful girlfriends, and Mery Jo and I were crazy about each other and him too. We were like three peas in a pod, spending virtually every minute of every day together. We had amazing chemistry, held nothing back, and disregarded all boundaries. During the next couple of months, we took trips to the Caribbean and traveled the coast of Peru. Everything was so incredible, magical, and fulfilling. We surfed, drank, made love, sang, laughed, and cried. Our life was a fairy tale. You know the old story: Boy meets girl, girl meets girl, girl and girl fall in love, boy falls in love with girls. I was living a wet dream. No one else existed outside our world of sex, sun, sand, and surf.

So why did this ever have to end? I mean, what could possibly go wrong in a perfect dream world? Reality set in and eventually led to our demise. It was inevitable that, at some point, one of us would fall harder than the others. Jealousy and resentment are hard emotions to ignore, especially when they're pumping through the veins of not two, but three individuals.

Somewhere along the way, I fell deeply in love with Mery Jo. It was far beyond my power, and completely out of my control. I never intended to hurt anyone, but that's what brought us down. Subconsciously, I began to pull further and further away from Wawa. I inflicted a great deal of pain on this man, and I will forever regret my carelessness. He loved me the way I loved Mery Jo—madly, uncontrollably, unwillingly. As I drifted away, he held on for dear life. Inevitably, Mery Jo began to pick up on the treacherous emotional inequality. She resented me for pulling away from Wawa and disturbing the delicate balance we all hung in, but still she couldn't bear to lose either of us. These feelings went on, unspoken, for weeks on end.

Until one day, when I walked in on Mery Jo and Wawa making love, without me. Normally, that would've been fine. But this time, seeing the two of them together didn't feel right. I became physically ill. I knew right then that, for my own well-being, I had to get out and move on. I ran back to my room. On the verge of hysteria, I booked the next available flight back to the States. Two days later, I was gone. We were over as quickly as we began.

We spent our last two nights together pouring our hearts out and coming to terms with the fact that it was truly over. We had fallen victim to a devastating, self-fulfilling prophecy. We had milked our polyamorous affair to the very last drop, like addicts chasing illusions of their first high. Until three people, once filled with so much love, had fallen to pieces.

It's been almost a year since we swept away the mess. We've all moved forward with our lives. We carry with us a new sense of strength and awareness. Yet, it took a long time for me to accept this experience and put regrets aside. I felt as though I had put myself through useless pain; that I'd have been better off never involving myself with either of them. For a long time, I didn't even allow myself to think about Mery Jo and Wawa. But I soon found out that pain and hardship carry with them an opportunity for growth. It's pretty ironic that I went to Peru with hopes of confirming my heterosexuality, and left the country one hundred percent homo.

Yet, without that drawn-out ménage à trois, I may never have pursued my current girlfriend. It hasn't been long, but already she's shown me love as it should be seen: wondrous, fulfilling, secure, and real. For the first time, I am truly loved by the woman who holds the keys to my heart. It sounds so simple, I know. But when you're a girl like me, struggling to come to terms with her sexuality, reaching this point can be, and has been, mind blowing and life changing.

When it's all said and done, it's amazing how profound a first-time experience can be. Personally, I would rather not think about the passionate friendship Katie and I shared. Or even think about my first love, the girl who tore my heart out of my chest. But, as I've come to realize, regardless of how embarrassed or devastated I may have been, this was all time well spent. My first passionate friendship, my first lesbian hook-up, and my first love brought me my first girlfriend. Without all these firsts under my belt, I'd never get seconds.

# deak

∙∙∙∙∙∙∙∙∙∙∙∙∙∙∙∙∙∙∙∙∙∙∙∙∙∙∙∙∙∙∙∙∙∙∙∙∙∙∙∙∙∙∙∙∙∙∙∙∙

My sophomore year in high school, I attended an alternative, artsy school. It was the eighties. I had a Mohawk, wore a ripped leather jacket, and sported a plethora of piercings. I fit right in, and I would eventually graduate along with the twenty-six other degenerates in my class.

I was dating one of the few jocks, a boy named Justin. Before me, Justin had dated Carrie. She was a freshman at Bryn Mawr, and Justin was still clearly in love with her. Justin and my best friend, Dave, would always talk about the "legacy of Carrie."

Despite dating a jock, I was involved in the performing arts at school. That Christmas, we performed *The Curious Savage*, some inappropriate play about people in a mental institute. I played the lead. On opening night, Justin came with Carrie. She was on break from Bryn Mawr. I knew she was going to be there, but I didn't know what she looked like or who she was.

I remember looking into the crowd and seeing this girl who was so amazingly beautiful. And it came to me all at once why these boys were so intrigued by her, why everyone was in love with her. It struck me so hard. It was this instant connection. I had never really had those feelings for a woman before. I didn't think much of it. I was only fifteen and didn't understand my feelings.

So, Carrie had a long winter break and we started hanging out. One night, I was having a party in my basement, which was what we did in high school. There was drinking, making out, and whatever else was going on. As I was refilling my red Solo cup, Dave pulled me into the bathroom and told me he needed to talk to me.

"What is it, man?" I asked.

"Carrie's really attracted to you," Dave said with a devilish grin.

I'll never forget that feeling; I never felt more alive in my entire life and I haven't felt the same way since. Words couldn't begin to describe the intensity of that moment. I knew, right then and there, that I was at least bisexual. I didn't want to be gay.

Cut to Carrie and me getting drunk together and making out, which led us straight upstairs to my bedroom. We lay down on my bed, and for the very first time, I made love to a woman. I'd never even kissed a woman before, let alone been naked in bed with one! I'd never even had sex with my boyfriend!

That night, I lost my virginity to a nineteen-year-old woman. Twelve years later, Carrie is still the most beautiful woman I've ever made love to—and, trust me, I've bedded lots of chicks in those twelve years. Emotionally, what I felt that night with Carrie was amazing, but, looking back, the sex was not. It was kind of scary. She popped my cherry. When we finished having sex, she called her boyfriend on speakerphone and told him what had happened. It was absolutely devastating to me. I wasn't exactly sure why. But I had fallen for this girl.

While she was away at school, I wrote Carrie an endless

number of love letters. She never responded. I didn't care that she was in college. I didn't care that she hadn't written me back. I was head over heels in love with this woman.

Once in a while, Carrie would come back to town. We made love a couple more times, but it was never quite like the first time. It just never is. . . .

# eileen

St. Patrick's Day—perhaps as heterosexual as a holiday can get, with all the green beer and drunken guys. When my friends and I decided to do an Irish pub crawl on March 17, I probably should have foreseen the ensuing night from hell. I hadn't yet come out to any of my straight friends. At the time, I had just two lesbian friends, and they were a couple. They weren't always eager to hang around gay bars and wait for some girl, any girl, to pick me up, and I certainly had no skills of my own. So, in a futile attempt to give the straight girl in me a fighting chance, I blew out my hair, put on my nearest pair of uncomfortable shoes, and caught the next Long Island Rail Road train to Manhattan.

I tagged along with my friends from pub to pub, but all I could think about was Henrietta Hudson's, the lesbian bar downtown. It was in that bar that I had kissed, and almost but not quite slept with, a woman for the very first time not so long before. So, about four bars into the night, and after I had given my inner straight girl ample time to assert herself amidst a bunch of smelly, sloppy, drunken men, I informed my friends that I didn't feel well and wanted to leave. I promised them I was perfectly okay getting home on my own.

I made it outside, jumped in a cab, and headed for the gay ole intersection of Hudson and Morton streets. In retrospect, I was thoroughly desperate. Walking into a lesbian bar alone is a daunting task, but I *needed* that atmosphere. I needed to see women kiss each other, to feel comfortable instead of overpowered and manhandled. I didn't care how lonely and wretched I felt or looked; I just wanted to *be* there.

I sat myself in a corner, ordered a drink, and looked around. Eventually, two women, one blond, one brunette, approached me. They were drunk and giggling. The two women began to ask me questions. What was I doing there? I didn't look gay, was I sure I was gay? Why was I there alone? Did I want to kiss them?

I answered all of their questions and, yes, I did want to kiss them. I wanted to get that feeling of softness back, the soft skin, soft lips, silky hair; that feeling of melting into someone else. I had never experienced that gentle passion until I kissed a woman. I assumed that it would accompany all of my future same-sex exploits. I soon learned that I was very wrong.

I was kissing both of these women—a lot—but there was no melting or burning desire. For twenty-three years I had wondered and worried if I really did possess a sex drive. I was scared I could never be both emotionally and physically attached to another human being. This lack of feeling in the make-out session disturbed me tremendously. I decided the only way to confront my confusion, once and for all, was to go home with one of these strange women and have hot girl-on-girl sex. That way, I figured, I'd know if I was a grade-A lesbian or just grade-B for bi.

The brunette asked me to go home with her. Once we made it back to her apartment in Queens, we talked for a while.

She asked me if I "wanted to." "Yes," I replied emphatically. We were in her bed, naked. She was completely hairless and very smooth. My mind was racing, trying to figure out why this still felt so wrong. Why wasn't I turned on? How could I not be into my first real-live lesbian sexual experience, when I had callously broken up with my boyfriend of three and a half years in order to experience women? After a heated online flirtation, and a few brief visits to some gay bars, I was certain the gay life was for me

When it was over, I lay awake for an hour or so. When it became light out, I jumped out of bed to find a train home. I shook her, told her I was sorry but that I had to get home. She woke up, walked me to the subway, gave me her number, and said good-bye.

I felt like I had just turned a trick. I wanted to take a shower, but, more importantly, I wanted to know what the hell was wrong with me. Why I was so revolted and turned off. I went as far as to consider joining the Peace Corps, where I could channel all of my latent sexual desire into making the world a better place.

Fortunately, it didn't take me much longer to figure out I still had plenty of same-sex desire. Soon, I was back at Henrietta's, this time armed with the newfound knowledge that when it comes to sex, lesbian or otherwise, physical attraction is far more complex than gay/straight or male/female. In the end, "sparks" almost always trump genitalia. So, my first time was a lousy one-night stand. Since then, I've had my share of meaningful relationships . . . and fantastic one-night stands!

## one more thing . . .

As the old joke goes, "It's hard losing weight when you're a lipstick lesbian. Can you imagine trying to eat Jenny Craig when you've got Mary Kay on your face?" All kidding aside, just beware: You may not fall in love with the first woman you sleep with . . . but you might just fall for the first *lesbian* you sleep with. The closeness of sleeping with another woman is almost addictive. You'll see. Like they say, if homosexuals are gay, then lesbians must be ecstatic.

4

CHAPTER FOUR:

# coming out

Closets are for clothes.

—Bumper sticker

Coming out of the closet is the most empowering step in a gay person's life.

You should come out when you are absolutely ready. Remember, you can disclose your sexuality at your own pace. Though this can be a confusing time, you are in complete control. Some women come out with a bang and some choose to come out slowly. The latter reveal their sexuality to a few people who are close to them. Next, they move on to friends and family. More often than not, the workplace is the last step. Being comfortable with yourself is contagious, and others are likely to follow your lead and become comfortable with you as well. Even though it takes a while to embrace your self-realization as a lesbian, one hopes family and friends are going to respond with joyous expressions of unconditional love. But, if you don't get the response you were hoping for, just realize that it may take some longer than others to come around. Try to be as patient with them as you were with yourself.

Coming out is like being born again. Steer away from letting your gay identity define you, but realize it is a new and important part of your life. Here are some pointers to help you learn as much as you can about yourself and what you want out of your new life.

## Take some "me" time

Many women spend a lot of time fearing other people's responses to their homosexuality when they come out. Instead of letting thoughts of rejection consume you, spend the time getting to know yourself. Don't become a recluse, but concentrate on your own well-being and emotions. This will make you stronger, more confident, and accepting of yourself. Be the same person you've always been, but take some quality "me" time to evaluate your transition.

## Friends and family

When the time has come to address family, friends, and the rest of society, say it like you mean it because you do. Be prepared for anything and try your best to tell people face-to-face, out of respect for yourself and also for your loved ones. Just remember, the longer you hold it in, the longer you are living a lie. How many times can you answer the question, "So, do you have a boyfriend?" with a runaround answer?

## Aftermath

Your friends and family should accept that being gay is just one part of who you are. But don't forget how long it took you to figure this out, and understand that it may take some people longer to embrace your revelation. Some will be easier than others, but everyone deserves some time. Remind them that your sexuality does not define you. You are still the same girl you were ten minutes ago, when they thought you were straight. However, you might find that, once you come out, you obsess over being gay. Is this a good thing? Not necessarily. Is it is a natural thing? Absolutely. Try to get out there and get involved. A new world is at your fingertips.

## It's not all about sex

When you come out, you may feel like people are visualizing you having sex with another girl—and they might be. Coming out and sharing your sexual identity will evoke sexual thoughts; that's just the reality of the situation. With friends, anything goes; that's what they are there for. Family, on the other hand, is a different story. No one wants to picture their parents having sex; why should your parents want to picture you having sex? Regardless of gender, it's never a comfortable conversation, so be sensitive.

## It's not set in stone

Just think of making any new commitment in your life; be it moving to a new city, starting a new job, or getting involved in a new relationship, these things take up major mental and emotional energy. We come out in many ways, over time. Coming out is about being free. It is about love and acceptance. Find what makes you happy, and take your best shot. You may conclude that you have to make a switch—or that you are a switch-hitter!

## Celebrate good times

As relieved and excited as you may feel, there is sure to be some precariousness about taking this new step. If you're a beginner to the gay scene, you may feel a lot of self-doubt; if you're an old pro coming out late in the game, it may be easier to adapt to a queer lifestyle. Don't forget that coming out should be a celebration of who you are.

## Coming out: May it RIP

Perhaps someday, people won't need to "come out." One's sexuality won't always default to straight. But, for now, it is a necessary step in achieving a happy, fulfilling, gay lifestyle. Make peace with the present, because nobody knows what the future holds.

Coming out is about readiness—a time of awakening and acceptance of one's own destiny in a balanced way. Currently, GLBT issues are in the forefront of political campaigns and the media, but it takes strength and a lot of courage to embrace your homosexuality. Take comfort in knowing that you can come out as whatever you like, to whomever you like.

# lauren levin

••••••••••••••••••••••••••••••••••••••••••••••••

Coming out is never easy. But, being able to date women and just be who I am is part of the reason I moved from Minnesota to New York. Liking girls was something I'd hinted about to a few chosen friends of mine, never with full disclosure. I tell everyone everything, and keeping this secret was brutal. I needed to tell people who I really was. However, I knew being true to myself meant being truthful to my loved ones. I was fed up with lying to my friends about dating women on the down low. I didn't want to hide any longer. I was bursting to come out of the closet, and to face the repercussions, whatever they might be.

In honor of Hanukkah, I gave a much-needed gift to myself. I decided to reveal my gayness to a different person on each of the eight nights of Hanukkah. The first night, I'd tell my two best friends, Kat and Alex. I was incredibly scared, but I felt they should be the first to know. We met for dinner at a restaurant in Chelsea.

"Could this place be any gayer?" Alex asked as she looked around the flamboyantly gay dining room.

Yikes, this was going to be harder than I'd imagined.

"Let's order some wine," I suggested.

"No, thanks, I don't really feel like drinking," Kat replied.

"We'll have a bottle of your finest cabernet," I smiled at the waiter, ignoring Kat.

After a couple of glasses of wine, I told my friends I had something major to tell them.

"You're moving," Alex said, deadpan.

"Hmmm, no." I stared at my friends. "Please know, this is incredibly hard for me to tell you guys."

"Just say it, Levin," Kat blurted out.

"Okay. Well, you guys, I want you to know that . . . I'm umm . . . I'm gay." I held my breath, anticipating their response.

Immediately, Alex grabbed my hand.

"That's wonderful," she said. "I love you no matter what and am so happy for you."

Kat continued, "Levin, that is fabulous . . . thank you so much for telling us. Alex is right—we love you. Oh, and by the way, I'm not that surprised!"

"Yeah, me neither. I hinted to my mom about you freshman year." Alex sighed.

They asked me a million questions I couldn't yet answer. We laughed the night away, and I felt as though a huge weight had been lifted from my shoulders. Alex explained that she'd always sensed I was looking for something to ground me. Finally coming out was what I'd been searching for all along. Turns out, being gay wasn't it. But it was a step in the right direction.

Well, I had tackled my first night of Hanukkah. Only seven left to go . . .

I'm pleased to say, the rest of the week went phenomenally well. Every single friend I told was outrageously supportive and proud of me.

I hoped my family could be as amazing as my friends. But, for some reason, I doubted them. My grandparents were so proud of their granddaughter in the big city, with the big-time job. I was their shining star and couldn't bear to let them down.

But the anxiety got to me. I was to go away on a cruise with my family in just under two weeks. Every night before vacation, I went out and got smashed. Every morning, I came into work with a hangover that could kill a small animal. Nothing got done those days at work, and my boss took notice. One day, I didn't even show up. That night, I received a call from my boss.

"Lauren, this is job abandonment. I don't know what's gotten into you . . . but, Lauren, you are fired," Tim told me.

Wha happened? I was a top salesperson at Google; they couldn't fire me. Tim went on to tell me my behavior was utterly unacceptable and could not be tolerated. I begged and pleaded with him, but it was no use. I had lost an amazing opportunity.

When HR called me the next morning, I explained what was going on. I told Brad, the director of HR, that I was in the midst of coming out of the closet. I was frightened to tell my family. Brad was enormously compassionate and told me he'd talk to my boss. An hour later, I was back on the job.

Vacation finally rolled around. It was the first time I'd be going on a family trip since my parents split up. I'm lucky enough to have two families who wanted to spend the holidays with me—one of the few benefits of their messy divorce. I would spend a week on a cruise with my dad's side, followed by a week with my mom's side on the island of Tobago. Surrounded by an inescapable body of water in both places, I thought these would be the perfect settings in which to share my news.

Instead of pulling each member of my family aside and telling them in private on the cruise, I decided to kill seven birds with one stone. My dad's side of the family sat around a large circular table.

"I'd like to propose a toast," I declared, lifting my wineglass in the air.

"Hear ye, hear ye!" cried a smiling Grandpa Al.

"This is to the most wonderful family, who provides unconditional love and support to everyone at this table. . . ." I caught my breath. "I'm gay."

No one said a word. You could cut the tension with a knife. Finally, the table behind us clapped.

"Did you hear what I said?" I asked my family. "I'm gay!"

"Yes, we heard you, Lauren," Grandma Jeanne replied. "But, just let this sink in."

Eventually, the table got louder, and everyone expressed their love and support for me. Later that night, my grandmother advised me to stop revealing so much cleavage. "You want to bring home a nice Jewish girl, don't you?" she asked. You can switch genders, but some things will always remain the same.

The next day, everyone expressed to me that they wished I'd told them individually, in private. I promised myself not to make the same mistake twice. I still had my mom's side of the family, the tougher, more traditional side, to come out to. My brother and best friend, Drew, still didn't know about me. He couldn't make it on the cruise, so I waited till we were in Tobago to tell him in person. I called him into my room and sat him down on the bed.

"Brother"—as I affectionately call him—"I've got to tell you something."

"What's up, Laur?" He looked nervous.

I looked him dead in the eye. "I'm gay."

"Seriously, what took you so long?" he asked, giving me a bear hug. "Thank God. This answers so many questions I've had about you," he said, as if the weight had been lifted from *his* shoulders. I guess those times I forced him to watch *High Art* over and over again had tipped him off.

I only wish my Grandpa Lloyd could've taken the news so well. His reaction baffled me. He told me it was just a phase.

I've always respected my grandfather's opinions immensely, so to hear him so quickly brush off my disclosure was demoralizing. What bothered me more was that I began to question my sexuality yet again. I could tell he really didn't mean what he'd said. Like the rest of my family, my grandfather just wants what's best for me. But he didn't know how to deal.

Ironically, Grandpa Lloyd has become one of the most supportive and accepting people in my life. He's definitely my only family member to ask if I'm a tit or an ass girl! I told him I'm a face girl (though usually I'm an ass girl). When I visit him and my Grandma Rhoda in Boca, they are always there to give me girl advice. Their advice to slow down and let the apple of my eye chase me has certainly come in handy.

Despite being a once boy-crazy teen, my family (minus Grandpa Lloyd) wasn't all that surprised that I'm gay. I'd never had a serious boyfriend or expressed sincere interest in finding one. Additionally, my friendships with girls had always been unusually close. There had been a lot of talk and speculation amongst my family before I came out.

After returning from vacation, and successfully conquering the most difficult step in my life, I did what any crazy lesbo-about-town would do. I threw myself a fabulous "I'm Coming Out" party at Hotel Rivington, the trendiest of trendy Manhattan hotels. Everyone and their mother showed up. My party was a hit, a perfect send-off to go out and conquer the girls!

## lauren blitzer

I think coming out to your family and friends is one of the hardest parts of being gay. Not only are you making the fact that you are gay "official," but you are hoping and praying that everyone will be as accepting as you have learned to be of yourself. It's out of your control, and you can't predict how people are going to react. Yet, since it takes most of us time to figure out our sexual identity, we must remember to give those around us ample time to accept the news.

Like most, my coming-out story is complicated and hard in so many ways. It was when I had come home from London. I felt as though I were on top of the world. I was in love and accepting of who I was. I felt grateful for my discovery. I never once thought being myself might be a bad thing.

As Sheryl Crow says, "If it makes you happy, it can't be that bad." And why shouldn't life work that way? Little did I know, loving myself would end up hurting the people who had always given me their unconditional love: my parents.

Growing up, you are led to believe your parents live by the mantra, "I just want my kids to be happy." Well, I think most parents want their kids to be happy. But, as I soon learned, there is a catch. My parents wanted me to be happy as *they* viewed happiness. What happiness meant to me became insignificant.

In a somewhat conservative Manhattan household, "being happy" is becoming a doctor, a lawyer, or an investment banker, and providing for yourself in the same way you have always been provided for. I wanted to make money and provide for a wife as much as the next nice Jewish boy. However, my parents weren't so down with this gender role reversal. It was something that they never considered. As far as baby boomers go, my parents fell into the "Did You Hear About Hugo and Kim?" *Bye Bye Birdie* category as opposed to the "Age of Aquarius" *Hair* camp. Boy likes girl, girl likes boy. End scene.

They weren't informed of my homosexuality until about a month after my return from London. I was having a really hard time being back in NYC, without Rachel. She had opened a door for me, and without her, I didn't want to function. I was driving myself to extreme dehydration from crying so much. Every morning, I woke up crying, and, every evening, I cried myself to sleep. I missed her so much. It got even worse after she came to visit in late August, just three weeks after I had left her in Brighton.

As expected, we spent the most amazing time together. She stayed with me while my parents were away at our country house. We immersed ourselves in one another. I told her not to leave, but she had to get back to work in London. At the airport, I watched her go through security and then waved good-bye, tears flowing from my eyes. I was a mess.

When I returned home from the airport, eyes swollen, devastated, I did everything I could to try and hide from my family. It worked for a few days. I went to my sister every time I thought I was going to have a mental breakdown. She tried her best to calm me down. She reassured me that it was going to get easier. With time, I would adjust to the pitfalls of being in a long-distance relationship. I was listening, but nothing she was saying helped. I felt helpless, torn between the happiness of finding myself and the misery of being so far from the woman I loved.

Finally, my mother confronted me about why I was being so distant and emotional. I didn't know what to say, but she was persistent in wanting to know why I had been crying for weeks. I asked my sister to come into the room, and as I sat there choking on my own tears, my sister said, "Lauren's gay. That's why she is crying."

My mother looked at us with astonishment. She wasn't sure what to do or what to say. I could see her mind running wild, and disapproval was written all over her face. A few minutes went by. "Wait, what do you mean?" she asked. Her words were so blunt, so to the point, so painfully raw. And hearing them come from my mother made me really uncomfortable. I was just getting used to telling people that I was a lesbian, and this was not a question I anticipated having to answer.

Julie repeated, "She's gay, Mom. Do I have to spell it out for you?"

"Well, I would have never guessed that was the case—never. You are so girly and love to shop. I mean . . ." My mother just sat there trying to come up with the words to make sense of this revelation. She kept trying to say something, yet nothing came out. I offered up a Valium, and she took one and went to her room. I knew my mother was in shock. I knew my sister was in even more shock: She had just outed me while secretly being gay herself.

Needless to say, the whole situation was extremely difficult and painful. Watching your family disapprove of something dear to you that you have no control over is a horrible feeling. My being a lesbian was hurting everyone around me, yet nothing I was doing was intentional. I wondered why just being me could drive the people I loved most to tears. I didn't feel like I had anything to hide, yet I felt wrong and ashamed.

I finally got myself to sleep that night. I talked myself into believing everything was going to be all right. I woke up crying the next morning, and tried to get myself together for work. As I walked out of my bedroom with my sunglasses on, I heard someone crying on the couch. My mother was sitting on the white couch in her robe, with her head in her hands. I sat down on one of the chairs and asker her what was wrong.

She looked up at me, tears streaming down her face, and said, "This is my fault, isn't it? I should have been a better mother. I didn't do the best I could."

"Mom, that's not it. This has nothing to do with you. You were great. You *are* great." I comforted her, tears rolling down my face too.

I went over to her and hugged her, but I could feel her disappointment. She was trying so hard to make sense of things, but nothing was working. What she didn't realize was that no one was to blame; this wasn't even an issue that required blame. It is just who I am. That was the hardest thing for her to come to terms with.

I sat there for some time, not knowing how to get up. All I wanted was my mother's approval, more than anyone else's. I left her on the couch and walked out of the apartment, feeling myself fall apart with each step I took away from the place where I no longer felt at home. After a few days, my mother couldn't carry the burden of knowing alone, and she confided in my father. My father was equally disappointed, if not more so. His avoidance of the topic and verbal disapproval were all it took for me to have an emotional breakdown.

All my life, I had worked hard to make them happy. I went to a great college; I was athletic, polite, social; and I loved my family more than anything. But, suddenly, none of that seemed to matter anymore. I was not a raging drug-addict-slut, pregnant at the age of nineteen. And, sadly, I think even that would have made more sense to them. Being a drug addict had a cure, and being pregnant by accident had a solution. Being gay had neither. And fighting against it was a waste of energy. But, what most parents don't realize is that if they try to fight it, they will feel their child slip right through their fingers.

I didn't want that for myself. My family had always had a strong foundation; I didn't want it to fall apart. I knew what I had to do, and it required some tough love. As much as my parents wanted to hear that there might be a ray of hope that I'd end up with a man, I couldn't give it to them. Sure, it would've softened the blow, but it would still have been a lie. I kept to what I knew was true, and wouldn't back down. I knew deep down that some-day they would be okay with it. They had to be, or else they would lose their daughter—and, one day maybe, both their daughters. I knew my parents would never let it get to that point.

That year was a tough one for my family. We had always been close, and now I felt such an incredible distance from them. I had to keep my personal life to myself. I really started to rely on my friends as my family.

If only coming out to my parents could have been as easy as coming out to my friends. They accepted me for who I was without thinking twice about it. When I came out, my parents were the only battle I had to fight.

It took them a few years to come around, but they finally did. Each day got easier, and being gay became a non-issue. It no longer felt like something that needed to be hidden or condemned.

My entire extended family has been unbelievably supportive. My grandmother's only comment was, "I love you." Once again, they began to see me for all my accomplishments and for the person I'd always been. They were so proud of the woman I'd become. My sexuality is a part of me, not a defining characteristic—just one permanent piece of the puzzle I like to call life.

## lauren m.

There was some unspoken rite of passage that I went through when I realized that, no matter how many times I sprinkled the occasional boy hookup in with all the girl hookups, I still wasn't "straight." It was around this time that I knew it was time for me to finally be honest about who I really was.

I had graduated from college and entered the corporate world. In the two years since moving to New York, I'd had one serious relationship. It was as normal and committed as any relationship I had ever known—and it happened to be with a female. We ran errands together, we went grocery shopping together, we fought, we laughed; we did all the things I saw my big brother do with his girlfriend at the time. We were together and in love, and so *not* straight. But, even though we weren't hetero, I still didn't understand what made our relationship any different from my brother's. Or from any of the other dysfunctional couples walking around.

But we had something to hide, something to prove, something that bonded us that they didn't have. It was our secret. Jen was my first girlfriend. It started off so intense and with so much magic that I didn't see any feasible way around her love. In retrospect, it was such a deep, dark, and reassuringly foggy love that I may have gotten lost in it. Jen was disarming and genuine at first, yet she had a kind of devilish and mysterious side. She was ambitious and outspoken, yet quiet and timid at the same time. We were together for almost two years, and I can now say, without any hesitation, that I don't regret it. She was the reason I realized I had no choice but to give myself to the next person I fell in love with, regardless of what I thought other people were going to say or think. Thing is, though, it took a lot to get me to that point.

After Jen, I left it up to a race of the genders: Whoever could "get" me first, whoever I could "get" first. I dated, and hooked up, and did that whole twenty-something entry-level mating dance. But the magnetic force that drew that me toward women was always much more powerful than the pull toward men. I could never seem to get myself to the emotionally vulnerable state with guys that I could with girls. No matter how hard I tried. I needed an urgency and an intensity that men couldn't provide me.

About seven months and a lot of gender hurdling later, I met the first girl I ever committed myself to. Verbally, at least.

I let her call me her girlfriend, and, more importantly, I let myself call her mine. Some of my friends nearly fell to the floor the first time I introduced her to them. "Helen, this is my girlfriend, Lauren" (yes, we were both Laurens). It was like I had decided, what seemed like overnight, to declare what they had known for well over a year, if not longer. Don't forget, just two years prior, Jen was always by my side, craftily dodging any signs of affection, but fooling no one. So, when the time came for me to finally admit my romantic relationship with a female to friends, the most common reaction was, "Oh, this girl gets the word 'girlfriend,' she must be important." And she was.

I'll try not to get into a laundry list of all the reasons I am with who I am with. All the girls in between, the guys in between, the times I got caught with my hand in the cookie jar; the times I had to lie to my family about why I was hung over or who I was out with, or explain that rugby wasn't only for lesbians, that being an English major and a rugby player and liberal-minded and a little bit crunchy did not make me a lesbian. Instead, I will say that, when the time came for me to acknowledge that what made me happy and at peace inside myself was to be in the company of women, the "coming out" scenario kind of just landed in my lap.

The setting was the Turks and Caicos Islands, on a family vacation in April 2005, three months into a pretty fast-moving relationship with my current girlfriend. The first girl I let hold my hand in public for longer than five minutes. The first one I really gave myself to fully, without restrictions, without rules, without guarding myself. Here I was, twenty-three years old, my twenty-six-year-old brother, his fiancée, my mother, and my stepfather. The setting was nothing short of picturesque. We had a week at our disposal, a blank canvas of time without appointments, schedules, meetings, or subways. For a family as busy as we were, this was unheard of.

My brother and his fiancée are both in high-pressure corporate finance positions in Manhattan. My mother is a pharmaceutical-sales-rep superstar who works long days and barely has time to make the transition between being "salesy" and slipping into normal mother/daughter conversation mode. If I call her Monday through Friday between the hours of nine a.m. and six p.m., I should not expect to speak with the woman who gave birth to me. Rather, I will be speaking with a saleswoman, complete with her "phone voice," the rushed conversational tempo she usually reserves for the doctors she calls on. She is brilliant at what she does; she just has a hard time turning it off. This makes emotional issues difficult to delve into without the help of a seven-day stretch of empty time laid out before us. And then there is my stepfather, who owns his own executive search firm (it's worth noting that he is the most hippie-hearted of the bunch.) The bottom line is, we were all busy, highly stressed, and really in need of this vacation together to reconnect and relax . . . and, apparently, to confront my sexuality as well.

One night, my mother telephoned the "kid suite" before dinner and asked me if I'd like to get a drink while the rest of the clan showered. Just her and me. Honest to God, when I hung up the phone and got into the shower, I knew that she had called more or less asking me to prepare myself for a conversational C-section. I knew we were going to order two rum-runners, move onto the beach, and sit, Indian-style, looking at each other, waiting for the other to make a verbal turn onto Lifestyle Avenue.

She initiated it. I just drank as fast as I could and braced myself. I had never been so quiet. She asked me how it was to be twenty-three years old in 2005. How I dealt with all the uncertainty and temptation in the world. She talked about how it was when she was twenty-three. How she hadn't had as much to think about, or as many options. My mother had married at twenty-four, was pregnant with my brother and living happily in the Midwest, working at the Mayo Clinic at twenty-five. Times were different, clearly. I was working in a big-girl corporate job in a city that never sleeps, having gone to college at a huge state school, having played every sport in the book, having been on lavish vacations—with the pictures to prove it.

But the most important thing she was trying to say was that I had the luxury of choosing whichever kind of person I wanted to be around, what kind of romantic pursuit I wanted to, well, pursue. She knew she was talking to a girl who was never really afraid to go against the grain. I think it scared her. Diversity was mine for the taking. She said that, when she was twenty-three, she had had an "experience." I almost choked on my straw.

I don't remember every word of our two-hour conversation on the beach that day. But I do remember that it only took her about twenty minutes and a quarter of her rumrunner to get right to the point. She was highly skilled and I was highly receptive. Her talking, talking, talking. Me listening, listening, listening. Then the boulder, a direct question that required the respect of a direct answer.

"Honey, are you in love?" my mother asked me.

Breathing, breathing, breathing. "Yes." I cried and cried and cried.

"It's Lauren, right?" Hugging, silence. Hugging, crying. Silence.

"Yes."

I was happy we did it, happy it was finally over with. We walked back up to the suite and, unbeknownst to me at the time, the remainder of that vacation was eerily indicative of the remainder of my twenty-third year and most of my twenty-fourth. There was lots of placating and not confronting. There were quiet nods of half acceptance, born completely from an unconditional love for me. The other half was the antithesis of acceptance: complete and utter denial and an unwillingness to take me seriously. I was going through a phase, they told me. This "other Lauren business" was immature, selfish.

I love my family more than anything on this earth. I tried to understand every contortion of every reaction they could have felt up to this point. And even if I don't *understand* every single one, I am *open* to every single one. I guess that's the difference between someone who struggles to be understood, and someone who never has to worry about being *mis*understood.

Am I happy I had my C-section on the beach in the Turks and Caicos? Yes. That day, I gave birth to a bouncy little thing I named "Honesty." Like most babies, she is a pain in the ass sometimes, but, mostly, she fills me up with pride and a sense of accomplishment. I feel free and less weighed down by my own obscurity. I hated the unnecessary stress that came from lying to my parents or my brother in casual conversations about where I was last Saturday night. I hated having to make up some reason why I couldn't hang out with Drew and his fiancée on a random Saturday afternoon. When they would call and, inevitably, I'd be sleeping in with my girlfriend or making her breakfast, like normal couples do. Still, I do miss their calls.

Ultimately, the stress and deceit that comes with having to constantly fib for the stupidest of reasons is not necessary. It wasn't necessary then, and it isn't now. I feel strong and independent and liberated. At least now, I have shared a little piece of myself with my family. They can now come and peck at the rest of who I am, bit by bit. This time, at least, they know that, whatever they ask me about, they'll get an honest answer. The only way to get where I'm going is through the truth. Do not pass truth, do not collect happiness.

# rachel

I never considered that I was born this way. I had boyfriends; I just never really liked them. No restrictions were ever put on me, or on my feelings. My family was very accepting. They always allowed me to flourish and succeed. Their nonchalance about sexuality is probably the reason I was able to recognize my feelings for someone other than my boyfriend at a relatively young age.

Like most gay women, I discovered my feelings for women when I noticed myself getting unusually close to my best friend, Gabriella. I was sixteen and had a boyfriend at the time. She did too, but most nights when the four of us hung out, it ended up being just her and me together. We talked, drank, and generally enjoyed each other's company. I had, for the first time, thoughts of being with another girl. I would get these intense visuals in my head, and I couldn't seem to stop. Even though my Latino family was more liberal than most, I didn't know what to do with these sexual thoughts. I literally slapped my hand, scolding myself.

Yet, as Gabriella and I got closer, I decided to fess up to my feelings for her. I recognized that what we were doing was somewhat of an unhealthy process. Two girls this close, not acting on their feelings, couldn't be good. Thank God, when I told Gabriella how I felt, she revealed the feeling was mutual.

It was amazing. I no longer had to pretend that my raging hormones didn't exist. We were inseparable, and Gabriella became my first girlfriend. We promised not to tell anyone, including the boy I was dating. Keeping silent made life hard. But I was finally really happy, in a way I had never thought possible.

Gabby and I were always together and so much alike, we'd constantly tell people we were sisters or cousins. It's not that we were ashamed, or embarrassed; we just weren't ready to take that step. We were still feeling our way through this exciting new relationship. But all of our privacy and secrecy would soon be put to an end. I auditioned for MTV's *The Real World*.

I had to start talking about it. I was going through the interview process and they wanted to know what my current relationship status was. I tried to be vague, but the network called both my boyfriend and what seemed to be my girlfriend. The producers saw the double life I led, and they liked it. I was dating this girl while still getting involved with members of the opposite sex. I was what they considered to be bisexual. Sure enough, I made the cut and was cast for the show. And I broke up with Gabriella. I'd decided to take on this experience alone.

Before the show aired, I decided to come out to my mother. When I say that Mom was supportive, I mean above and beyond supportive. She reassured me that the most important thing was that I was happy. My mother wished she'd had the same kind of happiness glistening in her eyes that I had in mine. I never had to gain acceptance from the most important person in my life. She loved me for me, and this sure as hell was me.

Most people have to come out to their family and friends individually. Well, I came out on national television in front of millions of people I didn't know. I was Rachel, the gay cast member. Once the show aired, not only did my friends and family embrace me, the gay community did as well. I didn't even know this community existed. I was exposed to this world of women who were just like me. Surprised and excited, I found many other girls with whom I could relate. I was so incredibly happy to be applauded, just for being me!

I got so much positive response from people in the Midwest, the South—everywhere. People saw past the gay thing and realized it didn't make me who I was; it was just a part of me. Being on the show spiraled into something amazing. It allowed me to open people's eyes to the fact that many lesbians look "straight." There is no one mold to fit in, in order to call yourself gay. I never sought acceptance from all those viewers who tuned in to see my personal life unfold. I was happy with the choices I'd made and with who I was. I wanted to come out because I was sick of hiding. Sure, I ditched the closet in the most dramatic way possible, but, hey, I'm a lesbian—I'm supposed to be a drama queen!

## one more thing . . .

You can come out as whatever you like to whomever you like. No matter your past, no matter your future, your sexuality is your own. Make peace with the present. Be more concerned with your character than with your reputation. Your character is who you are, while your reputation is merely what others think you are.

CHAPTER FIVE:

# 99 problems, but a chick ain't one: how to meet women

Introductions are tricky in a lesbian relationship. It's a word game. To my friends she's my lover, to strangers and family members in denial she's my roommate, to Jehovah's Witnesses at the door she's my lesbian sex slave, and to my mother she's Jewish and that's all that matters.

—Denise McCanles

As an "out" lesbian new to the scene, gay girls and curious girls alike may flock to you. However, you must always remember to check IDs at your door. One of Levin's first suitors ended up being sixteen. Though she was cute, some laws just aren't made to be broken.

After the immediate hype following coming-out dissipates, meeting chicks can seem difficult. There are times when you'll be envious of butch women, as every average Joanna assumes they are gay.

A questioning girl may approach a butch woman and flirt with her, assuming she is gay.

On the femme end of the spectrum, you walk down the street and no one even questions your sexuality. You look straight, so you must be straight. That's why it's critical to get your gaydar on point, girls! If you want to screw around with other feminine women, tweaking your gaydar is imperative to realizing who you have a chance with, and who will simply take your advances as flattery.

Good gaydar or not, the key to meeting babes is allowing yourself to do so. Just by putting yourself in the right situations, you dramatically improve your chances of finding love. Before you even go on a date, it's necessary to familiarize yourself with our short, but sweet

# sapphic rules and regulations to dating

**Tweet, tweet:** Women are nesters. At times, we seem desperate to mesh and not at all wired to date. We often get involved with one another for the wrong reasons. And most of the time, the level of compatibility isn't found out until much later in the game, when it's too late to casually say good-bye. Dating is healthy, and we should try to prolong it. It's a way to measure your compatibility with someone without having to figure it out a year down the road. Take your time, and enjoy the ride.

**Escape plan:** Whether you're at your apartment or hers, an exit strategy is a must. A sure bet for fleeing would be the family excuse, as face time at family events is nonnegotiable. You either have a brother's birthday party, aunt's luncheon, or cousin's graduation party to attend. It seems as though every weekend your family has something to celebrate! These excuses always leave you with a clean getaway, or at least will have her out the door, as you pretend to get ready for your familial function. Once you're alone, the relief sets in, and you can go about ordering your break-fast from the diner and enjoying your Sunday afternoon.

**Split the check:** It's nice to split the check, especially when getting to know someone. There is no need to expect to be paid for, or vice versa. Treating is always nice, and being treated is equally fun. If the date goes well, you can always pay in full, and suggest she get the check next time!

**Trim the bush:** I think this is self-explanatory.

**Follow the golden rule:** The lesbian world is small. You never know whose ex-girlfriend or best friend will be the next love of your life.

**Don't get overwhelmed:** There are many different ways to meet women, and in a short time, you can tap all available resources. Firstly, there are a plethora of online sites. Next, there is the more "traditional" way: bars. Lastly, get on the phone, girl. Mutual friends are sometimes your best bet.

# be educated in top and bottom theories

Lesbian dating is so complicated. You must try to come up with a consistent theory to apply to the behavior and dynamic between two women in order to understand the mating rituals. Our friend Kate is thirty-four years old, and it's taken her years of dating and relationships to make some accurate assumptions about the dance we girls call dating.

**Lucy and Ethel:** Don't make the mistake of succumbing to the text-book version of top and bottom. A perfect example of a top and a bottom would be Lucy and Ethel from *I Love Lucy*. Most people would think Lucy would be the top if the two of them were in a relationship, but, actually, she would be the bottom. Lucy is constantly getting herself into trouble and is quite a mess. Ethel is always helping her out, but in the end, Lucy gets credit for cleaning up her act. Yet, Ethel never makes Lucy feel like she should be given all the credit. She makes Lucy feel good, and in return, Lucy needs Ethel. Ergo, Ethel is the top and Lucy is the bottom.

**Boyfriend?** Many girls think they are a top because they like the role of being the "boyfriend." However, this stems more from growing up surrounded by heterosexual couples than what actually happens beneath the sheets between two women.

**Role play:** Clearly, being with a woman can be confusing. There is an instant feeling of being able to relate to a girl because you're one too, but it's not that simple. People get accustomed to choosing roles, because their parents did. So, you get involved with a woman and, suddenly, there is no husband or wife. Being aware of the dynamic between tops and bottoms is crucial to understanding lesbian relationships.

**Bottoms:** aren't what you think they are. A bottom can fix the electronics around the house or kill the spider the top is screaming about. It's all about control. The bottom is the one who runs the show. The top feels empowered by the bottom's need to take control. Bottoms make sure everything is in place and plans are made and confirmed. After that, they inform the top of the schedule. Roles develop from there, but they are not necessarily defined from there.

**Tops:** like to be in control of certain things. Whether it's driving the car, holding doors open, or handling the remote control, the top needs to have her jobs. It is just as much of a job for bottoms to make tops feel a certain way. As this job is somewhat taxing, bottoms love flattery. Their acceptance and reaction to it makes the top feel special and important. The two play off of each other perfectly. A good top knows exactly what to say to get to a bottom's heart: "I need you." We melt at those three words. The bottom feels important and needed and the top is taken care of.

It's no longer about what you look like; it's all about the way you function. The control you choose to delegate and the needs and wants you must have fulfilled will determine your Lucy or Ethel status. This theory is important and has proven successful.

# online dating

Thanks to the Internet, you can get laid! Online social networks can be about a lot more than just racking up your number of "friends." The online world of women is enormous, and it can do wonders for your love life. Creating a killer profile is key to online dating. Revealing your sexuality online can seem scary, but how else will other women find you? Once you check the "seeking women" box, you improve your chances of chowing box.

**Give good testimonial:** How can you be lovers if you can't be Friendsters? We lesbians tend to be quite a funny group of gals, so don't be scared to reveal that brilliantly witty side of your personality! After penning your winning profile, make sure to add a flattering and recent picture of yourself. Avoid profiles with no pictures, it's straight-up sketch. A no-show "female" could end up being a forty-five-year-old overweight man in Mississippi. Clearly, a no-go.

**Do your homework:** If you do in fact see someone who catches your eye, send her a message. It's always nice to mention something you read in her profile. Next, be sure to check on when she last logged on. This way, you can track when she reads your message. If she hasn't logged on since 'Nam, chances are, she won't be reading your message for quite some time.

**Location, location, location:** Friendster and Myspace are great sites for finding old friends and picking up new ones. However, in terms of online dating, the sites with romantic inclinations are best. The popularity of a site has a lot to do with where you live. Gays in the Midwest really like planetout.com. Here in New York, nerve.com is popular.

**You've got some Nerve:** Nerve is a more risqué dating site, and it is connected to the Spring Street Network, a dominant online dating network. They distribute profiles to most of the cool websites all over the web. But beware of selecting the option stating that you are seeking EITHER men or women. You may soon find your in-box filled with sketchy dudes looking for some hot girl-on-girl action to partake in. It is free to have your profile displayed on Nerve; however, sending someone a message costs money. Buy the cheapest package, and start sending notes and winks to girls galore. Replying to messages is freeżżżżżso send that honey a note back!

**Gay Friendster:** The gay version of Friendster is connexion.com. However, this site is more conducive to dating for gay men than gay women. But it's fun to check out, nonetheless. Connexion is growing rapidly, so don't be surprised if you get hit on in ten seconds flat.

**Oy vey, she's gay:** Our new favorite site is qjew.com. For all you Jewish dykes, this is the jdate.com for queers. Like they promise, the site is more fun than Hebrew school. Qjew is relatively new, but it's sure to attract the JAPs, and the ladies who love them, in no time. Before Levin came out of the closet, her grandma in Boca Raton offered to create a profile for her on jdate. Quickly, she declined. She should have had Grandma check out qjew.com!

**Do you have a light?** The most traditional of sites is match.com. Most of the women on Match are comfortable with their sexuality and looking for the real thing: commitment. There is also pinksofa.com, which we've found to be a waste of time. It's not user-friendly, and the girls tend to live outside the U.S.

# bars

• • • • • • • • • • • • • • • • • • • • • • • • • • • • • • • • • • • • • • • • •

**Is that sexuality you're wearing?** You can meet all sorts of women at gay and straight bars alike. One strategy for seeking "down" chicks at straight bars is to wear your sexuality on your sleevežžžžžiterally. Be an "Urban Outfitters" lesbian! Rock shirts that read, "No Boys Allowed," "I Go To 'N Sync Concerts To Get Pussy," or even a camouflage trucker's cap that says, "Bush Master."

**Make sure your gaydar is ON:** Even if your lesbo outerware doesn't proclaim your sexuality, it is, at the very least, a conversation starter. When boozing at straight bars, your gaydar needs to be on full-force. Check out who is checking YOU out. When you a spot a pretty lil' lady, if you're bold enough, walk up to her. Compliment her on her shoes or jewelry and take it from there. Many times, revealing your sexuality is not necessary. If you sense it might scare her away, don't bust out the flashing rainbow lights right away. If she starts talking about boys, you might want to move on. Next, please . . .

**It's a jungle out there:** At gay bars, of course, there is no need to reveal your stripes. Shit, girl, you're standing in a room full of Zebras. Welcome to the sapphic safari! At first, gay bars can seem intimidating. It can feel scary and foreign, especially when you're alone. But, if you have friends to accompany you, you may become an avid dyke-bar patron. Even if you're dating someone, it's still fun to go out and be surrounded by so many chicks that also dig chicks. Lesbian bars/parties can be a total meat market. Don't be surprised if what looks to be a really odd sorority mixer feels more like a frat party.

# mutual friends

Mutual friends are a favorite route by which to meet women. Your friends know you, and they know their friends. Right off the bat, they can sense whether or not there will be a love connection.

**Don't be cruel:** Of course, being set up through friends requires being out. See how great coming out of the closet can be! It is important to be sensitive to your friend's friends. Even if you don't like who your friend set you up with, you should always be polite. Clearly, what happens is going to get back to the matchmaker. If you ever want to be set up again, make sure you are honest with your date from the get-go. If you don't like her, let her down gently.

# booty calls

Booty call *n* 1 : the act of calling or contacting a person for the sole purpose of having sex. 2 : a person that is the recipient of such a call

**Play the field:** Booty calling is as apparent in the gay world as it is in the straight world. Some women might feel ashamed participating in this type of behavior. Still, homo or hetero, just "hooking up" is perfectly acceptable. Too often, lesbians come out of the closet and become obsessed with finding a girlfriend. Experiencing different types of people and different types of relationships is important. All too often, women yearn for experience with other woman after they are involved in their first lengthy lesbian relationship. You might want to get all of that out of your system before you decide to settle down.

**Just tell it like it is:** With regards to booty calling, there are some specific standards to which two women should adhere. Firstly, you should be up front with your expectations when participating in a booty call. If you're not up for a relationship with the other person, that person should be aware of your intentions. Booty calls are purely physical. When emotions get in the way, things become tricky. Of course, as the emotional beings women are, keeping a relationship purely physical between both parties can be difficult. Being a gay woman may not be more fun than being a gay man, but come on now, few people have more fun than our faggy brothas.

**Don't believe the urban legend:** Booty calls do exist! We know women who assign their booty call the speed-dial 69 on their phones. Many women bide their time with another woman while they both search for the "real thing." The biding of time can come in the form of a casual relationship or, simply, a booty call.

**Figure out your coordinates:** Before entangling yourself between the sheets with a lover, you should define to yourself where you're at in life. Are you needing to be single, and needing to have sex? Are you single and looking for love? Or are you just playing the field and feeling things out? It's important to know where you're at when becoming a member of the booty-call club.

Becoming obsessed with meeting someone and subsequently falling in love creates a path leading to utter disappointment if your goal is not soon attained. Keep your goal in mind, but detach yourself from it. Your experiences and memories will get you where you want to be, and they build character. Never miss out on life, and never regret anything. Your heart is an open valve; let loose, let go, and have a ball.

# lauren blitzer

The drama of the dating scene, the closeness of lesbian social circles, and the thrill of the kill is enough to make anyone run for the hills. Although intimidating at first, you don't have much choice but to jump into the dating scene, and get soaked in a sea of lesbos.

I had been in relationships for the first four years of my gay life. I met my first girlfriend in the London lesbian scene; my second, immediately thereafter, at a NYC lesbian bar; and the third, a "straight" girl who, two years later, is gayer than a rainbow triangle. Only recently have I borne witness to the true life of dating within the gay community. Everyone knows everyone, or so it seems. But, as with anything, you've got to dig deep for those diamonds.

Unfortunately, I was too emotionally scarred to dig too deep, and, for some reason, I didn't have much "game" when it came to talking to the ladies. In fact, I've been told my game is having no game. It works for me. Regardless, being approached by women I had no interest in, while watching women I wanted to talk to from afar, baffled me. I wondered how I was going to make this dating thing work when all I knew was the security of a serious relationship. From what I had heard, dating was healthy and fun. No commitment, no ball and chain . . . But I wasn't sure I was cut out for the single life.

Well, after giving it a few months, I finally learned how to disassociate sex and love. I became the fun and independent person I am at heart, and thrived in my new space. I was okay with being alone, and in fact, I was happy being alone. Once I realized and established this, I was ready to go out there and have some fun.

I met my friend Chris at a bar in Chelsea one night, along

with her girlfriend and a bunch of their friends. I was looking forward to going out and hanging with her friends, especially Thea. I had seen Thea at a party a few weeks prior and thought she was very good-looking. Thea had long dark hair, big beautiful eyes, and a very nice body. I wasn't sure how to talk to her or what my approach would be, but I did the best I could. I said hello to everyone, and gave Thea an especially nice, long hug.

I mingled with her friends, and kept my eye on Thea the whole night. Things were going well, and we were having a great time. Eventually, everyone got tired of the straight scene and wanted to go to Cubby Hole, a notorious lesbian bar in the West Village known for its cheap décor and fabulous jukebox. Thea and I took a seat at the bar. She had to know I was interested. I was being obvious about it, regardless of whether or not the feeling was mutual. I was a little buzzed, which took the edge off.

We talked for a while at the bar, each time leaning closer into each other, as her friends took breaks in their conversation to watch us. Everyone was eagerly anticipating the kiss, which seemed inevitable. But it was unclear who was going to make that first move.

So, out of nowhere, I leaned in and kissed her. I wasn't head over heels for this girl; I had just met her and she seemed cool. I knew I was attracted to her, but I also knew there was nothing about her that made me want to start a relationship. Most of the time, I know off the bat whether a girl is girlfriend material or not. But I figured this was what dating was about. And, yes, it was very fun; she happened to be an amazing kisser and I was enjoying myself. We continued to make out in the street, and in the car home, but I dropped her off and went up to my apartment solo.

The next day, I knew that I was on my way to being a dating machine. I liked Thea, but I didn't want a relationship with her. I wasn't ready yet. I was going out and meeting people, and it was amazing. I knew I had to be clear with her as my phone started vibrating with text messages from her the following day. This was all new to me, but I was going to be honest with her about my intentions.

As the lesbian world works, she moved in for the kill pretty quickly. She wanted to see me that night, and I decided that probably wasn't the best idea. But, when Sunday rolled around, I did invite her over. She came in dressed casually, smelling like Burberry. I sat her down and said, "I just want you to know that I am in no position to get involved in a relationship. I've been committed most of my life, and I really want to just have fun. I'm not sure what you are looking for, but this is where I stand."

She looked at me with a smile and said, "Wow, I am really happy we are on the same page." I sighed in relief; I didn't have to deal with someone wanting more from me than I could give. We hung out for the rest of the night, watching movies and talking.

Well, let me be the first to tell you, ninety percent of the time, people say they are on the same page as you mainly because they want to tell you what you want to hear. Once you tell a girl you don't want anything, all of a sudden, she wants everything. I didn't realize this until the following Tuesday.

I was at *Teen Vogue* doing my daily tasks as an assistant when a deliveryman came through the office, holding flowers. Everyone was looking around, hoping the flowers were for them. I definitely did not think they were for me. He asked aloud, "Do you know where Lauren Blitzer sits?"

"Uh, that's me," I said, turning a brighter shade of red than the roses he handed to me.

I walked back to my desk as my best friend and coworker, Perry, shot me a "Who sent you those?" look. I shot back a look of death as I opened the card, avoiding everyone's prying eyes. As I suspected, the roses were from Thea.

But, wait—hadn't I just had a conversation with her about not wanting anything? Was I in the twilight zone? I seriously pondered if that whole conversation we had was perhaps a dream. I was beyond confused, as I tried to decide how to tackle the issue. I called my older, wiser, lesbian friend Amy, desperately seeking an answer. She replied with, "Okay, say good-bye. You don't need this right now. Say good-bye . . . thanks."

In between fits of hysterical laughter, I realized Amy was right. This just confirmed that Thea and I were not on the same page, and that I was really happy being alone. Sure, I could have the comfort and security of a new relationship with Thea. But there was no way I was going to settle or move too quickly if it didn't feel right. And this didn't.

I kindly thanked Thea for the flowers and explained that this was not what I was looking for. She was an amazing girl, but I wasn't looking for anything serious. I felt bad, but we really weren't at the same place in our lives. She didn't put up a fight, and we've remained friends. The flower incident has even become a joke between us.

Fortunately, my short-lived relationship with Thea made me aware of how many women there are out there, once you just put yourself on the line. Whether you get rejected, reject someone, date, or fall in love, it's a risk that can, at times, seem scary. But in the end, dating should be something that excites you. It's all fun and games—until someone gets hurt. That's why you should be up front about where you stand. Women do tend to move in a little faster than men, so keeping to a slow, steady pace in the beginning does build a stronger relationship over time. It also maintains the excitement of seeing someone new, the butterflies and the longing. Take it slow; you've got all the time in the world.

# claire

●●●●●●●●●●●●●●●●●●●●●●●●●●●●●●●●●●●●●●●●●●●●●●●●

"I saw your profile and had to respond, but this is embarrassing" was my opening line to her. I was responding to a personal ad on a popular same-sex dating website, planetout.com. Yes, I'd caved. I gave Gay Big Brother my $12.95 for the chance to be writing this e-mail. It was my first time on such a site. Had I kept reading her ad, I would have noticed her personal e-mail address tucked away at the bottom, in code; it was the mark of someone more experienced and resourceful. And there I was, twenty-two, naive, and looking for my first date . . . with a dyke.

Growing up in north-central Wisconsin, I'd come out to myself somewhere around age twelve, but I didn't have any same-sex experiences until high school. Even then, I was just playing juvenile kissing games. The fear of rejection (or banishment) from our mostly white, Christian, suburban existence simply scared the life out of me. So, I enrolled at the University of Minnesota, a mere grain of sand on a beach of students sprawled over the enormous campus.

Throughout my freshman year, I dated one guy exclusively. At the same time, I was sucking face with sorority girls while checking out the bona fide lesbians walking the halls. I needed a meaningful relationship. My boyfriend and I broke up as soon as I told him of my deeper interests and needs. At that moment, I opened the door to my life as a lesbian.

"The Scene" can be very intimidating and daunting for a newcomer of any sort. But, when you are ready and the opportunity presents itself, you often find what many refer to as beginner's luck.

My roommate took me to a campus bar where I could pass security with my fake ID, and on the ticket that night was a local band fronted by a lesbian. It was like the clouds parted as

I found my way in, following the band and keeping my eyes open for other lonely baby dykes. For the most part, her show lived up to my expectations, and among the granola-eating uptown crowd sat the lesbos. A lot of them seemed older, more conservative, and tamer than I was. Even so, I thought I was starting to make some progress although I felt like there was something deeper and bigger that I was missing. I couldn't seem to find the younger crowd, the avant-garde kids, and more than anything, I was simply lonely.

Unfortunately, I started to lose steam, and confusion and insecurity set in. Maybe, with my long blond locks and girlie jeans, I wasn't lesbian enough. I felt I was being overlooked or simply ignored. I gave up for a while and fell into another relationship with a man. After my twenty-second birthday, I just couldn't take it anymore. I needed out once and for all. I was feeling so out of place, it was making me sick.

One fateful Friday night, when I just couldn't watch *Foxfire* one more time, I plopped down in front of the computer. I Googled something to the effect of "lesbian personals," and there it was: planetout.com, the website that would change my life.

As I searched the personals, I felt rather discouraged. Headlines as desperate as the mullet-dykes who wrote them jumped out at me. There were bi women, women with kids, women who were married to men. At one point I felt I was counting teeth. Wide-mouthed-bass T-shirts, four-wheelers, and mentions of deer hunting all made me cringe. I guess that, when you live in close proximity to "the North Woods," you have to expect these types. I knew what I liked, but I wasn't seeing it. I was looking for a soft butch who liked femmes, someone who looked edgy, wore black, and was open to tattoos and smoking cigarettes. *Ding ding ding!* I suddenly came across one who seemed pretty close to what I was envisioning. So I wrote to her (only after paying my $12.95, of course).

Shortly before my online endeavors, searching for some kind of acceptance, I decided to cut eighteen inches off my hair. I was trying to fit in and be recognized, a feeling that threw me back to middle school. As much as I want to say it didn't help, it did. Cutting my hair gave me confidence, and for the first time in years, I started to feel like I belonged.

When my online crush and I met, we clicked right away. As I anticipated, she was older, wiser, and more versed in the Minneapolis lesbian scene. She had been out for ten years, and I figured that, more than anyone, she would know where all of those elusive lesbians were lurking. The Crush started taking me to lesbian hot spots, and I felt like I was a boy going through puberty. There were women crawling all over these bars and nightclubs, and I just couldn't get enough. It didn't take long before my eye started to wander, and my pockets filled up with phone numbers. I embarked on serious crushes and endeavors with a number of women. When, one by one, they fizzled out, there was always another chick there to fill her shoes. Not only was I being accepted, I was being pursued. I was often jokingly referred to as "the fresh meat." I had no idea how absolutely aggressive some of these women could be, and I was becoming a little full of myself. It's said that it takes one to know one, and often that's true. You are just as good as the company you keep. Needless to say, it wasn't long before I found myself caught in the middle of some age-old dyke drama.

It's no small fact that people tend to move in circles. What I innocently overlooked was that there had been a lesbian dating scene way before my arrival. People knew people, people hated people, and everyone had dated a certain somebody. That girl's ex was my new love interest, but I was also interested in the person whom everyone had dated. It was neverending, and more confusing than I can express.

If you are familiar with Showtime's *The L Word*, you may recall the six-degrees-of-separation board that Alice keeps. Most lesbians would agree that the degree of separation in our community is roughly two. Two degrees of separation, and before you know it, you've got most of the lesbian community in your bed, simply by association. Despite warnings from friends who were privy to my crushes, I forged on in my quest to know as many facets of this world as I could handle. Consequently, I was burned more times than not, and I learned my lessons the hard way. Some called me a player, but I didn't know what I wanted, and I figured that gaining experience with different types of women would ultimately lead me to my life partner. I wasn't going to settle and I knew that I wasn't finding what I wanted in the bar circle. I decided to pull away from all the drama.

That original online crush really opened my eyes. In getting to know her, I learned about her experiences at the Michigan Womyn's Music Festival. It's a woman-born-woman-only festival that happens in the woods of eastern Michigan every August. My peers and I affectionately refer to it as "dyke summer camp."

Two years after our meeting, I went to the festival as a staffer, and once again, I felt my life changing. There were women from all over the world, from all different walks of life. The festival was twenty-eight years in the running, and was attended by the original founders as well as festie-virgins like me.

Since my experiences at the festival, I have been more aware of the women around me. I've noticed lesbian women throughout my community and have met love interests in the most random and mundane places. I've met girls in the grocery store, the place where I rent movies, at concerts, or just out riding my bike. After you've been out for a while, your gaydar becomes attuned to your environment. You are able to pick up vibes in the little things women do to show their interest in you. The butches strut; the femmes parade.

I first saw my girlfriend at a weekly event at a gay bar in the warehouse district of Minneapolis. As much as any adult can modify their behavior, you sometimes have to realize that you can't teach an old dog new tricks.

The date I was on that night brought me back to the middle of the lesbian social circle. I blissfully and drunkenly basked in the spotlight. This is where The Crush comes back into the picture. She was no longer my crush, just a friend now. She'd been dating a woman, Mara, whom I found myself attracted to. I was getting out of an on-again, off-again, year-and-a-half relationship when The Crush broke off her courtship with Mara.

Again, I saw a window of opportunity. Yes, sometimes being a lesbian can feel as though you're a mere pawn in a girlie game of Candyland, everyone racing to find their princess in the land of milk and honey. And it was bad judgment on my part to cross a line other women wouldn't even step close to; but then again, those two degrees of separation are hard to avoid. When The Crush exited both our lives by moving out of the state, despite any standing alliances, Mara and I started dating.

So there I sat in a little underground bar, with my ex's ex. We were being relatively introverted, and chose a table near the empty dance floor. A few minutes into our date, three other women filled up another table. One of the women caught my eye, but at second glance, she wasn't my type. I figured she was new on the scene, just having turned of age and still sporting Abercrombie & Fitch, head to toe. It was not until a few months later that I would see the young'un again, when my ex's ex, Mara, became *my* ex.

In ending the relationship with Mara, I was forced to take

stock of where I sat in my relationship life. With the faux pas of ex-dating, I had definitely hit the bottom of the barrel. I felt like I was out of options, and even contemplated a move myself. My job was stalling out and my friends were leaving town. I had been going out a lot, delving back into the bar scene.

While sitting in my friend Michelle's house, pulling off a bottle of cheap wine and watching *The L Word*, we decided to hit a ladies' night at a gay-friendly bar. We walked into the bar, half in the bag, and there sat the underage Abercrombie girl from the basement bar. Only now, she wasn't looking so Abercrombie. It dawned on me that she was the fresh meat now. She was mini-me. I played it cool, and my friends and I proceeded with our pool game, when halfway through it I realized the new girl was hovering over the railing, staring me down. A few drunken words were exchanged, enough to know that her name was Melissa. Despite some initial hesitation, I gave her my real phone number, figuring the only thing I had to lose was the pool game she was interrupting.

After a long Saturday night out, I awoke the next morning with what I thought was the flu. It had been three days since I'd given Melissa my phone number and she hadn't called. Soon enough, she became the least of my worries, as my physical condition quickly deteriorated. I was in and out of consciousness by the time my friend Michelle rushed me to the emergency room, the first in a string of visits that would eventually end in a diagnosis of toxic shock syndrome.

As I sat alone in my studio apartment, recuperating, I found my way back onto the Internet, again searching lesbian personals. I had developed an opportunistic infection called impetigo that had spread along one side of my mouth, creating a nasty scab. As if I didn't already look like hell after almost dying, I now had Mini-me to find and contend with.

Much to my delight, I came across Melissa's roommate on

one of the websites and sent her a message, telling her to have Melissa call me. Ironically, at the same time I'd posted the message, Melissa had signed onto the website and intercepted it. She called me, and for the next week we had marathon phone conversations. I began feeling better, even giddy, with this new connection with Mini-me. She assured me that she would overlook the repulsive scab if I agreed to finally meet up with her. Pushing my narcissism aside, I agreed to drive out to her apartment. The initial meeting was a bit rough, but a few shots of Jagermeister later, we were off to a gay bar, where we danced all night with some of my friends. After that night, I never thought of Melissa as Mini-me again.

The evening after our first date, Melissa and I spoke on the phone and expressed that we'd really like to see each other again—soon. The night was getting late, but I wanted to drive the twenty minutes to her apartment to see her. By the time I got there, she'd fallen asleep. However, I wasn't about to leave without seeing her. Repeatedly calling her proved futile, and throwing snowballs at her window was equally useless. Playing Columbo was a bit of a rush, giving me a shot of adrenaline that helped me ignore the freezing weather. I decided to sit patiently outside the security door until a tenant let me pass. I made my way up the stairs, finding her door unlocked. I knocked a few times, announced my arrival, and walked in. She was there, sleeping on the couch, with a little drool hanging on the side of her mouth. I startled her, she cursed at me, and the rest is history.

Melissa and I became inseparable. We've now joined the hordes of lesbians on the U-Haul mailing list. Early on, I knew she was a woman with intelligence, dignity, and self-respect. My life would be enriched simply by having her by my side. Everything I'd been looking for was materializing. Like today: There were laughs and fights, but always something to be learned. My journey to find my partner has come to an end.

But nothing about the journey has been storybook or without struggle, confusion, and, at times, desperation. Dating and meeting women in any situation can prove difficult, but always being open to new things, without losing sight of yourself, is an invaluable lesson to learn. The old cliché holds true: Unless you are able to love yourself, you will never truly be able to love someone else. Being proactive and taking charge of your life will pay off in more ways that just attracting a partner. Believing in yourself will take you as far as you can imagine.

# paige
...........................................................

My first night at a gay bar almost scared me straight. I was eighteen and questioning my sexuality. I was living alone in Boston for the summer, and decided to act on my burning desires. I thought I'd try my luck at a gay bar. As quickly as I stumbled in, I stumbled out. The majority of the women were mad-butch, and no one talked to me the whole night. I was the saddest girl to ever hold a martini. Moreover, I didn't even want these chicks to hit on me. They were *sooo* not my type. If this was what being a lesbian was about, I was as straight as they come.

Thankfully, I soon realized that being gay had to do with liking women, not looking "dykey." I came out at twenty-five. Quickly thereafter, I went to LA to visit my gay cousin, Brenda. Brenda is ten years older than me and has been out for a while. We were at a bar chatting up some chicks. Things were going well, and I could tell Bren was into the cute brunette she was talking with. Quite loudly, I threw out the fact that we were both gay. Bren gave me a little kick in the shin, and glared at me.

After the girls left the bar, Brenda turned to me. "Dude, that was *suuuuch* a rookie move," she screamed. "Here I was imagining walking my dog on a Sunday afternoon with that chick, and you go and lay out the gay-cards. So not cool."

In retrospect, my cousin was right. Who knows if anything would have happened with those girls, but my declaration of our homosexuality might have scared them away. Now that I bat in the major leagues, I try not to reveal my stripes too early.

Upon returning home from LA, I received a message from my friend Jenna. She told me she wanted to hook me up with a cute gay friend of hers, Nicole. After hearing about Nicole and looking her up on Friendster, I was intrigued. She was a couple years younger than me, from Boston, cute, and a graduate of Princeton.

We spoke on the phone, e-mailed, and instant-messaged before our first date. When the day finally rolled around, I was very excited to finally meet her. Dinner went well, and soon after, we were listening to Coldplay and making out at her place. We decided to meet up with some of my friends. An hour into our evening out, Nicole got out-of-control wasted. Her clinginess, sloppiness, and neediness completely turned me off. I wanted absolutely nothing to do with her.

The next day, Nicole called to apologize, and I decided to give her another chance. Lord knows, I've experienced many a night of making a total drunken fool out of myself. She came over with a long stemmed rose and we watched *Donnie Darko*. Unfortunately, I was way more into the movie than I was into Nicole. At work the next day, I IM'ed her that I thought it was best for us to just be friends. Nicole proceeded to put up weird messages like, "Once you see that your whole perspective is out of whack . . . maybe you'll love me if I fade to black." Well, Nicole certainly faded to black, but I never did love her.

Nevertheless, I almost lost my friend Jenna over the sticky situation. I learned it is necessary to be sensitive when fooling around with your friend's friends. I probably should've called her and let her down gently, instead of in a quick IM.

Sure, I've gone on some horrendous dates, but there have been many more phenomenal ones. My gay friend Jayson set me up with two of his lesbo friends, Dana and Tara. Dana and Tara were both cute girls, and they'd broken up with each other a couple months prior. As if there wasn't already enough lesbian drama, I was e-mailing and talking to both these girls at the same time. Shit hit the fan when they each found out. But Jayson had been right: I totally dug both of these chicks. After I calmed them down, they began to understand that I'd just come out and was only trying to make friends.

Dana is pretty, Ivy League–educated, butch, and undeniably hot. She's completely my type. Her ex-girlfriend, Tara, was cool but too feminine for my taste, as I was for hers. I might be a femme, but I love me some butch women.

I never went out with Tara, but Dana ended up becoming a very close friend of mine. Dana and I went out a couple times, but she wasn't feeling it. I was pretty sad about her rejection, but I soon got over it. The rest of Dana's friends were hot and androgynous looking. She set me up with her best friend, Michelle. Bingo! Had I never revealed my flaming lesbian status to Jayson, I'd never be able to call Dana a close friend, and Michelle the love of my life. It can be hard to put yourself on the line, but the easiest way to meet women is to come out and admit you like them.

## one more thing . . .

So, be it in a bar, on a website, or through friends, there are many ways to meet women. Just open your eyes, mouth, and heart and soon enough, someone special will come along.

CHAPTER SIX:
# the intensity between two women

We're sure you've heard the joke, "What do lesbians bring on the second date?" Answer: "A U-Haul." Like it or not, many times that exaggerated stereotype proves true. Most women long for commitment, so lesbian relationships tend to progress rather quickly. Our heterosexual friends laugh at us when we come to them with serious relationship problems after our third date with a woman. Women like to communicate; we love to talk. And be it by phone, e-mail, or IM, two girls who like each other are going to talk—A LOT. Come on—we already have "our song" picked out by the second date! From what we've seen, the time it takes two chicas to "connect" can be much quicker than with a man and a woman. The intensity in a lesbian relationship builds quickly. You may fall in love (or is it lust?) for a girlie so fast it will knock your socks off. Here are some things to keep in mind when getting involved with one.

## The epidermis affect
After you shed some clothing, the intensity will only increase. You may feel more connected to someone after you rub against their naked body. For this reason, it's best to hold off on having sex with someone you consider special, until both of you are sure you feel a

deep emotional connection. It is just as important to mesh well with someone outside of the sheets as it is between them.

## No means yes?

Intensity is what makes sex between women better than chocolate. However, it can sting you just the same. Rejection is hard, and for many women, it only fuels our desire for what we can't have. Women will try anything to win each other over, time and time again. We may send each other flowers or the lyrics to romantic Air Supply songs. With regard to lesbians, no hardly means no.

## You've got a great set of emotions; wanna cuddle?

A basic difference between men and women is the male propensity to rank sex and sexual attraction as integral components of a relationship. For many lesbians, the role of sex is minor. Instead, holding and caressing are the more highly valued physical activities. In those cases where making love *is* a critical component, it is often because of the emotional intimacy sex symbolizes. The propelling "drive" in some lesbian relationships is to meet emotional and nurturing wants and needs, and these yearnings tend not to be sexualized to the same degree as in male homosexual relationships. For the female homosexual, oftentimes "emotional attraction" plays a more critical role than sexual attraction.

## Avoid being a suction cup

In a loving relationship between two girls, there is a capacity for a particularly strong attachment. However, some women's behavior indicates a fragile relational bond riddled with fear and anxiety. For example, we see fears of abandonment and/or engulfment, struggles involving power (or powerlessness), and desires to merge with another person to obtain a sense of security and significance. Additionally, many women choose a partner they not only admire, but also literally want to *be*.

## Believe it or not, before her you were still you

During the course of a lesbian relationship, one might find the "highs" to be very high, and the times of conflict, extreme. Excessive time together, frequent telephoning, disproportionate card or gift giving, hastily moving in together or merging finances—these are some of the ways separateness is defended against. It is not uncommon for lesbian lovers to have a "can't live, if living is without you" kind of feeling toward each other. One friend told us, "In the beginning, she made me feel little. I wanted to be noticed by her, I wanted to be special to her, and that want took over my mind. I don't know how I would live without her. Before she came into my life, I was so empty."

## SWF didn't end well, did it?

For anyone, this extreme dependence on someone else's love is scary. Yet, both of us have fallen prey to it. You may feel like you can't breathe or your heart physically hurts because you need this woman so badly. Before getting involved with someone, it is important to take a step back and reflect on your lover's qualities, not on what is lacking in your own life. You should be in a relationship for the right reasons. Don't succumb to pressure, premature ultimatums, or your own fear of being alone.

## So good they should make it illegal

Although the intensity between two women can turn obsessive, it is the best thing about being a gay woman. We crave the closeness, and can only seem to find it with another girl. From conversation to sex, the bonds between girlfriends makes everything (except breakups) better.

Intensity is harder to ignore than a slap in the face. It's amazing, life-altering, and all-consuming—in other words, it's wonderful. As with everything, keep your priorities and perspectives straight, because you clearly are not.

# lauren levin

If anything makes me gay, it's the butterflies in my stomach and the incessant pounding of my heart that I feel when I fall in love with another woman. Daniela made me feel that way. She made me feel light-headed and heavy-hearted. I could never get this girl off of my mind.

Daniela took me by surprise. The girl I'd been looking for never appeared in one of the many gay bars I frequent: She showed up in my in-box. We went to high school together, and the news of my coming out had clogged the phone lines and e-mail boxes of everyone I'd encountered since age eight. It bothered me that something so important to me was the subject of petty gossip. And then I got an e-mail from Daniela.

Daniela had just returned to Minnesota from a year away, surfing, in Peru. While there, she'd fallen madly in love with a woman—the woman she was now trying to get over. She was still in the closet to her family, and to some of her friends.

In our first round of e-mails, Daniela pretended not to know who I was, that she had stumbled across my MySpace profile randomly. Later on, however, she revealed that she'd known me in high school. When she heard I'd come out, she was intrigued. It's not every day a girl from Edina comes out of the closet, let alone a "popular" girl. D told me it took her a month to garner the courage to send me a friendly e-mail, and I was glad she finally did.

The intensity between us was like nothing I'd ever known. We pined for each other; every day, our longings grew more pronounced. We had phone sex, and we liked it.

I believed that upon reuniting with Daniela, when I kissed her for the first time, everything would suddenly make sense. Our desire for a relationship, long distance though it would be, wouldn't be so much a decision as a powerful act of fate neither of us could deny. We were both ready to fall in love again.

As much as our intensity lured me, it scared me all the same. Having the opportunity to get to know someone before laying eyes on her as an adult is rare and special. We valued our deep connection and reveled in its uniqueness. Still, it was difficult to communicate strong feelings without being able to stare into each other's eyes. It had only been a month, but already we had endured some major ups and downs. One week, I told D I needed distance. Sure, there were thousands of miles between us, but I needed more. The next week, she told me not to come to Minnesota. Finally, we found a balance between our desire and our fears. We agreed not to hook up with anyone else. We admitted to falling in love with each other.

When Daniela said "I love you" for the first time, it was the best thing I'd ever heard. No one I'd been so enamored with had ever reciprocated my love. Turning to her was like falling in love when you're ten. We read each other's minds. It was both a blessing and a curse.

My arrival in Minnesota was to be a surprise. D thought I was coming to town on a Wednesday, but I was actually arriving on Tuesday. I spoke to her friends and endlessly planned our first encounter. They were to take her to a bar, where I would arrive soon thereafter. We'd said before that this would be the best way to meet, since we both wanted to tip a few back before a potentially awkward introduction.

Much to my dismay, my plan went haywire. Being that D and I spoke all throughout the day, she knew that if my phone were turned off, for even just four hours, I couldn't be anywhere but on a plane. I guess she didn't buy my "I've got meetings all day" alibi.

D arrived at the bar and told her friends that she knew I was in town. She wanted to punk me. D called me up and said she was heading to a bar, The Independent, to meet up with some friends. She told me she was wearing an all-red outfit.

"An all-red outfit?" I asked hesitantly.

"Yeah, babe, tonight I felt like sporting red shoes, red pants, and a red shirt," she said, sounding serious.

At this point, I didn't know D knew I was in Minnesota. I bugged out. I didn't want to meet this girl in an all-red outfit! I mean, other than Meg White and Elmo, who wears all red?

Hastily, I called up D's best friend, Taylor. "Taylor, I just got off the phone with D. She said she's wearing all red. Does she do that?"

Taylor began to laugh.

"What's going on, T—does she know I'm coming? Tayyylor, tell me," I pleaded.

"No, she doesn't know," Taylor replied unconvincingly.

"Taylor, tell me. Come on," I begged.

"Fine," he said. "She knows."

Ugggh. I was disappointed; there would be no surprise. However, I was relieved to learn that she was probably kidding about the red outfit. Surprise or no surprise, my friend Kelly and I were going show up at that bar to meet my girlfriend.

Kelly and I looked all over for D and her friends, but they were nowhere to be found. Finally, I glanced toward a pool table in the back of the bar. I saw a girl with long dark hair, wearing a vintage Stones tee and a snowboarding hat (cocked to the side, of course), and holding a pool cue. Not only was this girl the hottest chick in the bar, she was one of the most striking girls I'd ever seen in my entire life. I prayed it was *her*.

I turned around to inform Kelly of my hopeful hunch. Suddenly, my phone rang . . . it was D. I picked it up and turned around. The girl with the pool cue walked toward me;

she held a cell phone to her ear. We spoke as we approached each other, then slammed our phones shut and embraced. She smelled like the D&G Light Blue perfume that she said was her signature scent. She told me I smelled like mine, Stella. We stared into each other's eyes for the first time. And just like I'd hoped, everything suddenly made sense. I knew it would all be okay.

I bought D a drink at the bar and felt my legs shake and my palms sweat. Her beauty and confidence intimidated me; I was nervous and excited. D exceeded my expectations in so many ways. She held my hand all night, introduced me as her girl-friend, and was very affectionate overall.

That night, D came home with me, to Kelly's house. We both laughed as we entered the guest room. Kelly, the straight-est of all my friends, had been kind enough to set up our room as a lesbian lovers' lair. There were candles, rainbow coffee mugs, and the local gay magazine.

D sat down on the bed and pulled me toward her. We kissed. My entire body tingled. We made out like horny sev-enth graders discovering themselves, and each other, for the first time. The only thing that came off were our shirts. Falling asleep next to her felt so right and so natural. Waking up next to her felt like a gift from God.

We stayed in bed all day long. In fact, we stayed in bed all week long. We hardly ate, let alone came up for air. I felt child-ish and in love. Every day we went further, eventually doing anything and everything two girls can do. D was the first per-son I ever made love to. She opened my eyes to the difference between sex and love. She told me she was obsessed with my stomach; I fell in love with her dimples.

I was so happy doing absolutely nothing with someone. I could have sat in five hours of traffic with this girl and had the best time of my life. We traded all sorts of clothing, like only two girls can do. She wore my board shirts, I wore her T-shirts.

On my last night in Minnesota, we got motivated to finally go out on our first date.

D held my hand over the table. "You're looking at me differently tonight," she said midway through our meal.

She was right. I didn't realize it at the time, but I *was* looking at her differently. That night, I saw a sophistication in D I had not yet seen. Our conversation was deep and intelligent. We had gotten past the point of just getting to know each other and talking about how amazing we were together. We spoke about religion and politics. For the first time, I saw Daniela as the woman I loved, not just my cute little girlfriend. From the way she ordered the wine to the way her hair fell smoothly against her shoulders, everything about D turned me on.

"I *am* looking at you differently tonight," I told her. "I'm just so in love with you," I said.

"I am so falling in love with you, baby." D smiled.

Hearing her say that meant everything to me. I knew she loved me, but she had told me that it takes time to "be in love" with someone . . . like, months. She might have been right. Looking back, we were both falling fast, but I don't believe we were really "in love" with each other at that point.

We simply loved each other which was better yet. People fall in and out of love at the drop of a hat. Being in love is fun, but unreliable. When you really love someone, it doesn't matter if they bother you; you're still going to be kind and considerate. Being passionately in love with D is something that would happen in due time. I knew it would happen, and I looked forward to it immensely.

A couple days after our three-month anniversary, it finally did. Daniela had come to visit me in New York, and we'd had a rough week. I slowly learned the meaning of lesbian drama, as we started to fight about the littlest things. Two girls with their periods confined to a one-room studio, surviving on little food, is dangerous, to say the least. Both of us were broke and couldn't afford to leave my apartment. We lived on the eggs she cooked. I was on deadline, writing all day long. I couldn't lie in bed all day with her. I couldn't have her listening to music or TV while I wrote. Essentially, reality had set in. We had to function together as productive human beings, and do more than just make love.

One night, we got into a fight, the most explosive fight in our short herstory. As intense and amazing as the highs with Daniela were, the lows, and the fighting, were just as bad.

I can't even remember what that fight was about. But I will never forget the hour of silence that followed it. I knew there was something eating away at her; I just didn't know what it was. When I finally asked, Daniela told me.

"I don't love you as much as I loved my ex. I don't love you as much as you love me. I've been thinking this for a while," she said somberly.

My heart sank into my stomach. "What does this mean, Daniela?" I asked, not wanting to know the answer.

"I can't hurt you. I care too much about you," she said, still not looking into my eyes.

"Are you trying to break up with me?" I asked.

"I don't know, but I know things are not even, and I know how important balance is to you," she replied.

She called her best friend from home, who said she'd pay for Daniela's flight back to Minnesota. I called Julia, my best friend.

"You girls are crazy," she said. "One of you needs to be the guy in the relationship. Lauren, calm her down, tell her she's being irrational, and work this out. Love is not quantifiable, and every relationship is different."

I hung up the phone. Daniela didn't want to leave, and I

didn't want to let her. We could work through this. Although her words were painful, there was too much at risk not to listen. She assured me that she loved me, that the love we had was more fulfilling and pleasurable than anything she'd ever experienced. She loved her ex immensely, but it was a precarious kind of love. A love that had lasted a year: She'd gotten herself out of it just two months before we met.

Here we were, just three months into a long-distance relationship. I wanted to let her go because she didn't love me as much as the girl who had held her heart for a year. I'm impatient, but I had to give it time. She fell harder with each passing day, and I had to give her a chance to love me the way I loved her. I had nothing else to compare us to, and I couldn't hold the fact that she did against her.

The rest of the week was better. I tried not to think about what she had said. When it came time for her to leave, I shed some tears and kissed her good-bye. Two hours later, she called me from the airport. As her flight to Minnesota was boarding, she decided not to get on the plane. She made up some story about meetings to attend. She pleaded with the ticketing agent to let her stay one more night. Somehow, he was sympathetic to her needs and changed her flight, free of charge.

Daniela called me, excited, to say she'd be coming back home. She'd be back at my place in an hour. I rushed to borrow money from a friend, in order to pay for her bus back to the airport and a bottle of wine. I wanted to surprise her with something romantic and special.

Hastily, I cleaned my studio. Considering I'd been living in sweats and a ponytail all week, I cleaned myself up too. Two girls can tend to get comfortable together, forgetting to spice things up and even dress up for each other.

As I lit the candles on a folding dining table I'd never used, it hit me. All of this behavior was new to me. I'd even drained my bank account to support her while she was here.

I broke out my aunt's good china for a dinner consisting of tuna fish sandwiches and a six-dollar bottle of wine. On the stereo, I played the CD she'd made me, filled with love songs that reminded her of me. Watching the way Daniela pulled the best out of me was gratifying. I was good at being in love.

Daniela and I cried a lot that night, even as we made love. She admitted to being on the same level I was, head over heels in love. She'd come out of the closet; I'd changed her life. She turned my world upside down, and for the first time, I realized she loved me for the person I am. Girls have a tendency to jump the gun. We think we're in love, because we want to be. But it's nothing you can predict or control. It just happens.

With each subsequent visit, I fell deeper and deeper in love. When she'd leave New York, I'd become a bawling mess. I am not a crier, never have been. Yet, with Daniela, sometimes I would just look at her and cry. I couldn't believe someone so beautiful, funny, smart, and amazing was mine.

For so long, I believed I'd never find what I'd always craved: an all-powerful, knock-the-wind-out-of-you kind of love. Making love to Daniela was the best thing I've ever known. She brought with her a lot of *bests* into my life. My best love, my best relationship, my best friend, my best sex. That was intense. That was love.

# lauren blitzer

• • • • • • • • • • • • • • • • • • • • • • • • • • • • • • • • • • • • • •

The intensity between two women is hard to describe. Before falling in love for the first time I'd never felt such desires, urges, or longings in my life. It's like a deep and powerful undertow that pulls you down. It comes in waves, and when you fall beneath one, you feel as though you can't breathe without that person.

You might not be in love, but you are deeply infatuated and bursting with lust. If all that remains is this intensity, well, then, girl, you've got yourself something good.

I will be the first to admit, I've felt that intensity quite a few times. The first time, it was intense feelings that quickly turned into falling in love . . . harder and quicker than ever before in my life.

It was four Gay Prides ago, otherwise known as my first. I had been out for a year, and was very excited to join the gay community for a fun-filled weekend of parties, parades, and an overall sense of togetherness. My first year out of the closet felt rather lonely. I had no sense of community. Still living with my parents on the Upper East Side of Manhattan for the summer, I was far removed from the neighborhoods in New York that were flourishing with gays and the bars they drank in. Gay Pride '02 was to be my formal introduction to fags, queers, trannies, and everyone in between.

My sister Julie and I looked up lesbian bars online, and Henrietta Hudson's caught our eye. So, with our best friends Annabel and Emily in tow, we piled into a cab and headed to the West Village.

The bar was as empty as the night was cool. We settled in a corner section and scanned the place. I noticed two women at the bar, one with terrible teeth, the other very attractive. The woman with the teeth looked at me and smiled, almost laughing. I couldn't figure out if this woman was joking around with fake teeth, or just terribly unfortunate and possibly British.

Apparently, Emily was thinking the same thing. "No way those teeth are real. I'm serious. That's just not right."

"I know, but . . . no, they can't be her real teeth. They are so messed up and her face seems actually really pretty," I blurted out.

"Whatever. Maybe she's just trying to be funny, but I don't get it," Emily said, heading to the bar for another drink.

I continued to watch the woman at the bar. Aside from the obscenely grotesque teeth, she was captivating, even from across the room. A few minutes later, I was overjoyed to see her remove the fake teeth from her mouth. She put them in a tissue and smiled at her friend. I prayed they weren't a couple, yet didn't have the nerve to go over to her and do anything about it.

I tugged at Emily's shirt and pointed. "Look, they aren't real. She's beautiful, really beautiful." My reaction surprised me.

"Ha-ha. Aren't you lucky? Plus, she's got a wicked sense of humor," Emily affirmed.

That's the great thing about going out with my straight friends: no competition. As we broke out in fits of laughter, the woman and her friend came over to our side of the bar. Somehow, we all got to talking. The hottie made me incredibly nervous, and with each word flying out of my mouth, I tried to be funny and light.

"So, you guys should come to this Shescape party with us tomorrow night," Fake Teeth said.

"A cheesecake party?" I was puzzled. Fake teeth, and now pastry parties?

The woman laughed. "No, a *Shescape* party. They take place once a month and are really fun."

I couldn't imagine what this bash entailed, but it was being thrown at a hip lounge, Metronome. I was down. I needed to see this woman again. I couldn't pinpoint why or what it was, exactly, but her every movement lured me in. I know, I know: I fall fast. She introduced herself as Maria and I gladly shook her hand. She smelled sweet and clean like soap. Her hair was blond and straight, and she was casually dressed in jeans and a black T-shirt. On her way back from a Cher concert, she'd come into the bar for a nightcap. Her apartment was conveniently located above the most notorious lesbian bar in the city.

She didn't stay long, but I felt okay watching her leave. I knew I had a very good chance of bumping into her the next evening. We left the bar shortly thereafter, and I found myself thinking about her beautiful face for the rest of the evening. And the following day. Wanting to be close to her and to get to know her preoccupied my thoughts. I barely knew this woman, but it didn't matter; that created even more of a mystery. I loved and hated it all at once.

The evening of the Shescape party, I was anxious. As Julie and I finally approached the venue, I literally could have thrown up on the street. Instead of vomiting, I walked in, wide-eyed and dry-mouthed. The dark lounge was packed with women. Upstairs there were separate rooms, and a balcony overlooking the entire place. I grabbed my sister's hand and led her to the staircase to help me spot Maria from the balcony.

Julie and I hit the upstairs bar and spent half an hour leaning on the railing, looking down on the crowd. It seemed as though there was someone for everyone there that night. But I knew who I wanted, and I kept my eyes peeled.

As another hour crept by, I nearly gave up. Then, suddenly, out of the corner of my eye I saw her, her skin glowing as if she'd spent the day in the sun. As Maria greeted friends, I pinched my sister to let her know I'd spotted my prey. We made our way downstairs and found a spot at the bar beside her. She was chatting with a friend, and I figured she didn't remember me. Why would she? I tried to look available, but not too available, as I sat alone, while my sister ordered another martini.

"Hey, when did you get here?" I turned, and there was Maria.

"What's up? Just a few minutes ago," I lied. "My name's Lauren, if you don't remember." I instantly regretted what I'd said.

She smiled at me sweetly. "How could I forget?"

I looked into her dark eyes and smiled. I was beyond flattered. I either wanted to kiss her or run away in fear of messing this up. There was something gentle and honest about her face that felt so familiar to me. It was official. I was infatuated beyond belief.

We got to talking and I found out we had much more in common than I'd thought. Both of us were athletic Tauruses with a love of sushi. It was loud in the club and I could barely hear her, but with every word she said I became more and more immersed in her.

At around one a.m. she asked if I wanted to go to Henrietta's with a bunch of her friends. Of course, I said yes. I grabbed Julie from the dance floor and all of us headed down to the West Village. I ended up in a cab alone with her. I was undeniably happy.

We reached the bar, where Maria was a regular. We cut the line and skipped the cover charge. As we headed to the back bar I looked around, finally feeling the sense of community I had craved. Halfway there, she grabbed my hand so I wouldn't get lost. I looked at her and smiled.

We reached the back bar, and comments about my age were thrown left and right. I suspected Maria was older than me; I just didn't know how much older. She was so beautiful it was hard for me to tell. Moreover, I couldn't have cared less.

I let it slide, and all decided to head over to her friend's apartment, just down the block from hers. When we got there, I lay down on the couch, indicating that I was fading a little, and Maria did the same. We were alone in the room, and I could feel my body literally heating up. She was so close to me. That exact moment was what had consumed my thoughts all day. Our hands were playing with each other's as she looked at me. I closed my eyes but could still feel her stare as I turned toward her and went in for the kill. It was a first for me, but the craving that comes along with the intensity threw my inhibitions for a loop; I acted purely on physical instinct. What my body did felt almost out of my control.

I wanted to cry as my lips touched hers. I felt so much emotion at once. I kept it together as we kissed. My breathing got heavier; with her lips on mine, I was becoming more turned on by the second. After a few minutes, I had to take a break. I was overheated and lost in her kiss and in her eyes. I thought I'd never find my way home.

We soon realized it was four thirty in the morning and probably time to go. She asked me if I wanted to spend the night, and suggested we just snuggle. I was incredibly tempted to let this woman hold me all night, but I had to be up in two hours to go to a bat mitzvah in Westchester. I would have killed to have spent the night with her, but I got in a cab with my sister and we headed home.

I glanced out the car window to find the sun beginning to rise over the pink-and-yellow skyline. I rolled down the window and took a breath of fresh air; all I could do was smile. I couldn't get over what had happened that evening. I looked at the torn receipt Maria had written her number on. I was delirious and in heaven. Maria was beyond unbelievable.

That night was the beginning of a yearlong relationship. We took things slowly, really getting to know each other. One of the first things I found out about Maria was that she was thirty-seven years old. I was twenty-one. There was a sixteen-year age gap between us. I didn't care. My friends cautioned me to stay away, but after seeing how happy we were, they let it go. Maria was intellectual, passionate, caring, and beyond gorgeous. I was whipped. Thankfully, she felt the same way about me.

Our entire year together filled me with nervous excitement. Every single time with her, it felt like the first. She was the one for me. No one else existed in my world. I would just wait for her beautiful face to light up the dark bar. She made me smile from ear to ear and without even saying a word. Maria drove me crazy without my even being near her. Watching her from the opposite end of a room, talking to a friend, laughing, warmed my heart. From across a crowded party, she'd give me that devilish smile, and I'd literally have to turn away. I was scared my smile would give away the "I love you" I'd wanted to say for months.

Throughout the first nine months of our relationship, there had been plenty of times I wanted to grab her and tell her I loved her with all my heart. But, knowing she didn't want to rush into anything, I waited. I hinted to her that I wanted to hear it, but she made it clear that when the time was right, the L-bomb would drop.

By our tenth month, I started to feel like it was never going to happen. We booked a trip to Miami with a few of her friends. I wanted so badly to tell her I loved her before we left. I'd look into her eyes over dinner and feel nothing but love, yet I forced myself not to utter the three fateful words. She meant everything to me. I was completely, utterly, madly in love with this woman. I couldn't sleep if my foot or part of my body wasn't touching hers. Maria made me feel safe, warm, and loved, but I wanted to hear the words from her lips.

The day of our trip to Miami finally arrived, and after a few hours of traveling we were in the hotel getting ready to head over to the beach. Maria had been quiet that morning, and I was starting to wonder if she were having second thoughts about me.

After all, this was our first big trip together. We walked out of the hotel room, hand in hand, and got into the elevator.

She looked over at me. "You know what?"

"I've got the suntan lotion. I don't think we forgot anything," I told Maria.

"No, that's not it," she replied, with a glisten in her eye.

"Then, what?" I said.

"I love you." She looked deep into my eyes and straight into my heart.

I turned toward her. If anything was ever true in this world, it's the next four words I uttered in that elevator to my girlfriend. "I love you, too."

I dropped the bag in my hands. In the tiny hotel elevator, I wrapped my arms around Maria, not wanting to forget that moment. That day, she made me feel complete.

At the lobby, we stepped out of the elevator, both of us grinning ear to ear. Hearing her say she loved me was such an intense experience, I wasn't sure how to function, as people stared at my telling facial expressions. I knew it was love. I'd never felt so strongly. No other words ever rang so true. It was what everyone talks about, only better.

Right off the bat, I fell hard for Maria. Despite the wide age gap, we managed to have one of the healthiest relationships I've ever witnessed. We connected on such a deep level. From the first day we met, the intensity I felt for her only increased, up until the day we broke up. Making love to her brought me to tears, it was just so damn intense. I loved her with all of my heart and never held back. I wanted absolutely no distance between us. The end was painful and heartbreaking, but I wouldn't give up what we had for anything in the world. For two people to reach that level of intensity is so incredibly unique and special, it should be forever treasured . . . no matter what the outcome.

# ashley

We stumbled into my studio apartment. It was eleven p.m., but it felt like four in the morning. We had been out drinking with work friends since midafternoon, and the night had progressed to drinking games, uncontrollable laughter, and typical Friday-night debauchery. We'd met only a few weeks prior, but we'd become best friends instantly. Alex was one of those people I knew I would be close with the minute I met her. After only a few weeks, I couldn't remember what my life had been like without her in it. We understood each other. We talked incessantly. We laughed until we could not breathe. There was a reason we'd met.

That night, during a long, drunken heart-to-heart about God-knows-what, we'd both started laughing. Neither of us could complete a full sentence. We stared at each other, and at the huge, untouched and unnecessary glasses of Ketel One in front of us. "Bedtime?" I asked.

"Sure," she'd replied.

We lay as far apart from each other as a queen-size bed would permit. I remember wishing that I had bought a bed more appropriately sized for my studio. Why didn't I get the full bed? Hell, why didn't I get the twin? I knew that we both felt something, but for a few minutes neither of us moved. Finally, I inched closer and closer. Our first kiss was amazing. It was uncoordinated, self-conscious, and inexperienced, but it was laced with an emotional intensity that I had never felt before. For two women in their mid-twenties, we were acting like twelve-year-old children. It was perfect.

We spent the entire weekend together. Actually, we spent the next three months together, until she moved away. I fell in love. I knew every curve of her body. I knew what made her smile and what made her tick. I could glance at her across the room and know exactly what she was thinking. And I could rip her clothes off and feel how badly she wanted me. I knew Alex's morning routine and her bedtime ritual. She knew mine. Everything about us just worked. Except that she was married, and I had a serious boyfriend of eight years.

Jeremy and I were high school sweethearts. We started dating in the ninth grade. We looked like Barbie and Ken; we were motivated students and good athletes. We came from loving families and had a million friends. We fit like a puzzle. We constantly held hands, cuddled, and giggled. We were that nauseating couple, the one everybody wanted to be part of.

Jeremy and I went our individual ways for college, but the physical distance was all that separated us. Our emotional bond continued to intensify, even if we casually dated other people. Jeremy and I grew together. Following college, I applied to law school and Jeremy applied to medical school. A lawyer and a doctor . . . every Jewish parent's wet dream! We returned back home, to Chicago, for school. I rented the studio and Jeremy lived across the street. A year later, we bought a condo and moved in together.

Looking at my life in retrospect, I think that, to some extent, I always questioned my sexuality. When I was eleven years old, I had my first real kiss. It was a Saturday night, my parents were at a wedding, and my friend Julie and I had "late-night" plans. Patrick Swayze and Jennifer Grey were mid-mambo, "I've Had the Time of My Life" was blasting, and Julie scooted near me and grabbed my hand. We understood each other with a force well beyond our innocence. My only recollection of being eleven was simply of kissing her. Passionately French-kissing her! For years I tucked that memory away in my secret vault.

In college, my friends nicknamed me the "cock tease." For

four years, I went to bars and fraternity parties, met oodles of guys, talked to them for hours, flirted, and rarely did anything more than kiss them. I justified my immature actions to myself and my friends by the logical explanation that I did not want to hurt Jeremy. My friends believed me. In fact, for years I believed me too. And to some extent, my reasoning held truth. But it wasn't only Jeremy that held me back from experiencing other guys. More importantly, it was the fact that I would rather drive cross-country with hemorrhoids than come in close contact with a frat boy's blue-veined junket pumper. Hindsight is twenty-twenty.

Until I met Alex, I was convinced that God had created me without a sex drive. Jeremy and I had sex, but I never really wanted to. My lack of desire terrified me. More than anything in the world I wanted to make Jeremy happy, but I constantly found myself inching away from him. The never-ending period, the "I'm too tired," the terrible stomachache—I used every excuse in the book to avoid sex. In fact, I was relieved that there was little opportunity for us to have sex in college, as we only saw each other a few times a year. Thankfully, medical school was so stressful and time-consuming, even Jeremy lost a little bit of his libido. I would have sold my soul to the devil to want to rip his clothes off the way he always wanted to rip off mine.

After nine years of dating, and four months after Alex moved away, Jeremy proposed. Our friends and family were ecstatic. My mom and the wedding planner immediately kicked into high gear. Dress, date, venue, florist, band, photographer, videographer, makeup artist—this was going to be a wedding even Martha Stewart would envy. A three-hundred-guest black-tie extravaganza, a night to remember. Nobody was going to ruin perfection.

After Alex moved away, I convinced myself that my relationship with her was mere happenstance. I forced myself to believe that I was only experimenting, I was not gay, I was meant to marry Jeremy. I'm a great lawyer; even I found my argument somewhat compelling.

When Jeremy and I got engaged, I truly believed I wanted to marry him. But as time went on, and the wedding plans became more and more intricate, I cracked. I knew that I needed to explore my sexuality before I could walk down the aisle, but I didn't know how. I felt trapped, alone, and terrified. I only had fourteen months to figure out the rest of my life.

It was a cold Monday morning in Chi-Town. I woke up, threw on work clothes, and rushed out the door in my typical still-recovering-from-the-weekend frenzy. At nine twenty, I robotically found myself picking up the phone and calling Jeremy.

"We need to talk," I said.

"Is everything okay?" he asked.

The tears started pouring down my face. My breathing got heavy. My voice shook. "We just need to talk. Okay?"

"Do you want to meet for coffee?" He sounded nervous

"How 'bout dinner?" I suggested. I knew there was no chance in hell I could come back to work after the conversation we were about to have. I could feel his heart pounding through the phone.

That night, Jeremy and I sat down to dinner. I took a deep breath, then a few gulps of my Ketel One, cracked a nervous smile, and stared into his sweet and innocent eyes.

"I love you. I have always loved you and I always will," I began. "And I want to marry you more than anything. I want a white picket fence and adorable kids. You are going to be the best father in the world."

"Of course, Ashley," he said.

"I just don't want to go into this with any reservations. I've never been anything but honest with you. And so I want to be honest with you now," I continued. "I'm having hesitations . . . and it's not you . . . it's me. . . . And it's scaring the shit out of me."

"Is this a joke?" my fiancé asked.

"I'm questioning my sexuality. I'm sure it's just the nerves and the what-ifs speaking, but I'm questioning who I am," I confessed.

"You want to make out with girls?" Jeremy looked puzzled.

"Maybe." I looked down at my drink.

He spoke quickly. "Well, I don't want anything to do with that. But you do what you need to do. Be with who you need to be with. I don't want to hear about it. Just figure it out before the wedding."

We didn't tell anyone, and I spent the remainder of the year in deep self-analysis. I dove headfirst (no pun intended) into the lesbian community and simultaneously worked on my relationship with Jeremy. As time went on, however, I realized that my relationship with Alex was not just a phase. I found myself attracted, attached, and connected to the women I met. More so than with any man I knew, including Jeremy. In the back of my mind, I knew I shouldn't get married. But the wedding was quickly approaching, and I couldn't get myself to call it off. How could I? How could I hurt Jeremy and my family? We'd be the talk of the town.

After nearly a year of planning, twelve days before I was set to say "I do," I called off the wedding. I met Jeremy at Starbucks. We started crying the minute we looked at each other. We both knew this was the end. After almost a decade together and countless "we're doing this, we're not doing this" conversations, we officially called it quits. We talked for hours that Monday morning. We laughed, we cried, we held each other tightly. We called our parents and our friends. I called the party planner, the band, and the photographer. We cancelled the honeymoon. We shocked our world.

The day I left Jeremy was the hardest day of my life. The following weeks only proved more difficult. We sold our condo and our car. We separated our bank accounts. We returned our wedding gifts. In one fell swoop, I managed to lose everything I knew. I lost my best friend and my security blanket. I lost my second family and my picture-perfect future. I felt empty. But for the first time in years, I didn't feel numb. Despite losing all these things, I knew I had something more to gain.

Since leaving Jeremy, life has been somewhat chaotic. The rumor mill had a field day with our big news. We tried to cite nondescript irreconcilable differences for the breakup, but gossip travels fast. I officially came out to my friends and family. I told people at work. I started dating women.

Sometimes I fear I gave up the only great thing in my life. Sometimes I worry that nobody will ever love me the way that Jeremy did. At times I wonder if I should have taken the easy way out, and gone through with the wedding.

But more often than not, I have moments of clarity. I know that no matter how high my highs are or how low my lows are, I made the right decision. I am no longer floating through life blankly. I am skipping through life with my head held high. Finally, I am allowing myself to embrace the emotional intensity that I can only feel when loving a woman.

# jill

When it comes to intensity, one moment in my life strikes me as more poignant than all the rest. For twenty-three years, I followed the typical—or should I say expected—path set out for me. I am a nice Jewish girl from Long Island. I grew up in a comfortable home and did as I was supposed to do. I excelled in high school, attended a good college, and continued on to law school. By anybody's standards, especially my parents', I was living life just as I should be. The only thing lacking was a loving relationship. In fact, that aspect of my life had always been pretty much nonexistent.

Whenever I fielded questions like "So, do you have a boyfriend?" or "Are you seeing anyone?" I'd get so uncomfortable, my face would turn a bright shade of crimson. Christ, when did brunch with my grandparents become the Spanish Inquisition? I always had a hard time understanding why I was reacting so adversely to such simple questions. Lots of my friends were single, but they answered these questions with grace and ease.

I guess you could say that, in terms of dating, I was somewhat of a "late bloomer." In high school I'd hooked up with a few guys, and even had some crushes, but nothing serious ever materialized. When I got to college, I casually dated men, and I had some satisfying experiences. But, when presented with a situation that could lead to something more, I always found myself feeling uncomfortable. If I was alone with a guy, my mind would wander to my roommates; I'd wonder what they were up to. I'd go so far as to create situations where my best guy-friend would be the one I'd fall for, knowing full well nothing could ever come of it. Despite my guy issues, I always had enough going on with one boy or another, and my friends never thought to question anything.

Dating women was never something I really thought about, or, rather, let myself think about. I always assumed I'd never met the right guy, but that when I did, I would feel the so-called "love" that everyone always talked about. I believed I was meeting the wrong men, or just not opening myself up enough to let anything happen.

But then things changed. Emily, a good friend of mine from college, had a best friend from high school who had recently come out as a lesbian. I had met her friend Sarah a few times during college, but hadn't really ever spent any quality time with her. When I graduated and moved back to New York, I saw Sarah a handful of times. We always had a great time. I was just so happy whenever we hung out.

As a single girl in Manhattan, for Valentine's Day I decided to throw a little cocktail party for my other single friends. Thinking it would just be an ordinary "chill" night, I invited a few girlfriends over. Later on in the day, Sarah called to say she was coming. And after hanging up the phone, I couldn't deny the weird sensation rising up in my stomach.

The night came and Sarah and two other friends of mine showed up at my apartment. We had some cocktails, some dinner, and an overall great time. As the drinks started flowing, I let my guard down. I just stopped overthinking everything so much. All of a sudden, I found myself on the couch with Sarah. I was just lying on her, being extremely happy.

We all left my apartment for a bar down the street. As soon as we got there, Sarah and I found ourselves talking alone. I started firing questions at her. I asked her when and how she knew she liked girls. And then it just happened. Never in my life had I felt like this before. Let me preface this by saying that I am typically an extremely passive person. Throughout my life, it took a lot for me to speak my mind. I had always just let things slide and was never in a million years the one to make the first move, especially in a circumstance that might ultimately have a dramatic effect on my life. Like this one. But in this instance, I couldn't let the moment pass. As we were standing there, I felt this intense energy. It was as if a force field overtook me, and if I didn't say something, my head would literally explode. All of a sudden, I found myself saying, "Okay, I don't know what it is about you, but I'm extremely attracted to you." In response to this, I got a sort of smirk that said, "Okay, that's cool." And then the bathroom incident occurred.

We wound up in the bathroom together and probably shared one of the most intense kisses I've ever experienced in my life. I felt this overall elation and didn't know what to do with myself. We left the bathroom and tried to play it cool. We ended up not going home together, which, looking back on things, was definitely for the best.

The next day, I went to brunch with Emily and two other friends. I had never had a more stressful, awkward day in my life. I knew it was possible that Emily knew what had happened, but I held my tongue the entire day. It wasn't until I was alone with her, after I wouldn't let her leave my side for the entire day, that I spilled the beans. "Okay, Emily, I have to tell you something. Something happened Saturday night."

"What, did you try coke or something?"

"Um, no, not that. I kissed Sarah."

"Oh, whatever. She's always had a crush on you."

Now, I have to say, I thought this would be the biggest deal on the planet. But an "oh, whatever" was NOT what I was expecting. As a Jewish girl from Long Island, I'd expected a bit more backlash than that, but for the most part, my friends could not have been more supportive. Needless to say, I got a call from Sarah later that night. She just wanted to make sure that I wasn't completely and totally freaked out by what happened. The thing was, I wasn't freaked out by what had happened. I was more freaked out by the fact that I wasn't freaking out.

After a serious game of phone tag, Sarah and I finally ended up getting together again. We started to see each other a couple of times a week. We were taking things pretty slow, but never in my life had I felt like this. I was excited every time she called, nervous calling her back, and more nervous than I'd ever been to actually see her. My usual game with guys was that I'd hook up with them once and then never return their phone calls. Now, I was anticipating the phone calls, upset if they didn't come, and completely unraveled about how quickly my feelings were progressing.

We saw each other for about a month with nothing really being discussed relationship-wise, except that we liked seeing each other. Really, I'd never thought that kissing someone could be so satisfying. Lord knows how frustrated she was with me when we started dating, but, really, it was like I'd never been with anyone before and was discovering the human body for the first time. Kissing her was so soft and gentle and so much better than kissing any guy I'd ever been with. And then she went away for a week.

My best guy-friend, whom I thought was the love of my life, came to visit me during his spring break. He stayed with me for a few days, and I don't know if it was that I wanted to deny what I was feeling for this girl or to see if he really was the love of my life, but one thing led to another and I ended up hooking up with him. And then it happened. Almost immediately after things started I found myself saying, "No, I'm sorry, I can't do this." It just didn't feel right. It wasn't as if I was in a committed relationship with Sarah, but whatever I was doing with him was just extremely wrong. Then, a few days later, I went on what I thought was a friendly movie-going experience with another guy that turned out to be a date. As the night ended, he leaned in to kiss me, and again, it felt all wrong. And then Sarah returned.

I just can't be anything but honest with her. So, when we met up, I started to spill my guts about the two encounters I'd had, and followed up by saying that I felt it was all wrong and I was thinking about her the entire time and I couldn't do it. And then she spilled the beans. Turns out, she wasn't just on vacation, she had met up with her ex-girlfriend. Girlfriend . . . I don't even know what they're called in Europe. And although they definitely hooked up a bit, she found herself feeling uncomfortable about the situation as well, because of me. So, then things took a turn, and I found myself in the first "relationship" that I'd ever been in.

So, what's intense? Intense is what I felt whenever I was with or not with her, eating, breathing, sleeping, studying, or anything else you can think of. Nothing in my life had ever progressed so quickly. After that conversation, we acknowledged that this was something we both wanted. I wanted to see her all the time; if I wasn't seeing her, I was thinking about her. Never in my life had I thought I could feel this way about someone.

Everything she had to say was like it came out of Einstein's mouth; if I was speaking, I felt like I'd never had a better audience. Things were amazing. It was the first time I had ever felt anything "real." I finally got what people were talking about when they spoke of love and desire. But I soon learned that along with intensity come both the good and the bad.

After a while, things got a little *too* intense, and I'd go from feeling like a million dollars one minute to feeling like I had just been hit by a Mack truck the next. My life became a rollercoaster. It was like happy and sad were the only things I could feel. And for a while, I was miserable. However, I now realize that this was the greatest thing that could ever have happened to me. Because no matter how difficult being in a relationship with her was, it was a relationship. It was the first time in my life that I was able to feel something other than the continual apathy that had plagued me. Having this experience awoke something in me. I always thought I would just go through life on that path I was told I should follow. Now I know that you don't feel anything, be it good or bad, unless you're willing to take risks.

Being with this woman was one of the most, if not *the* most, fulfilling experiences of my life. She taught me so much about myself, about other people, about relationships, and just about life in general that I could never in a million years have learned without her. The truth is, although I've been hurt and have struggled a lot since making the conscious decision that I like women, I wouldn't trade a day of my life now for a hundred years of how I was before. It was like I was going through my life living a lie. It made so many other things clear as day, and "regret" is not and will never be a word in my vocabulary.

## one more thing . . .

Beware: If you do indeed fall for someone, and she falls for you, the intensity between both of you will become the hook that draws you closer. Just don't be surprised if you feel stronger about a woman you've known for two weeks than a man you've known for years. It happens; just have the number for U-Haul handy.

# passionate friendships

7

> When my mother found out I was gay, she sent me to juvenile hall. That's smart. Sending me to live with five hundred girls who can't get out!
>
> —Kat Howard

The tightrope between friendship and love is a tough one to walk. Passionate friendship is defined as "friendship that doesn't allow itself (due to inhibition/lack of recognition/lack of language/societal sanction) into a 'proper' relationship." These types of relationships are very common among women, gay and straight alike. The majority of women experience a passionate friendship in their lifetime. For a lesbian, this friendship with a straight girl could be the most crushing relationship she'll ever encounter. When a platonic relationship blossoms into love, it can be a stormy sea to navigate. Here are some things to consider before getting on board.

## She stops you dead in your tracks

If you've had a passionate friendship, you know that the phrase "takes my breath away" literally applies. She will be all you have ever dreamed of. Stop planning out your commitment ceremony until she reveals her sexual preference.

## Won't you be my Valentine?

Even in the nineteenth century, female friendships were considered "romantic" because they included almost all of the aspects of a modern, intimate, heterosexual relationship. Girlfriends would exchange verbal expressions of fondness, love letters, and romantic poems. Nowadays, IMs, text messaging, and e-mail have replaced the old expressions of love.

## Filling out the questionnaire

You've befriended the girl of your dreams; now it's time for the interrogation. She might want to know everything; blushing and thrilled, she'll ask who pays for dinner, who wears the pants, and "what defines sex as a lesbian." You will answer honestly as she mentally takes notes. You've shown her the door to your world; now, let's see if she wants to come in. Even if you don't know what your world is yet, this girl will rock it.

## Hold on, let me ask my wifey

It seems you have it all, but something is missing. Oh, yeah, that's right: the sex. She knows your every move and you love it. Check-ins, holding hands, snuggling at night, dinners, brunches, and fights, but no sexžžžžwell, I guess that does make you sound married. This is normal, and happens so much more often that not. You guessed it right: You've got yourself a passionate friendship. She drives you crazy and you're in debt from calling Ms. Cleo. You need someone who's able to read her mind.

## Irreconcilable differences

If one night your dream comes true, you might actually have the relationship you've always wanted. But you might not, and what used to seem fulfilling feels more and more empty. You want more and she can't give it to you, not the way you want it. She's not Burger King, but you do deserve someone who gives it to you your way. Hopefully, she'll understand, but it definitely won't be easy.

These days, it seems that everyone has a passionate-friendship story. Depending on how intense you let things get, passionate friendships have the capacity to end in disaster or become a funny time you like to reminisce about with your buddy, whom you now refer to as your ex-wife. Try to avoid getting in over your head. But if you do get crushed, it will probably teach you to avoid falling in love with your best friend again!

# lauren levin

· · · · · · · · · · · · · · · · · · · · · · · · · · · · · · · · · · · · ·

My first passionate friendship occurred my junior year of college. I always knew of Samantha and thought she was just some sexy, crazy, cool senior girl. It was only on our spring break trip that Samantha went from being an acquaintance to my first love.

On a sunny day in Mexico, eight of my friends charged the pool bar for rounds of tequila shots and margaritas. Soon enough, we were all drunk, and Samantha and I began to make out. We continued to converse and play the remainder of the day. As the sun set on the beach and we both came down from our buzz, Sam and I got into a deep conversation. She revealed to me her struggle with depression and attempts at suicide. I couldn't understand how this beautiful, smart, creative girl could hate herself so much. How could she not see herself for the amazing girl I saw each time I looked at her? We spoke for hours, and from that day on we were inseparable. Together we were crazy and intense. Our relationship looked like something straight out of the film *Thirteen*.

That vacation took a romantic turn for both of us. We rode horses at sunset, took long walks on the beach, and danced the night away. Although we never made out again that week, our friendship progressed into something incredibly passionate when we returned to school. Never before had I experienced such longing. I felt a deep, unwavering desire for my new best friend. Despite not being able to physically express my love for Samantha, I felt passion every day I was around her. Sure, it was painful, but I wouldn't have traded the way she made me feel for anything in the world. Although Sam had a boyfriend for most of the time I was in love with her, we were still all over each other, and we enjoyed many platonic sleepovers. I could've watched her sleep for hours. I dreamt of the day she'd turn toward me and kiss me, releasing all the sexual tension that bound us so tightly together.

There is a fine line between friendship and love. I walked that line every day for six months, and almost lost my balance on a number of occasions. Loving Samantha led me to do crazy things. One night out at the bars, Samantha slipped me a Xanax. Afterward, her boyfriend, Tom, had an after-hours party at his house. Sam came over to me and beckoned me into Tom's room. When we got inside, she began to undress me. I was so excited, I didn't know what to do with myself. So what if her boyfriend was going to be there too? I was finally going to get to be physical with the girl I loved!

Samantha and I began to kiss. I tingled all over as passion scorched through my veins. Being that it was a threesome, Tom inevitably entered the picture. Tom's attention was clearly focused on me, and only me. At one point I began to pet Samantha's hair just to make her feel a part of things. I wanted to get closer to Samantha, but Tom began to hook up with me almost immediately. In a matter of minutes, Samantha exclaimed that I had to "bounce," as she was so incredibly jealous—of whom, I still don't know. I threw my clothes back on and ran home crying. I didn't want Samantha to be mad at me for being intimate with her boyfriend. Christ, I did it because

I thought she wanted me to. It never even crossed my mind that Samantha and Tom had taken advantage of me.

The following morning, I was scared to death to see Sam. I told my roommates what had happened, but they were hardly sympathetic. By this point, my friends had had it up to here with me. Since spring break I had ditched all of them to be with Samantha. They thought she was a manipulative bitch who had pulled the wool over my eyes. I thought she was an angel. Thankfully, when Sam came over the morning after my first ménage à trois, she was tearful and sorry. I accepted her apology and was just happy she wasn't mad at me.

Yet, in retrospect, my friends were right. I almost lost every meaningful relationship in my life in order to maintain my passionate friendship with Sam. We were never good with others, but we were incredible by ourselves. Samantha and I finished each other's sentences, read each other's mind, and all that good stuff that is so hard to come by.

After Sam graduated, I went back home to Minnesota. She broke up with Tom and moved home to Westchester, N.Y. We spoke for hours on the telephone and missed each other immensely. Samantha said things to me that made me question the nature of our friendship. For graduation I sent her a framed photograph of us. When we got off the phone one night, she told me she was going to go masturbate to our picture. Clearly, I had done this before and never told her, but were the sexual feelings finally mutual?

A couple weeks later, I moved into the NYU dorms with my friend Julia. Julia was not so happy about this living situation, as I had all but disappeared from her life for the past four months. Three weeks into that fateful summer, Samantha went to Italy with her family. My friends staged an intervention. They took me out to dinner and gave me an ultimatum: It was either her or them. I was torn. I loved Samantha, but I would be going back to school in a few short months and I needed my friends. It felt wrong to love her like I did. Despite how much it would hurt, I knew I had to "break up" with Samantha.

When she arrived back in the States, Samantha showed up at my apartment with dried flowers, a bottle of fine Italian champagne, and poetry she had written for me. Three weeks before, I'd have been ecstatic at her romantic gestures. However, I knew I couldn't let her gifts sway me from my decision. I needed to end our friendship. There was no other way. When a friendship grows that passionate, it's all or nothing. You can't maintain any form of moderation when things get that extreme. That night, I told Sam she couldn't sleep over, and she was clearly hurt. My friends made fun of the presents she'd brought me, and I laughed along with them. Really, though, I was crying inside.

But Samantha was bad medicine. She was like a drug I was addicted to, and I needed to wean myself off of her. Instead of being up front with her about it, though, I acted immaturely. I stopped returning her calls. I thought she would just get the hint that this phase in our lives had ended, but my pulling away only seemed to fuel her desire to be with me.

Samantha would call me from unknown numbers, knowing I wouldn't answer if I saw her number on the caller ID. She acted like nothing was wrong the times she'd catch me off guard on the phone. Hastily, I would make up an excuse for why I couldn't talk right then, and hang up. Samantha began to follow me out to nightclubs and bars. When we spoke, she pretended like nothing was wrong. It was sad, bizarre, and excruciatingly painful for both of us.

One July night, my friends were all away for the weekend and I really wanted to go to a cool new club that was opening. I caved. I called Samantha.

"Everyone must be out of town, huh, Levin?" she asked, annoyed.

"No, Sam, I just miss you and want to see you," I replied sincerely.

Fifteen minutes later, Samantha was in her car on her way down to the city. We went out that night and hardly spoke at all. When we got back to my apartment, Samantha asked to use my vibrator, a favor she'd asked of me back at Cornell. I gave her my vibrator, went into the bathroom, slid down against the door, and held my head in my hands. I rocked back and forth, trying to restrain myself from entering the room and hooking up with her. Finally, she called out my name.

"How was it?" I asked. "Did you come?"

"Nope," she replied, pulling me into bed.

Sam held me tightly in her arms. I sat on my hands. I wanted to kiss her so badly, but I knew that if I succumbed to my desires, I'd never get her out of my system. Breaking off this passionate friendship would become virtually impossible. Moreover, I never wanted any of my friends to know my intense feelings for Samantha. I suspected she'd use our night together against me, accuse me of being a lesbian, and tell my friends we'd hooked up. I rolled over and fell asleep in her arms. Holding myself back from physically expressing my love for Samantha was incredibly difficult.

The next day, our friendship came to a screeching halt. We got into a huge fight and I revealed to Samantha all the terrible things I thought about her. She cried and cried, and asked why it felt like we were breaking up. She didn't even realize we were in a relationship—how typical for a relationship that never really happened. She went on to rip apart all my pictures and smash the CDs I'd made for her. She begged for forgiveness, but I remained strong and told her I could never see her again.

Samantha and I didn't speak for four years. Yet, I never

stopped thinking about her or fantasizing about her. Worst of all, I never stopped thinking about that night. I wished I could take back the night and make love to her. It still hurts that I never acted on the one opportunity to really hook up with Sam. Even though I dream of going back in time and changing the way that night went down, deep in my heart I know it wouldn't have been a good idea.

She never loved me the way I loved her. Her attempt at seduction was a last resort to get me back. She knew that by giving me all I had ever wanted and never had, she could win back my friendship. Samantha, my passionate friendship, was an intense heartbreak. It took me three years to get over it, and another year to finally realize why.

# lauren blitzer

It was one of the hottest summers I can remember. I had just returned from London and come out to my parents, and was beginning my junior year of college. As I waited outside my first class, my eyes wandered aimlessly over all the new faces passing by in the hallway. And then *she* walked by.

I stared as this dark-haired exotic beauty glided by. The mysterious girl chatted up the two boys on either side of her. It wasn't her tight green T-shirt that caught my attention so much as her wild eyes and hair. They seemed both mysterious and curious at the same time.

Suddenly, she looked away from the boys and directly into my eyes. Beads of sweat began to gather on my brow. I quickly looked away from her, fearing I would expose the rapid beating of my own heart. She continued to waltz right on by me and into the room I was waiting to enter. Score! The hot girl was in my class!

I walked in minutes later and proceeded to spend the entirety of my first Ancient Art class staring at the back of her head, wondering what she smelled like. Armed with a new found acceptance of my own sexuality, I was no longer afraid to confront my unshakeable curiosity. I wondered where she lived, who she hung out with, and what she ate for lunch. I couldn't decide where to take it from there. There was just something about her that drove me crazy, and I hadn't even met her yet.

I needed to get to know her and become her friend. Another week like this passed when my professor announced a required field trip to The Metropolitan Museum of Art. Finally, I'd be with the object of my lust in an environment other than the depressing gun-metal gray of an NYU class-room. And not just any old place, for that matter. I'd be with her in my favorite museum, surrounded by beauty.

The morning of the field trip, I got on the train with my friend Maggie and positioned myself strategically near my crush, so as not to strain my neck trying to catch a glimpse of her face. She stood with those same two boys, hands around the pole in the middle of the car, leaning backward, allowing her hair to fall onto her bare shoulders. She laughed, throwing her head back every so often, gesturing to the two boys. The girl was intoxicating. I was in a trance.

I turned to Maggie. "What's that girl's name?"

"It's something weird. . . . I can't remember how to pro-nounce it. I think she's from Morocco or something." Two sec-onds later, Maggie stood up and headed straight over to ask her name.

*Oh no*, I thought. *Where's she going?* As I looked on, morti-fied, I saw Maggie point directly to me, her lips moving. I looked at her, and with my hands reaching out, mouthed "What?" like an eighty-year-old Jewish man who is hard of hearing. In hopes of redeeming my coolness, I walked over to them, and Maggie introduced me to Miriea.

I can't even remember what words flew out of my mouth, as I realized I found this woman utterly flawless. Even her not-so-perfectly-spaced-teeth seemed the perfect addition to her face.

From that day on, our contact with each other increased. By the time exams rolled around, we were studying together in the library, sitting closer and closer together with each study session. We'd even share the earphones on my iPod. Miriea looked at me in a way no one else did, and I looked back at her with equally curious eyes. For both of us, seeing each other became a rush. Still, I wasn't sure what it all meant. Miriea didn't know I was gay, nor did she bother to ask.

Once exams ended, we were both relieved, yet also reluctant to see our time together end. She was heading to Morocco for Christmas break and I was going skiing upstate with my family. We exchanged e-mail addresses and phone numbers, and said we looked forward to seeing each other next semester in our Italian Renaissance class.

I knew it was time for me to come out to Miriea. Even though she'd never asked me about boys, I still felt it was necessary for her to know who I truly was. At that point in my life, coming out to new friends was always hard for me. Coming out to the girl I was infatuated with would be even harder. I meant to tell Miriea that I was gay in person, but I chickened out and waited till she'd been in Morocco a week to send her an e-mail.

And I told her everything. I wrote to Miriea about Rachel, about coming out to my family, about everything I'd gone through since my fateful trip abroad. I wondered what she would think about all of this. Would she assume I had been hitting on her for the past two months? Had I been?

However, whatever her take on my sexuality might be, I prepared myself for it. After all, if you can't accept me for who I am, then you're not worth being part of my life. After calculating the time difference between New York and Morocco, I waited a good twenty hours before checking my e-mail again. And there it was in my in-box: an e-mail from Miriea. I began to read, and couldn't believe that her best friend had recently come out to her as well. She was completely accepting, and felt special that I'd confided in her.

Never before in my life had I counted down the days till classes began. I'd felt unusually close to Miriea since exchanging a few very open and sincere e-mails with her over break. We planned to meet for lunch with some of her friends the first day back, and as I rounded the corner to the restaurant, I tried to act cool. I didn't want to seem too excited or at all nervous to see her. After all, she was just a girl—a straight girl.

Well, my stiff approach got tossed in the gutter when Miriea excitedly jumped up from her chair to give me a hug. Her arms wrapped around my neck, and mine around her waist. It felt right, and my day was made.

From there, our friendship took off. She called me the following weekend to invite me to a loft party her friend was throwing. I had to constantly give myself reality checks that this girl was not interested in being anything more than just my friend. However, in the back of my mind I wondered why her attentions seemed to increase after I told her I was gay. Maybe she felt like I had opened up to her and now we were closer? Perhaps she was curious about her own sexuality? Or maybe it's that she just liked me as a person? I stuck with the latter and tried not to overthink it at all.

As I stepped into the loft party, I was feeling confident, put together, and hot. I spotted her immediately. She was wearing a tight red T-shirt, jeans, and boots. Her long hair hung loosely on her shoulders. Her strong hands gripped a red plastic cup, and I noticed how perfectly shaped her toned arms were. Her head turned and our eyes met. For about five seconds, neither of us moved a muscle. Miriea looked me up and down. When her eyes made it back to mine, she smiled at me mischievously. I walked over to her and bent in to kiss her warm cheek, as she put her hands on my hips and whispered "hi" in my ear.

A few seconds later, I bumped into my friend Justin, whom I had fooled around with in high school. He was clearly hitting on me; after all, I was all dolled up for Miriea, who stood a few feet away, not once taking her eyes off me. She rolled her eyes sarcastically when I glanced over at her, and I sensed her jealously at the attention I was receiving. The way she was looking at me felt amazing. I desperately wanted this girl to fall for me, and in some ways I felt like she was. I knew Miriea had never experienced being with a woman, and I'm not sure she ever wanted to. But that night started something for both of us.

A few minutes later, Miriea approached me and grabbed my hand. We walked out the door, and back to her apartment. We talked for about two hours about nothing in particular, our legs touching all the time. It was six a.m., and I was starting to get tired. She noticed my yawns, stood up, and threw me a gray T-shirt and pajama bottoms. I put them on and followed her into the bedroom. Since it was a dorm, the beds were singles, but her roommate wasn't there. Miriea got into bed, and I stood there confused, not knowing where to go.

Miriea lifted up her covers and invited me in. "What are you waiting for?" she asked. I smiled and ran over, jumping into the bed. She insisted I sleep on the inside, by the wall. Christ, I would've slept on the floor just to be near her. Nervous and awake, I lay still as she passed out on her side. I watched her, looking at the back of her head and neck, her bare shoulders peeking out from the sheets. I stayed in my corner all night, practically hugging the wall. I wondered what would happen if I had enough nerve to move closer to her and wrap my arms around her waist. Five hours later, I woke up sweating and cramped, but I was in heaven.

The ice was broken that night, and we felt more comfortable around each other. Progressively, we spent more and more nights sleeping together, either in her tiny bed or mine. I fell harder and harder for her everyday. It almost felt like we were in a relationship. My friends would comment on how not normal my friendship with Miriea was. They didn't sleep in the same bed with their friends nearly every night, they pointed out. I ignored them, yet in the back of my mind I wondered if they were right. How bizarre was this? I felt like I was in a relationship that just happened to be missing a crucial component: sex. I tried to just go with the flow, but that became exponentially hard as Miriea and I grew closer and closer.

One night after drinking and dancing in Soho we decided to spend the night at my place, which was closer. We walked the three blocks to my dorm, holding hands, laughing the whole way home. Every few steps, we'd glance over at each other and smile. All I wanted to do was blurt out, "I love you," grab her face, and kiss her. But I held myself back.

We got upstairs and Miriea grabbed her favorite pair of my sweatpants and a wifebeater. We crawled into my tiny bed. The room was pitch-black. My head was spinning; I was drunk with my desire for Miriea. She climbed on top of me. She was breathing down my neck, and then she gently kissed it. My hands didn't know what to do; they just started to tickle her back. I lifted up her tank top and gently ran my fingers over the small of her back and up to her neck. She shivered with pleasure as my fingers explored her skin. I thought I was going to explode. This wasn't normal behavior between friends, yet I still wasn't convinced that she wanted me to go further. The last thing I wanted to do was to make her feel uncomfortable or jeopardize our newfound friendship. I continued tickling her back until we both passed out. She eventually rolled off of me and spooned me for the rest of the night. Occasionally, she'd wake up and kiss my shoulder, her arms wrapped around me, safe and warm.

That night sent me into a frenzy. Each time we hung out, I looked at her seeing only beauty and perfection. She drove me crazy. Every time she grabbed my hand on the street or my body in bed, I felt myself melt. I was caught up in my fantasy of kissing her.

We both craved each other, yet I wasn't sure we craved each other in the same way. In our own messed-up fashion, we were dating. Neither of us saw anyone else the rest of the school year. Every day, we'd check in with each other, and almost every night we spent together. My other friends became jealous and threatened by her, as she was of them. Her friends would poke fun at us, asking how the happy couple was doing.

Summer in the city was soon approaching, and that meant only one thing: Miriea would be off to Morocco for nearly two months. The thought of being apart made us weepy, but we made the most of our time left and tried to have as much fun as possible. That last night was approaching fast, and we made big plans for a proper farewell.

In all this time, still, nothing had happened between us. Night after night, she'd lie intertwined with me, her face so close to mine — but never a kiss. Each morning, I walked away with regret, mad at myself for not gathering the nerve to actually do something about it. I figured, if something was meant to happen, it would. Maybe this intense flirtatious behavior was all I was ever going to have with her.

We had dinner with all her friends and then continued to barhop. The crowd got smaller and smaller, until finally, it was just me and Miriea. The clock was approaching four a.m., and we decided to walk to her sister's place to say our final good-byes. We reached her building and I sat down on a bench out front. I turned toward her, legs up, hugging my knees to my chest. She sat next to me, grabbed my legs, and put them around her waist. She pulled me closer as a few random passersby stared at the moment we were sharing. Miriea started to shake a little, and I hugged her tightly. She was crying on my shoulder. I didn't know what to do, except join her in those tears.

"I'll come visit you in Morocco. Really, Miriea, I will," I told her, tilting her chin up with my fingers.

"Yeah, but all my friends say that," she said, as I brushed a tear away from her eye.

"But, I'm different," I stared straight into her eyes.

Finally, after the sun came up and we'd been laughing and crying for hours, we stood up and walked to the front door. I grabbed her waist tightly and she held mine, leaning into me. My fantasy was becoming a reality. She was about an inch away from my face. I could feel her cool breath against my lips. Miriea shut her eyes and leaned her forehead against mine. It was now or never.

I looked down, and her lips hit my forehead. Did I just miss it? Was she finally going in for the kill and I gave her my fore-head instead of my lips? I was confused and sad as I hugged her one last time. Seconds later, I knew I needed to walk away. It was all too much. I turned to leave and she just stood there watching me; tears streamed down her cheeks as I got into a cab and drove away.

The next few weeks, I cried about the smallest things. I was constantly irritated, but knew it was just because I missed her. My love for Miriea drove me to book a flight to Morocco, just so I could be with her on her birthday. She couldn't believe I was actually coming. We talked on the phone as often as possible and e-mailed three times a day. When I finally got to Morocco, we had an amazing time. We were still touchy, but I came to accept that nothing romantic would ever happen between us.

I loved Miriea: I still do. But I need more from someone. I need someone to want me as much as I want them. I didn't want either of us to be able to control it. When I returned from Morocco, I started going out more. I met other gay women and actively searched for something both sexual and emotional. Miriea was still on my mind, but I knew in my heart things were going to be different between us. We'd grown out of whatever we'd had, and maybe it was for the better. Miriea will always remain an incomplete chapter in my life. We broke up, without being together. Fortunately, our friendship remains.

# alessandra

It was in the seventh grade when I first realized I loved a woman. She was beautiful, with big blue eyes, long blond hair, and a gorgeous smile. The woman was my teacher. It was weird, but every time Miss Jennings approached my desk or called my name, blood rushed to my head. And when she held my hand, I just wanted to die.

At thirteen, I didn't realize what was really going on inside of me. It was all these new feelings my friends and I were starting to have. That tingly feeling, that ardent jealousy, those raging hormones . . . But mine were different. Unlike my friends, I didn't have those feeling for the guys in my class. I had them for Miss Jennings, our beautiful teacher. I would try to bump into Miss J all the time, even outside of school. I'd run to her classroom, located on the top floor of the four-story building, just to have one minute alone with her. I'd get so nervous around her. I loved it; I loved her. I daydreamed about her. I even joined every club she supervised, like the community service one. The woman had me feeding the homeless on Saturday mornings.

I am now eighteen and live in a small, immensely wealthy community in Lima, Peru; the rest of the country's population is impoverished. There is hardly a middle class. But since my dad is Lima's most successful doctor, I attend the most exclusive private high school in the country.

In this small community, everyone is alike. They don't necessarily look alike physically, but the way they live their lives is all too similar. From a very young age, children know what is expected of them. It's like everyone at my school was handed the same step-by-step guide on how to live your life the minute we left the womb. It's a very traditional lifestyle, in a modernized city. The typical Peruvian woman is expected to become a great housewife and care for her children and loving husband. And that's it.

Living in a small, high-class community isn't so easy all the time. Everybody knows everyone's business. If you misbehave or stray from the ordinary, you won't only ruin your own reputation, but your family's as well. I fear that if I were to come out of the closet today, it could ruin my father's practice.

Gay? That's only for drug-addicted men here in Peru. Watching Bette and Tina on *The L Word* is the closest I've come to seeing an open lesbian couple. As I've grown up, I've started having more and more of those weird feelings I had for Miss Jennings. I started looking around for people that experienced or shared the same feelings I did. I couldn't find anyone. I felt so lost, so different, so alone. I had to hide myself, because the only thing I perceived about my feelings toward girls was that they were wrong. I could never do anything to upset my family. I'm just not capable of disappointing them.

I've always been a sporty surfer chick with an offbeat yet funny sense of humor. I get good grades and have a hot surfer boyfriend who's finishing college. I'm cute, popular, and the captain of the varsity soccer team. What else could I want?

How about the ability to feel comfortable with myself, for one. I feel fake. I act fake. It's a tug-of-war competition between who I am and who society wants me to be. I'm not satisfied, and I'm not myself.

Sure, I have a boyfriend. And he is the best boyfriend ever. But he's more of my boy friend than my boyfriend. He is the most loving guy, and we have the best time together. We love the same sports and the same music. We've been together for about two years. Sexually, we have fun together. And even after those random parties where I find myself drunk and desiring, he is a proper gentleman who would never ask or demand anything from me that I wasn't ready for. It's very confusing, my craving for woman and my love for him.

Every time I think of being with a woman, my whole body feels different. I feel those butterflies in my stomach, that tingly sensation, that desire for touching and being touched. Women are incredible, who wouldn't want to kiss the finest lips, the softest skin, to hold perfection and vulnerability simultaneously. Just by watching them, women send me vibes of pleasure. That feeling of excitement is unique and rare.

I constantly try to deny the fact that I cheat on my boyfriend. I've had several encounters with other girls while dating him. But it's different, or at least I want it to be. I want it not to count. But sometimes it feels like it's another me who is doing the cheating—the me that wants to be with a woman. My boyfriend doesn't even care when I tell him I made out with other girls. He thinks I do it just to joke around. I couldn't disagree with him more, and it breaks my heart not to tell him the truth about myself.

When I entered high school, a lot of my friends started the whole "experimenting" phase. We would go to parties and make out with each other, just to go along with a dare. For my friends it was just a game. But for me it was a glimpse into my future.

One of those crazy nights, I found the most amazing friend in a girl named Luana. Luana was the most exquisite girl at school. Although I knew her as a casual friend, this particular night the friendship I found in her was on a different level. She has the most amazing body, and incredible features. Luana is blond, tan, and funny as hell. We got along so well, loved to party together, and would always flirt with each other. We danced closely at clubs and held hands. We had never kissed, but I hoped that's where all this was leading. One night, at a friend's party, we got really drunk, and that's when my passionate friendship with Luana began.

She called me into the bathroom and I followed her. Luana closed the door and switched off the lights. Through the moonlight that shone through the small window, Luana looked at me. "I've been wanting to do this all night," she said. My heart pounded a million beats per second as she slid one of her hands onto my waist and gently pulled me toward her. With her other hand she pulled my head toward hers and pressed her lips against mine. She gave me a tasteful try, then slid her tongue into my mouth. Luana kissed me. It was so passionate, so rhythmic, so perfect, and so incredibly different from any other kiss before. We were so good together.

From that day on, we were hookup buddies. These secret encounters grew frequent, as we really began to enjoy ourselves. During final exams, we took bathroom breaks just to make out. Luana would sleep over and snuggle with me.

However, we couldn't really be together; we were just "close friends." One day, Luana told me that she had met a guy, and that she was really falling for him. I prayed nothing between us would change.

Sadly, Luana and I did in fact grow apart. But it wasn't so much about the boy. Luana's family moved to the States. We still remain good friends. And even though we don't get to see each other often, every time we do, we slip back into our savage little secret. I guess you could call us "casual lovers." Over time, it's been great to have Luana as both a passionate friend and a lover. We've experimented and experienced many things together. Doing so has allowed me to discover my sexuality. When my heart skips a beat each time I lay eyes on Luana, how can I deny who I am?

# catie

This is all about that aching need. It's about dabbling and jumping in headfirst at the same time. This is about being in love with your best friend. A passionate friendship will throw you on your ass, literally. I'm straight . . . always have been, always will be. But, like many girls, I've swum in that gray area. It takes the gay and the straight, the love and the friendship, to find that dangerously passionate mixture.

I remember knowing who Carmen was since way back in the sixth grade. She was the little Spanish girl with the accent. We had Math and Science together, but we never really talked. To be honest, I was a lot cooler than she was. She'd always laugh at my jokes, though; and, well, I'd always laugh at her. She was a quirky little gal and I found her quite amusing.

At the age of fourteen, I hit a slump. It's not that unusual when eighth-graders begin to slam their bedroom doors and respond to everything their parents say with: "You're ruining my life!" It's like hormones gone wild, but for me, it was more like hormones gone mad. Those screaming arguments with my parents and their attempts to "ruin my life" had tipped me over the edge, and into a deep depression. I blamed everyone for everything; I thought that the whole world was out to get me in some way. I began to isolate myself without even knowing it; I don't remember a time when I felt more alone. I felt fat, although I wasn't. I threw up, because I believed I needed to. I felt worthless, unloved, and completely unable to control anything around me. Whether it was a savior sent to me from God or an entire bottle of Paxil shoved down my esophagus, I needed something to help me through this funk.

I never sought out God or a psychiatrist for my problems. But help did find its way to me. It actually came along on my first day of U.S. Government class. My teacher was Ms. Meryn, a strange lady. The first thing she said to the class was that she believed in aliens. I hated her already. Great. I hated everyone in this class. I took a deep breath, subtly rolled my eyes at the crazy woman, and peeped over my left shoulder to see who was seated behind me. I saw a very warm and comforting face. It was good ole Carmen! I felt like I hadn't seen her in years. We were never really friends, but for some reason I felt refreshed when I saw her face that day.

"What a pleasant surprise," I whispered.

"What up, Catie?" she responded, with a half-assed smirk.

Carmen had blossomed. She looked great, and she no longer spoke like a Brazilian. As the weeks went by, we managed to team up and nonchalantly ease our way into becoming Ms. Meryn's worst nightmare. It was incredibly fun. Carmen understood me. She didn't care, just like me.

In a matter of weeks, our friendship grew. Soon, we were skipping U.S. Government class altogether. Instead of learning about the Constitution, we chain-smoked cigarettes in the woods behind the school. I had never met anyone quite like Carmen, and yet, she seemed so much like me. She made me feel important, needed, and loved; three things I had not felt in a very long time.

We became inseparable, and obsessed with each other. Before long, we had created our own little world, with slang, nicknames, and rituals. Aside from the never-ending fun we shared, we also created a very strong emotional bond. Carmen helped me battle my eating disorder. I was so happy around her that I lost my urge to purge.

We had sleepovers every weekend and we slept incredibly close. We did things most eighth-grade girls didn't do. We kissed on the lips and held hands under blankets. We constantly talked about how much we loved each other and how pretty we found each other to be. I was fascinated by the way she loved me. It was almost as if she were filling all the voids I had in my life. She took care of me like a parent, believed in me like a best friend, and kissed me like a boyfriend. I loved her for it. I just loved being loved.

Our friendship grew and remained strong until high school. Somewhere between eighth and tenth grade, she nursed me back to health. But our relationship changed. I didn't need Carmen the way I used to. She still wanted to partake in our bedtime rituals, but I had grown out of them. I began to notice many cute boys in the hallways at school. I eventually landed an amazing boyfriend, and, almost immediately, Carmen began to slip away. She resented my boyfriend, and although I never really understood it at the time, she was heartbroken.

When Carmen turned twenty-one, she came out of the closet. She explained to me that she had loved me differently, passionately. I loved her, too, but not like that. Carmen was strong and confident when I was not. I latched onto her, and she loved being needed by me. I've spoken to some of my other friends, gay and straight, about Carmen. I was surprised to find that a lot of them had encountered similar seminal relationships. In most cases, the story was the same: young, strong gay girl meets weak straight girl. At the time, sexuality is not an issue, but eventually it leads to the relationship's demise.

I never suspected Carmen was gay; she didn't even realize it back then. Had I known, I would've let her down gently. I wouldn't have stopped speaking to her because she acted bitchy around my boyfriend. I loved Carmen and never wanted to hurt her. Carmen's love for me was pure and innocent.

In college, I had my fair share of drunken make-out sessions with other girls. But none of them were gay. I guess I learned my lesson about fooling around with lesbians. Like the Indigo Girls say, "The hardest to learn was the least complicated. . . ."

## one more thing . . .

You may have experienced a passionate friendship and just never realized it. It is only natural to want to take a friendship to the next level if you yearn to know every facet of your friend. You may fall in love without even knowing it. Extracting yourself from the pseudorelationship you have created is painful, but when you get the attention and passion you deserve, you'll know it's real—and, most importantly, mutual.

CHAPTER EIGHT:
# heartbreak

'Tis better to have loved and lost than never to have loved at all.

—Alfred, Lord Tennyson

No one wants to talk about heartbreak, let alone go through the experience. Each situation has different consequences and bares different feelings, and how you deal with them is your own decision. We just want to offer a few helpful tips as people who have been there and know what it's like to hit rock-bottom. We bounced back and so will you.

## You had a life before you met her

You used to go out to brunch with your friends before she was around. You spent countless nights watching movies and falling asleep alone before her. She hated stupid teen movies, so go see three in a row. She hated that black shirt you used to wear all the time, so wear it for a week underneath everything. Do what you loved to do that you couldn't do. It's liberating. Get back in touch with what you like.

## Questioning your sexuality?

If girls make you hurt this much, maybe they aren't worth it. You might venture to the other side for a night of sloppy, drunk, heterosexual hooking up, only to find that wasn't what you were looking for at all. You are quickly reminded that girls do it much better. It wasn't a mistake, just a part of the healing process.

## Anything that reminds you of her goes in a box. No, not that box—the shoe box

Photos, notes, cards, tickets, gifts, ANYTHING that was given to or reminds you of her should go in a designated box. You might want to burn it all or throw everything out. That's okay; desperate times call for desperate measures. But if you can see a future of reminiscing, try a box with a lid. Hide it somewhere in your closet or under your bed; you'll soon forget what that damn shoe box was full of anyway.

## Put down the crack pipe

Like a drug, she is something you need to wean yourself from. Your structure and routine with her no longer exists, so life feels unstable and time seems immense. To fill the gaps, try to organize dinner parties with friends, taking turns as host. This will give your week some structure and a chance to be around people you love. If you feel it necessary, go to a therapist. Chances are, you and your girlfriend did a lot of talking. Shrinks are great listeners. Unfortunately, they charge by the hour.

## Stop being creepy

If you are both on MySpace or Friendster, stop checking her profile, get off the Internet, and remember what daylight feels like. Erase her screen name and phone numbers. They are no longer of use to you. Avoiding her for a while is your best bet.

## Treat yourself to something good—Dairy Queen, perhaps?

If you want those shoes you've been eying, go buy them. You deserve them. If it's a facial or massage you need, go for it. It's only money. It's time to be selfish. Put your needs first; chances are, you've been putting someone else's first for a while. Embrace your independence and focus on you!

## Get back on the pony

Letting go and accepting that it's over is like a breath of fresh air. Now it's time to get back on the field. It's a small community, but you can handle it. Don't let familiar faces and places cause you to regress; you're doing just fine. She's not the only one for you; there are like fifteen, no matter where you are. So get out there and find the other fourteen.

## Take your time

Healing is the most important process in getting over someone and getting healthy. Grieve, remember, cry, and text her when you're drunk. It's okay—we've all done it. You'll learn what not to do next time.

# lauren blitzer

· · · · · · · · · · · · · · · · · · · · · · · · · · · · · · · · · · · · · · · · ·

When it comes to heartbreak, I've been to the depths of hell and back. And each time, the one thing I realize over and over again is that time heals. Yes, it will be painful for a while, but, no, I won't die alone with ten cats. I will survive.

Maria, my second girlfriend, was quite a few years older, but still, we managed to have an incredibly balanced and healthy relationship. We were approaching our one-year anniversary when things started to go downhill. Slowly, with each passing day, I felt her pulling away. I didn't know what to do. The more I tried to get closer to her, the further away she got. I swallowed my emotions and gave her the space to figure out what she was battling.

I kept my distance, stayed at my own apartment more, and let her come to me. I had invested so much in my relationship with Maria, all I wanted was for it to work. All my belongings were at her place; I had practically moved in with her. When she went out of town, I was there to make sure the dogs were fed and walked. When she returned, I would greet her with open arms and a spotless apartment. I did anything and everything to show her I was everything she was looking for, and so much more.

For a while, it seemed to work. We hardly fought, never got jealous, and agreed on almost everything. We laughed, loved, and were there for each other at all times. She was sixteen years older than me, but her age never seemed to be a problem for me. Maybe my love for her blinded me to the point that I never really thought about our future together. We were what we were. But my age became an issue for her—one that she couldn't ignore any longer.

Things were getting progressively worse. The distance between us was immense. Even the way we slept was a reflection of the widening gap. For the first time in nearly a year, I slept without any part of me touching her. That morning, I knew I had to find out what was going on.

Prepared for the worst, I looked at her and said, "Maria, something's not right. This isn't working anymore." Tears started to build up in my eyes. I didn't want to cry, not yet. Damn it.

"I know. I just don't think I can do this anymore." She couldn't even look into my eyes.

"Why? You need to tell me why," I almost screamed, so frustrated for getting myself into this mess.

"It's the age thing. I can't seem to get over it. I just can't," she said, her face visibly upset.

"Fuck you, Maria! Seriously, fuck you. It's been a year of you loving me and now you tell me you can't do this anymore. Why can't you just get over this?" I bawled. I felt like my heart was being torn from my chest. I got out of bed and screamed, "I hate you!"

In the name of drama, I walked into the bathroom and slammed the door. I hated Maria for making me feel the way I did. I sat on the edge of the bathtub and cried my eyes out.

I sat there for a while. I thought of all the showers I had taken in that bathroom. All the mundane times I'd brushed my teeth and washed my face before getting into bed with her crept into my mind. All the baths I'd taken with her, the woman I loved. After soaking a roll of toilet paper in tears, I found her still in bed wearing a Yankees hat, hiding her face.

I walked over and sat down next to her.

"I don't hate you." I cried softly.

She lifted up her cap and quietly said, "I love you."

I lay down next to her and she held me. My body shook hard, wanting to stay in her arms forever. I prayed that, if I didn't move, then all of this would turn out to be a bad dream. I couldn't stand the distance or the fear I saw in her eyes.

Going into the relationship, I knew that Maria had issues about getting close to people, a fear of intimacy. I just never realized how powerful that fear really was, that it could lead to our relationship's demise. I eventually got up from her bed, afraid of getting too comfortable in her arms.

I didn't know what to do with myself. I paced the apartment, ripping all my clothes out of the drawers and putting them into bags. She was lying there crying, and all I wanted to do was hold her. But Maria had already let me go. Not only had I lost the woman I felt was the love of my life, I had also lost my best friend.

I finally got up the courage to leave Maria's apartment. I regretted having gotten involved with her in the first place, knowing she was bursting with issues. But as the weeks went by and she called to talk, I started to feel lucky to have had this experience, lucky to have fallen into a love so blinding. It was the end of a relationship, not the end of my life.

# hallie

. . . . . . . . . . . . . . . . . . . . . . . . . . . . . . . . . . . . . . . . . . .

I met Jane years ago, and from the moment of our first kiss, the straight lie I was living was forever curtailed. We met at a party. As soon as she walked into the room I knew it was love. I had had crushes on women my whole life, but something about Jane struck a different chord in me. It's as if I knew that this woman would be the one who would change my life forever. Turns out, I was right.

Jane and I became fast friends. Almost instantly, we were obsessed with each other. We talked every minute of every day, fulfilling the lesbian stereotype that two girls fall in love before really getting to know each other. It was the most exciting time in my life. Eventually, we began spending every waking minute together. Sleeping alone was no longer an option, and keys were exchanged within weeks. My days in the office were spent behind closed doors, whispering sweet nothings into the phone: "No, YOU are so cute . . . ," "NO, Jane, YOU, are. . . ."

Jane was my one and only gay relationship. I couldn't believe that my lifelong dream of having a girlfriend had finally come true. But, more importantly, that someone else felt the same way I did. Growing up as a Jewish girl in Scarsdale, New York, being a lesbian was unheard of, and quite taboo. Knowing I was gay my whole life, I feared being ostracized if my secret were let out, as documented in my third-grade journal.

I've heard women tell their stories about coming out in college, even in high school, and I envied their courage. Unfortunately, I never had the nerve to deal with my feelings. By the time I met Jane, I was so ready to experience women that I fell headlong without any protective gear. I never once looked back. Jane became my muse; she was my way out of traditionalism. She simply didn't care what people thought, and led me into a world that, until then, I had been afraid to experience. I wasn't sure if she were really gay, but I was determined to find out.

A few weeks into our relationship, we headed over to a random bar, and Jane did something that completely floored me. Perhaps it was due to both of us getting those "first-love jitters," or maybe the excitement of wanting to share our relationship got the best of her. In either case, the cab dropped us off, and as we prepared to go in, she looked at me with a huge smile and said, "Ready, girl?"

A little confused, I smiled back. Jane slowly reached over, took my hand, and led me into the bar. Normally, two girls holding hands wouldn't draw much of a crowd. But Jane stepped right into the middle of a circle of strangers, and yelled, "Everyone, listen up! Hallie is my girlfriend." She kissed me on the lips—a real kiss—and I almost fainted. The rest of the night was a blur; we spent it making out.

This bliss, however, did not last long. After just a few months, Jane began to question if she could really be with a woman for the rest of her life. (Yes, we had discussed marriage and being together eternally.)

Thus began her emotional roller coaster. Soon enough, my life completely revolved around hers. We no longer stayed at my house because "my shades were too light in the morning," or because of her fear that my roommate would find us (even though my roommate pretty much lived at her boyfriend's house). I found myself obliging every one of her requests, regardless of how it affected me. Behavior I would never have allowed in a relationship was tolerated for fear of losing her. For instance, Jane had no qualms about checking out men when we went out. I would even see her periodically making out with them on the dance floor, right in front of me. She also went on a few dates with men during our courtship. All of these were, of course, to my dissatisfaction, but I wouldn't dare bring it up with her. I feared that the fire it could spark might extinguish this dream that was finally becoming a tangible reality.

Our first breakup came just five months after we got together. Jane couldn't handle the intensity of our relationship; she was overwhelmed. Jane's first tactic was to cut me off completely. The phrases "Can't do this anymore" and "I should have never gotten into this," knocked the wind out of me. I was speechless, shocked; life as I'd come to know it was over.

That's when the endless cycle of heartache began. For more than two years, we would break up, then get back together again a few days later. A month of no contact would pass, and then Jane would call me. I'd fall back, paralyzed, at her mercy. On and on this went, like a car alarm. With each reunion I believed our situation would be different. I convinced myself that she really did love me, and that being gay wasn't the issue, she was just scared. You know how they say love is blind? Well, I was blind as a bat.

During our on-again, off-again relationship, we spent a lot of time just lounging around. One night at my apartment, Jane and I rented a movie, and as we lay close together I really sensed her distance. She never wanted to talk about our relationship, always brushed me off or changed the subject. For whatever reason, that evening I decided to push her to the limit, all the while knowing it would end in disaster. It was building up inside of me and I couldn't hold it in any longer. As I spoke, I began to cry. I told Jane how much I loved and needed her, even though I knew it would push her away. She looked at me, held my face, and told me she had something to tell me. Immediately, I sat up and wiped away my tears. I suspected what I was about to hear would not be pleasant.

"Hallie, I have a date next week with a boy," she said, half smiling.

I stared at her blankly, not knowing what to say next. "What? Who? When did this happen?" My stomach dropped. I felt betrayed. As far as I was concerned, her dating a boy was worse than another girl. I figured he had what Jane wanted, something I could never give her.

"We met him last week, remember? That guy I was talking to at the bar." She went on, but I couldn't hear a word she said.

My mind flashed back to the week before, recalling Jane talking to a tall boy who bought her a drink. That happened so often, I hadn't thought twice about it.

"He called me, and I said I'd go out with him," she said carelessly.

As the words sunk in, I was hit with that all-too-familiar feeling of devastation. I went to sleep that night knowing that I deserved to be treated with respect by someone I loved.

My reunions with Jane became less frequent. I decided to move on and get her out of my life, once and for all. I took her off my Instant Messenger, deleted her phone number, and threw away anything that reminded me of her. The past two years of my life went straight into the incinerator.

Finally, as ironic as it sounds, it was the intolerable heartache that cured me. I turned into the typical breakup junkie, hiding myself from the outside world. I was in so much pain that I wouldn't let anyone in, fearful they would hurt me just as much as Jane had. I wouldn't call people back, and I was constantly in a bad mood. To top it all off, I was moonlighting as a heterosexual.

My parents and close friends became increasingly aware of my post-Jane depression. The pressure eventually became too much, and one day I just burst. I told all my friends and family what had happened, one by one, and thus the healing process began. By finally coming clean and letting everyone in, I was able to breathe again. To my surprise and relief, I was showered with moral support and acceptance, something I had continuously looked for in my relationship with Jane and never found. I was relentlessly looking into an empty barrel when all along there was a full one right next to it. In the end, after a long grieving period, it was time that healed my wounds. I learned that the only person you can control in a relationship is yourself, and that I will never live my life for anyone until I am truly happy in myself.

# dakota

I had dated a handful of guys throughout college, but never really fell for any of them. It was pretty rare for anyone to keep my attention for more than a month or two. After two months, I was already looking for a way out. At the time, I was the Number Two singles player on the women's tennis team. Back then, the combination of my sexual ADHD and lack of spare time convinced me I was not going to meet anyone special. I never bothered to try.

When I first met Jen, I liked her immediately. It was undeniable; we clicked right away. I've never had trouble making friends. I'm outgoing, fun, and athletic. But with Jen, it was more than just your average "fun new friend" thing. We talked a few times a day. I always set aside time to call, and whenever my phone rang I subconsciously hoped it was her. When we hung out, I felt nervous at times, a feeling quite foreign to me.

Late one drunken night, I kissed her. And so began the next two years of my life.

Before our hookup, we had already planned on sharing an apartment. We'd signed a lease a couple of months prior. This made for quite an interesting living situation: a three-bedroom apartment with Jen, me, and a third girl who was completely clueless to the nature of our relationship. Despite the awkward environment, the next year was absolutely incredible. Sure, we were sneaking around in our own home, but I didn't care. I felt so strongly for Jen. I hadn't known I was capable of loving someone so entirely. I didn't want to do anything without her. Thankfully, I didn't have to. Jen played Number One singles, and we traveled together most of the time.

The intensity of our relationship was something I imagined happened only in the movies. I honestly never thought I could be that crazy about someone. Jen was a year older than me, and when she graduated, she began traveling a lot for her job. I was still in college, and at that point, we hit the first test of our love. Before that, we were in our own bubble—always together, no distractions. When Jen began traveling, she grew insecure about us, since our relationship was not out in the open. That's when the problems started.

In the meantime, I told my mom what was really going on between Jen and me. I couldn't lie anymore to the person I was closest to about something so amazing. While my mom was supportive at first, the whole girl-on-girl thing began to wear on her, and it tormented me. The thought of someone I love so much losing sleep over me sickened me. She wasn't going to cut me off or anything, but it just killed me that she couldn't understand.

Over and over I heard my mom say, "But you're not gay. Why would you do this to yourself?" I couldn't get through to her that, yes, I had only been with guys until Jen, but I'd fallen hard for someone who happened to be a girl. It was like I was speaking Chinese to my mother, and the fact that she didn't understand tortured me. I didn't expect her to be able to relate to me, but I wished she could just try to understand. My mom was a wreck, and I was a mess knowing I was breaking her heart. Oddly enough, my mother was my first brush with heartbreak.

Unfortunately, all this was going on all while Jen was traveling and stressing about our changing relationship. I felt suffocated. I started listening to my mom. I would think to myself, *Well, if I'm not gay, where can this go in the future?* The next thought that popped into my head would be: *But I cannot envision my future without this girl.* My head was constantly spinning. It didn't help when I'd get a call from Jen telling me how hard it was to travel while I was still a "college girl." After hanging up with her, I'd inevitably get a call from my mom, who was clearly upset and out of sorts. All I wanted to do was run away and hide.

When Jen was home with me, things just weren't the same between us. The spark was fading, and we were no longer in a state of bliss. Reality had sunk in; she had a job, and she couldn't plan her days around my whereabouts. I was more confused than ever. We fought constantly, near breakup after near breakup.

Eventually, I caved. I watched her pack her bags, both of us bawling. As much as I wanted to dive on her bags and tell her to stay, I kept telling myself, *It's better for your future. Just let her go. . . .*

And so she left. Jen was destroyed. In her eyes, I had just gone and quit on her. Sadly, the problems we had were not just in her head. I had crushed her, and thrown away the best thing that had ever happened to me.

My way of dealing with this was not remotely healthy. I

went out every night and got drunk with my friends. I wanted to numb myself to avoid dealing with the pain. When I was drunk and around my friends, I didn't have to face my loss. However, when I came home alone, I'd lose it.

Jen dealt with our breakup in a different way. She was just as distraught and heartbroken as I was, but she wanted a distraction in the form of a person. She got herself a rebound fling to travel around with her on her job. At the time, I didn't know about Jen's girl. Yet, I began to realize that I had failed, and in a moment of weakness, I let go of the person closest to my heart.

I couldn't handle living without her. And when I got wind of the fact that she had already rebounded, I really lost it. The thought of Jen with another person made me want to vomit. I did everything I could to win her back. It took about a month to convince her that I wasn't going to cave again. That I had messed up, and didn't care anymore what anyone said or thought about us. While I wasn't marching through Gainesville with a rainbow flag draped around my body, I would tell the people I cared about that Jen and I were in love.

She finally let me back in, but it was never the same. For the next eight months, it seemed as though I were dating a completely different girl. She kept telling me to give her time, that she loved me but needed to become her old self again. I completely understood and would've given her all the time in the world if that's what she needed. But the fiery passion was gone. Jen still had intense feelings for me, but she had her guard up. In the back of her mind she thought, *How do I know you won't do this to me again?*

The same girl who used to sometimes cry as we made love, now had me crying while we were hooking up. When I looked into her eyes, I saw hurt and emptiness. I couldn't handle it. Letter after letter, talk after talk, crying session after crying session, my heart was in her hands. She had all the control in the world over me. I waited and waited. I did every little thing in my power to win back her heart entirely, but I was fighting a losing battle.

Jen had always been a stubborn girl; in her eyes she was never wrong. But her behavior went above and beyond stubborn. I would tell her, "If you aren't ever going to come back to me, what am I fighting for? Yes, I fucked up. But, Jen, I am doing everything I can to show you that people screw up, and it doesn't make them bad people. If you'll never move past this, am I just wasting my time?"

Her reply was always, "In time it will be fine, I'm just still hurt."

Well, eight months passed, and still, it seemed like I was a burden to her. I felt like I was being annoying trying to win her back. All the cute little things I did to make her smile or realize how much I loved her weren't even acknowledged. The talks began again, and we both seemed to agree that our relationship was not getting better. We'd almost break up, but the intensity would temporarily come back and we couldn't let go. Things would be okay for a few days, but eventually they'd slip back into the norm.

Finally, I went home for the summer, and we called it quits. I'd given every little part of me to making this relationship the best it could be. But I could not change the repercussions of that first breakup. Her answer to everything was, "If you hadn't broken up with me in the first place . . ." After months of a nonstop guilt trip, constantly being reminded how much I stomped on her heart, I just couldn't take it anymore.

We briefly saw each other once that summer and hooked up. It was natural and out of habit, but I just didn't feel it anymore. Suddenly, she "realized she was wrong all those months." Jen begged me to come back, told me she was still in love with me. But I wasn't happy; I did not want to get back into this again. I had just moved to New York and she was still in Florida. Her timing could not have been worse.

She'd tell me, "I gave you a second chance the first time around. You should be giving me one now." What she didn't realize was that, night after night, for eight not so "straight" months, I gave her chance after chance. Most people would have been too hurt and rejected and called it quits a few months in. In my most humbling moments, when I would pour my heart out and rip myself apart for being so weak, she'd react to me with coldness. I was so emotionally drained at this point I just couldn't walk back into her line of fire again.

I needed time alone to figure things out. I needed to be by myself and let things play out naturally, without forcing them. You can't really make sense of what happens in a breakup until you suffer alone. You can't talk about it with your friends and expect them to understand your situation. Unless they were behind closed doors with you and your girl, they can't possibly give you perfect advice. You can't go out and get wasted every night to numb the pain. And you sure as hell can't pick up the phone and call your ex in a moment of loneliness.

Post-breakup, Jen and I took very different routes in how we dealt with our broken hearts. It's the reason we each stand where we do today. I was in a new city, beginning a new life. I lived alone. I needed new distractions, but I needed my space to be able to deal with things. I didn't do the usual breakup stuff—tear apart photos, remove her screen name from my buddy list, erase her number, et cetera. I left it all there, so I could deal with it.

God, did it hurt at times; but I stayed strong. All the times I cried and wanted to pick up the phone and hear her voice, I resisted. I didn't want to start dating, or have random hookups just to hook up. I just wanted to be alone. I believed I'd never feel what I felt for her again, so why try to find it?

Until I was fully ready to let my baggage go, I was not going to unload that upon anyone else. I met a few people here and there, both guys and girls who held my interest for a short period of time. Yet, anytime they showed interest or actually "liked" me, I went back to my old ways and ran away. I was like some shady guy who wouldn't call back and just dropped off the face of the earth. I just could not be bothered with anything. The last thing I wanted was to feel something good, because that would mean that I might have to go through losing it again.

Thirteen months later, here we are. I have not seriously dated a single person, because, when the time comes, I want them to have all of me. Jen and I don't speak anymore. We've tried a handful of times, but it always ends in a fight. We'll try to bullshit, but in the end, all we can talk about is the first breakup.

Our intensity created a vicious cycle that has not yet stopped. But, very recently, I have started to feel like myself again. I let the hurt stay with me. I hear about Jen and her new girlfriend going here and there. Jen invites our mutual friends to their new house to spend time with them. I just let it sink in and don't vent about it to my friends. Friends serve many purposes, but they are not psychologists.

The last time we spoke, Jen interrogated me. "So, you're just totally fine now? You mean you can actually hear about things in my life? How did you just move on?"

It hurt me. I couldn't understand why she did not want me to move on. Was I supposed to be on her back burner? She was living her own life and involved in a new relationship. I don't know what her thought process was, but I do know that she has not taken the time to deal with our past. When you roll right into a new relationship, it becomes a placebo for your pain.

How can you deal with the past when you have someone new attached to your ass every minute of the day?

I could rant about this for hours, but the bottom line is this: Deal with it. Don't mask it. Don't numb it. I've done it all, in one long relationship. The partying to numb it, the loneliness forcing me to call, the hooking up when you're not together . . . all of these things are temporary. They will never mend a broken heart.

Nothing puts things into perspective like time alone. Everyone I've known who has been mature and independent enough to suck it up and deal with the pain is better off today. From what I've seen, a girl-girl relationship brings with it a heightened level of intensity. But just because you crave that passion doesn't mean you should immediately go looking for it.

The best things come along when you're feeling good about yourself, your life is drama-free, and you're not looking for anything. Enjoy yourself! You've got all the time in the world. Don't force something that isn't there. There is no better remedy for a broken heart than patience and time. You can't change the past or predict the future. Stay honest with yourself, and the heartbreak will get better with each passing day.

## one more thing . . .

Life existed before you had a girlfriend and will continue to now that she is your ex. It takes time to adjust to not having the sweet smell of her perfume on your pillow, or kissing her lips before you go to sleep and after you wake up. It's painful, but you won't die of a broken heart. With time, you will heal.

CHAPTER NINE:

# hooking up with straight girls

Some women can't say the word lesbianžžžžževen when their mouth is full of one.

—Kate Clinton

I t's inevitable: If you do decide to go gay, you'll see more experimenting come your way than a seventh-grade science fair. Curious straight girls will flock to you. You may even try to convert straight chicks to "the lifestyle." Don't be surprised if you attempt more conversions than a rabbi in Martha's Vineyard.

For most budding lesbians, it's the straight schoolgirls who surround us that turn us on. A quick glance at the hottie changing next to you in the locker room, a late-night massage with your best friend—these are the experiences that confirmed for us what we wanted and who we would become.

So why are hookups between gay women and straight women so widespread? We know we should stay away from the straight and narrow, but sometimes they're just too hot to resist. The myth of the "do-able" heterosexual—or its twin urban legend, the deep closet case just waiting for the right same-sex key to unlock them—is everywhere in gay culture. Here are some tips on navigating the straights.

## Finding the chewy center

Straight girls are just like Tootsie Pops. Some lesbians take the slow, wear-down-the-hetero-crush approach: teasing, flirting, lengthy touching, and phoning until the other woman gives in. Others go right in for the kill. Really, now, who has the patience to wait around?

## Grand prize, an ego boost

The idea that you have enough sex appeal to "turn" a straight woman on for some same sex nasty may be one of life's greatest ego boosts. After all, gay sex remains one of straight people's biggest taboos, so you must be all that and a bag of chips if you snag a breeder.

## Looks are everything?

If a chick sets off your particular, inexplicable sexual radar, you're likely to lean over to your pal with little hesitation and say, "Check her out: hot!"—or the more discreet equivalent, "Babe at two o'clock." It's only after we attempt to size up a girl that we consider her sexual preference.

## The flock of the curious

Some straight-chasers win, some lose, and some end up with black eyes. But the next time you set your sights on some sexy straight chick, ask yourself something first: What kind of opposite-sex invitation would you need to make you switch teams? More and more, straight women are dabbling in sex with other women. From the Madonna/Britney kiss to the lesbian affairs on mainstream shows like *Ally McBeal* and *Buffy the Vampire Slayer* to the popularity of *The L Word,* the media has relied on lesbian make-out sessions to boost ratings.

## The proof is in the plethysmograph

Plethysmograph studies point to a biological basis for differences in male and female sexuality. (A plethysmograph is an instrument that measures physiological arousal.) Heterosexual women hooked up to a plethysmograph showed symptoms of arousal in response to lesbian porn; even those women who denied having interest in sex with another woman showed physiological arousal in these tests.

## Reality bites

But you've got to be realistic: Hooking up with a straight girl will likely be a one-night stand. As they say, the difference between a straight girl and a gay girl is four beers. The hetero chick may be drunk, up for some sexual experimentationžžžžand then want nothing to do with you the next morning. If you want more than a one-night stand, you probably shouldn't hook up with her in the first place.

## Don't let straight girls become your vice

Hooking up with a gay woman is complicated enough. With concern for your mental health, we plead with you not to let straight girls become your vice. We have friends who played the straight-girl game for quite a while. In the end, most went back to lesbians. It's nice to be with a woman you don't have to worry will ditch you for a dude. Making a habit of converting heteros can make a lesbian feel like little more than an open buffet, which can be damaging to her self-esteem. More likely, it will remind her to adhere to lesbian rule Number One: Don't tease or feed the straights.

## Safest sex possible? Impossible sex

The assertion seems counterintuitive, but often it's true: Chasing after the straight ones gives us all the pleasures of fixation without the danger of acquisition and the risks of a relationship. It's non-threatening lasciviousness without follow-through. For the commitment phobes out there, what better way to bypass "I do" than to say "I'm only attracted to heteros"?

## Predator or prey?

Of course, the gay girl is not always the predator in these types of situations. Many times, we are the prey. Like everyone else, straight women enjoy being lifted onto a lusty admirer's pedestal. They know there's a wealth of wooing to be had if they flirt, even if only ever so slightly, with their gay friends. A straight girl will lean in and coo to her gay friend, "What's it really like to be with a woman?"

## How can you be friends if you can't be lovers?

If you can handle not ever seeing this woman again, then, by all means, show her what you had in mind in the bedroom. However, if you can't, beware. Friendships have been lost over experimentation. The repercussions of the hookup are more important than the cause. What if your friend falls in love with you and you weren't looking to do anything more than rid your friendship of sexual tension? Or what if it's the other way around?

Just as hard as it is to not feed the animals at the zoo, staying away from straight women can be near impossible. If you take it as seriously as Paris Hilton takes engagements, you'll bypass potential disappointment. But tread very lightly, or someone might get hurt.

# lauren levin

• • • • • • • • • • • • • • • • • • • • • • • • • • • • • • • • • • • • • • •

I used to believe everyone to be "hetero-flexible." Yeah, right—wishful thinking. On the cruise ship, when I first came out to my family, I went on a bender. I was a make-out bandit with all the curious chippies onboard. I even Frenched two sisters—at different times, of course. However, upon my return to New

York I learned that, much to my dismay, there are girls who really are straight. Thinking otherwise is as ignorant as saying gay doesn't exist.

It saddened me to learn that girls who thought I was cute and cool didn't want to hook up with another girl. Yet, despite some minor heartache at not being able to physically express my feelings for some of my straight friends and acquaintances, I moved on to girls of a "hetero-curious" nature.

There was my friend Molly. In high school, Molly and I were friendly. When I learned she lived in New York, I contacted her and suggested we go out for drinks. I'd had a minor crush on Molly in high school, but thought nothing of it at the time.

Molly came over to my apartment for cocktails and hung out for a while. She looked smokin'. I wanted a piece. However, she was heartbroken over some dude and kept rambling on about it. Being that we had nothing else to do, I suggested to Molls that we go to a lesbian bar. I was pleasantly surprised that she was down for going out gay.

We hopped in a cab and went to the big lesbo party bar in New York, Nations. After a couple vodka sodas and shots of SoCo, we both felt a little warm and fuzzy. We wandered up the stairs to the plush purple couches in the corner. Molly and I sat close, our legs brushing up against each other's. I didn't think of making a move on her, since she'd been going on about guys too long. Even for a liberal thespian like Molly, attending your first lesbian party is a big step; I didn't want to press my luck.

In the midst of a conversation about nothing in particular, Molly turned to me and said, "Do you think it would be weird if we kissed?"

*Score*, I thought. *This chick is coming on to me!*

"Weird? Not all," I replied, touching her leg. "I think it'd be hot."

I looked into Molly's eyes and kissed her gently. She sighed and grabbed my hand. She was into it, so I didn't hold back. We continued to kiss softly, gently. Even though the party was packed, I felt like we were the only two people in the world. I pulled her on top of me and kissed her neck. She moaned and I wanted more. I put my hands between her legs, right over her jeans. This time, she moaned louder. I could tell she wanted to come. I tirelessly caressed her sweet spot, the friction between my hands and her jeans building quickly. Molly threw her head back and gasped for air. A couple moments later, she screamed my name. I did it! For the first time in my life, I made a straight girl cum! I couldn't have been more happy if Lindsay Lohan was going down me.

We stumbled out of the bar. Molly and I hopped in a cab and I asked her to come home with me.

"I will another time, but I'm not fully groomed down there right now, and I don't want you to see me like that," she said, laughing.

"Oh, come on, I don't care," I told her. Even though I probably did care a little, I wanted her to think I was down with the punani, hairless or not.

"Well, babe, I care. Another time, for real." She squeezed my hand and told the cab driver we'd be making two stops. "Cheer up, Lauren. You not only brought me to a lesbian bar for the first time, you made me cum. I can't say that's happened to me at a straight bar before."

When she put it like that, I felt victorious. I fell asleep with a smile on my face. The next morning, I woke up wondering if anything would happen again between Molly and me. We spoke on IM that week and when Friday rolled around we met up at a random bar in the East Village. A bunch of kids from our hometown were in the city, including Molly's ex-boyfriend, Zander. When Molly grabbed my hand and pulled me into the single stall bathroom, I knew what was about to go down. Hastily, I slammed the door behind us, and threw her up on the sink.

This time, our kisses were quick and needy. I wanted her badly and she wanted me, too. Neither of us had forgotten the last time we hung out, and I needed to hear her orgasm again. She guided my hand right to the crotch of her jeans. I rubbed her deeply, in little circles, back and forth. Making Molly come was like learning to riding a bicycle. Once I knew how to do it, my body could never forget the motions. In ten minutes it was over. We kissed and opened up the bathroom door.

"What the fuck took you two so long in there?" Zander was pissed.

"Um . . . we were just . . . going to the bathroom," Molly lied, flustered.

Being that Zander was a friend of mine, I panicked and sketched out of the bar. I didn't want to stick around for any more drama. As Molly and Zander fought, I left the bar without saying good-bye. For a bit, things were a little awkward with Molly, but we've continued to remain friends. Last time I heard from her, Molly had a new boyfriend. I had a girlfriend. Our sexual tension was as good as gone; it never reared its ugly head again.

# lauren blitzer

Ahhh, straight girls—where do I begin? At first, I think of my ex, Sharon. And then there's my best friend from college, Victoria. She considered herself to be straight, which I've found equals, at the very least, bi-curious. V and I would occasionally enjoy a romp in the bathroom of some bar or club in New York, her boyfriend sighing all the while at how silly it was that girls always have to go to the bathroom together. Ha! If he only knew . . .

The more typical response I get from straight girls regarding being gay is, "Wow, I didn't know they came that way"—meaning my way. The stereotype of women who look and act like men is still rampant, even among the most educated of people. After the shock dissipates, a look of curiosity and mischief appears on most of these women's faces.

The most recent physical encounter I've had with a straight woman happened in, yet again, a lesbian bar. There are so many "straight" girls in gay bars these days, they might as well just throw lesbo parties at Victoria's Secret. Anyway, it was one of those steamy June nights where you can't seem to do anything, let alone breathe, without sweating profusely.

I was meeting my beautiful co-author at the popular Tuesday-night lesbian party, Snapshot, at Boys Room in the East Village. We just planned on discussing some business over one drink. Aside from the fact that the heat was killing me, I was tired and had to get up early for work. Regardless, I built up some momentum and hopped on my bike. I skipped the drink special at the door, intending to have only one drink, some conversation, and then home to sleep. God, if only I had a nickel for every time I said that and then ended up in a completely different predicament.

I found Levin and we chatted for some time, but it became harder to hear each other as the bar grew more and more packed. In walked lesbians of all shapes and sizes. We noticed our friend Laura, her girlfriend, and a gaggle of what appeared (and was confirmed to be) straight women. We approached Laura and began chatting it up. I strayed over to the bar, and noticed that next to me was one of Laura's girlfriend's straight, very hot, friends. I introduced myself and she did the same.

Her name was Danielle. She turned out to be married and straight. Normally, Danielle's marital status would be a clear indication of her being there solely in support of her lesbian friend and the promise of a seven-dollar cover for an open bar. Well, this time my assumption proved false . . . and it ended up getting me some ass!

We got to talking and she told me she had been married for five years, but she'd been with her husband for ten. Danielle was thirty-five, with dark hair, blue eyes, freckles perfectly placed on her face and nose, and a beautiful smile. As we got a little more buzzed, I asked her if she had ever been with a woman.

Danielle looked me dead in the eye and said, "Yeah. Who hasn't?"

She told me about a quasi-gay experience she'd had while studying abroad in Brazil. She described it as awkward and mechanical. I told her what a shame that was! And she laughed. I was starting to really feel the booze, and I asked her what she thought of lesbians—a question I would pretty much never ask.

She replied quickly, "They're hot!" Danielle smiled at me with her eyes and lips.

I blushed and turned to her, a little surprised. "Really??"

"Yeah, of course. I think girl-on-girl action is hot. Women are beautiful. They are soft, warm, and delicious," she shot back. Better than I could have described it myself.

I replied with a sly smile, "Well, yes. I couldn't agree with you more."

She looked at me. I looked at her. She grinned at me with what appeared to be bedroom eyes. The music was all I could hear and her face was all I could see. I wasn't sure what was happening. I hadn't really allowed my head to go there . . . she was married, for Christ's sake! But I was drunk and couldn't keep my hands from sliding down to her hips every few minutes. It wasn't appropriate at all, but she got closer to me each time I touched her. She was practically sending me a personal invite into her pants!

Danielle continued. "I think that all women are bisexual, if not fully gay. Every woman who is in touch with her sexuality must find it hot to think about, or actually be with another woman." For a split second, I couldn't decide who was speaking, me or her.

"Again, I couldn't agree with you more," I said jokingly.

"No, I'm serious. I have been married for five years and I love my husband more than anyone. But from a purely sexual standpoint, I think women are hot. I've always felt that way. I just can't imagine being in a relationship with one." Her voice was slurred.

"Wow, that's exactly what my ex said the night we met." I laughed and followed the comment with a quick, "Not that I am comparing the two of you at all."

Danielle just looked at me and said, "Hypothetically, what if we went to the bathroom together?"

I nearly spit out my drink. "What do you mean?"

"You heard me. What if you and I went to the bathroom, together?"

She was propositioning me. I didn't know how to react. The woman was basically spelling out the fact that she wanted to have her first "real" lesbian experience with me. I did the only thing any level-headed single lesbian could do at the moment.

"I am going to the bathroom." After a long pause I added, "Are you coming?"

Danielle got up from the bar stool and followed me into the bathroom. I walked in with her following me like a lost puppy and locked the door behind us. The bathroom was a surprisingly large single. Just my luck. The lighting was fluorescent, but it didn't matter. I turned around and pushed Danielle against the wall. I put my hands on her face and kissed her hard. She dropped her purse and put up her hands in surrender. This was my time to be aggressive and have no inhibitions. The woman didn't know me, and I assumed I would never see her again. It was a one-night stand. I could be whoever I wanted to be.

We kissed passionately for a while, just like I'd wanted to all night long. She made little noises as our tongues intertwined together perfectly. Each kiss was better than the last; I didn't want to stop. It felt so good. . . . I was dizzy and hot from the drinks and the thrill of what was happening. This woman was older, married, straight, and, most importantly, it was her first time. She was kissing me as if she'd never kissed with such passion in her whole life. Danielle totally turned me on. I was enjoying myself to no end.

My left hand undid her pants while my right unclasped her bra. Nothing had ever gone so well in my entire life. I thought about how smooth she must think I am, when in reality I'm so not!

Danielle let out a moan as I took off her shirt and let it drop to the floor. She couldn't contain herself as my other hand ventured down south. It was getting ridiculously hot and sweaty. I had forgotten that we were in a bathroom, with a long line of lesbians waiting to use it. God, if they only knew what was going in there, they'd let me be!

The knocks on the door became louder and less sporadic. I didn't care and neither did she. Loudly, Danielle screamed, "Back off!" to the stranger on the other side of the door. I pushed her against the sink and used my hand to make her moan. Within minutes, she was having an orgasm. I wasn't sure if it was what I was doing, or the sheer pleasure and naughtiness of the scenario, but, whatever it was, it made me hot. And it was certainly working for her.

I turned the faucet on cold as we continued to kiss. I ran my hand under the freezing water and dripped it all over her back and shoulders. Her skin shone with hints of a new summer tan. She rested her head on my neck, in shock and pleasure. It was so hot in the windowless bathroom, and our actions had just cranked up the heat by about ten degrees. I was comfortable with her head resting on my shoulder.

As Danielle tried to button up her pants, one last, loud knock on the door jolted us both back upright and back to reality. She looked at me with her beautiful hazel eyes and said, "Wow."

No other words were spoken about what had happened as we went back to the bar, exhausted and ready to go home. I said good night to her and we exchanged e-mail addresses.

I got in bed, pleased with myself. I had finally taken sex and love and put them in two separate places. Previously, they were one and the same. Now I was living. I was happy. I assumed I would never see Danielle again, and, to be honest, I was okay with that. What happened that evening was the kind of thing you see on television shows like *The L Word,* or in the movies. Straight women don't have one-night stands with lesbians in the bathroom of gay bars, do they? I began to wonder how many married women out there fantasize about that very thing. Danielle couldn't be the only one! The thought made my head spin. I fell asleep smelling of Marc Jacobs perfume and cheap vodka.

I woke up the next morning to the vibration of my BlackBerry. A little envelope appeared on the top-left corner of the view screen. It was Danielle. I was pleasantly shocked. What the hell would a married woman want with a cute lesbian, the day after they had fooled around? I was sure she was done with me, and I wasn't sure what to do with her. I was about to find out. as I scrolled down the screen.

*I have three words for you, oh my god. . . . . . . . Danielle*

I smiled and blushed as I put my BlackBerry down and proceeded to fall back asleep for fifteen more blissful minutes.

Danielle was safe; she was already hitched, which made flirting with her fun. I was still heartbroken from my ex, and in no position to be in a relationship. She was a perfect distraction for me. The previous night burned images into my head, sending me into a sweat. It was as if I were watching the whole thing from above; I was so aware of every moan and facial gesture she made. Just one flashback to last night sent me into a frenzy.

She was sweet and unavailable—right up my alley. I wondered if she was down to have a repeat of the previous night, this time horizontal. I perform much better when I'm in not such compromising situations. I allowed myself to fantasize about getting an amazing hotel room and conquering this woman for hours.

After a few hours, I decided to write back. I kept it equally as simple, except I couldn't help but wonder if she had told her husband about our little rendezvous. Instead of wondering, I just asked her in the e-mail; I didn't have much to lose. It took me a while to hit "send," as I read the e-mail over and over again, making sure I hadn't made any horrible spelling or grammatical errors.

Danielle responded quickly. She laughed at my honesty, but told me that, as much as she wanted to have a repeat session, this time it would have to involve her husband. It was my first real invitation to a threesome, and to be honest, I considered it for about two seconds. But I had to break the unfortunate news to her, which she had assumed would be my answer.

We e-mailed back and forth for a few days, flirting and teasing about the idea of me joining the happy couple in the sack. We both knew I'd never go through with it, but part of me was curious to meet her husband. I needed to see what I was up against! Danielle pushed the idea of a threesome every chance she got. She told me how badly she wanted me, but not at the cost of her marriage.

My curiosity was piqued when Danielle told me she was

going to a party with her husband and her lesbian friends. She asked me to stop by. "Just meet him," she said. "There's no harm in that, right? You can just see the man I love, and maybe, just maybe, you'll want to go home with us," she said, half kidding.

"I don't know. I'm really not into that, but hanging out with you guys won't do me any harm. I'm sure he's a great guy. I'm just not sure I want to be in bed with him. I decided that a long time ago, actually. It's not you or anything," I replied.

"Then, unfortunately—and this kills me to say—it's nothing," she said sadly.

The tone in her voice was borderline weepy. I decided to show up at the party with plenty of friends to back me up, and mostly make it seem like I wasn't there to meet the next two people I was going to sleep with.

I couldn't understand why I was so nervous, and for no good reason. In my head I had decided that I was not going home with them, even if her husband looked like Brad Pitt. That's not what I'm about.

So I got on my bike, a little tipsy (not safe), and went to the Chinese restaurant/bar in the East Village where the party was. My friends were there when I arrived, so I got a quick drink with them at the upstairs bar before venturing down to what felt like a setup. I took those steps toward the room they were in feeling like all eyes were on me and everyone knew why I was there. I finally looked up to see Danielle smiling at me, but with no man in tow. Thank God. She came over, gave me a kiss, and whispered, "You smell so good."

I blushed an undetectable shade of red and we sat down on the soft leather stools. She looked amazing, as she always seems to, and I felt like I was on a dating show. I eyed every man that walked by, thinking that he was her husband. It became a game to me. She was talking away as I scoped out the room. Finally, a man with light brown hair, a striped button-down, and nice jeans came over and put his hand on her head. She looked up and smiled. I knew it was him. Danielle turned to me and said, "This is my husband, Chris." I shook his hand and introduced myself.

Apparently, he had heard a lot about me. I had to say the same back to him. I felt awkward talking to him, knowing that we were both into the same woman, except that he got to go home with her every night. The conversations were sparse and uncomfortable. I took the initiative and got up to get another drink, and of course she came over for a status report.

"So, what do you think?" she asked, like a little girl awaiting her new puppy.

I replied with as much enthusiasm as I could muster. "He seems really sweet."

"Oh, I get it. He's just not your type," she said, her eyes to the ground.

"Honey, I'm gay—of course he's not my type. I wish I was interested, but I'm not," I whispered honestly.

"I know, I know. A girl can dream, right?"

"Of course she can, and I will about you tonight," I said sweetly.

She looked at me and smiled, then offered to walk me out. We walked up two blocks and she took my hand. I hailed a cab, and as I was getting in, she grabbed me and kissed me one last time, long and passionately. My knees went weak; I felt like a soldier going to war. It was one of those closing-scene movie kisses where you know it will be the last kiss with that person. I got in the cab and headed home, reliving my cinematic ending. And then laughed, remembering that I'd left my bike locked up outside of the bar I was just at!

I was glad to have had what I did with Danielle. There were no strings attached and no possibility of a future with her. She was gorgeous, smart, sexual, and straight. I considered that evening in June to be a hallucination, given the heat, but came to grips with the fact that it was all real. Just thinking about it sent an empowering rush of confidence through me.

Straight women are funny that way; they end up being the more aggressive ones, once they realize what they want They remain somewhat of a mystery to me, but God bless them!

# falon

I came out when I was fifteen years old. It was in 1996. If you recall, being a lesbian in 1996 was very different from what it is now. Girls weren't experimenting at such a young age. There was a definite shortage of hot "bi-curious" girls in my high school. Nor were there a lot of hot, out, femme lesbians for me to choose from. In fact, I was probably the only out femme lesbian to step foot in my school. I have nothing against butch women; they just aren't my type. Throughout most of my teen years, I thought that the majority of lesbians were butch, and that I was only attracted to "straight" girls.

Naturally, I started going for the straight girls I was attracted to. Sometimes they ended up being bisexual, but for the most part they were straight. But I didn't care. I was attracted to them, and that's all that mattered to me. At a young age, I realized that a lot of girls call themselves straight because they want to feel normal, even if "straight" doesn't encompass their true desires and/or experiences. These girls want to have lesbian experiences without their lives being defined by them. Wouldn't that be nice?

In 2000, I took a class in college called "Lesbians and Gay Men in Society." It was in this class that I met my current girlfriend of five years. Before you flip back to the beginning of the chapter, to clarify that you're still reading "Hooking Up with Straight Chicks," hold tight. My girlfriend, Erica, was at that time, based on her experience, a straight chick. I saw her on the first day of class and thought she was the most beautiful girl I had ever seen. I interrogated Erica as to why she would choose this class, and after a while I accepted that she wasn't there to cruise. She was just a really progressive, straight, open-minded person.

That began our very intense, passionate friendship. Erica and I had so much in common. We came from similar families, and we hit it off from the very beginning. We became inseparable. Everyone (including her) knew I had a huge crush on her. I didn't deny it, because I did! I got a lot of flak for committing so much time and energy on someone who wasn't "gay." My friends predicted that Erica would ultimately waste my time and never reciprocate my feelings. Most of this talk came from my gay girlfriends and my then-closeted roommate. Everyone was very concerned about how far over on the Kinsey scale she slid, but it didn't matter to me. What mattered to me was that I'd found the girl I'd been looking for since I was fifteen. What these people didn't know was how I felt Erica felt. Deep down, below the fears and the risks, I felt she liked me too. Her feelings mattered more to me than some arbitrary labels I felt were too limiting to describe anyone, including myself.

I didn't see the "gayness" in Erica. It may have been one of the reasons I liked her so much. After having dated women for the previous four years, it was kind of a relief not to have to deal with the repetitive lesbian problems I'd encountered with card-carrying members. There was no U-Haul on the second date, no figuring out which girls we'd both hooked up with, and no "I love you" after one week of dating. Better yet, no tapered jeans, ever! Bringing Erica over to our team wasn't easy; it took me three years, but it did spare me all of the above.

In our first couple of years, Erica was a Straight Girl Who Fell in Love with a Lesbian. After a few more years of dating me, it was hard for Erica to exclude her own experience from that title. So now, if forced to be labeled, she would consider herself bisexual. Before we met, she had a genuine attraction to men, and still does. I'm totally okay with that, because I have a genuine attraction to women! At this point, Erica feels comfortable talking about being attracted to other women. But, like everything else that comes along with hooking up with straight chicks, it took some time to get there. We try to avoid labels altogether, but, since most people's understanding of sexuality is limited to straight, gay, or bi, it is hard to never use them.

I'm the only woman Erica's ever slept with. Does it scare me that she's only been with me? I get asked this question a lot. Actually, I'm really honored to be the only woman in Erica's life. She's a beautiful girl who could have anyone she wanted, yet she chooses to be with me. I find that fact alone really significant.

She's had the option to be with men, and let's face it, it's easier to be straight. There are no complications getting married. You can introduce your partner to the members of your family without explanation. So, when we decided to become a couple, I never forgot that Erica could've taken an easier route. I knew she must really love me to "come out" for the sake of being my girlfriend.

Fear is the emotion that holds us back from what we truly want. If Erica had let fear overpower her love for me, we'd never share the incredible life we do today. Don't ever let labels, or other people's perceptions of sexuality, dictate your experiences in life. Otherwise, you might miss out. I'm sure glad I didn't.

# Maya

There's something about being someone's first lesbian experience that's very exciting. In fact, it's borderline addictive. There is this knowledge that you're introducing her to a world unknown, a place thought about but not yet explored. You feel this arrogant yet surprisingly altruistic sense of pride in being in this position, as if you're doing your civil duty as a gay woman. I feel good about being a part of furthering someone's understanding of herself. But let's face it: The fact that no one else will be her first, that you have facilitated her initiation into a place where her desires and fantasies can come to fruition, is totally hot.

One of my most intense experiences occurred with a woman named Jill. She was someone who had never been intimate in any way with another woman before. Jill was a college friend of my close friend Karen. I only had the pleasure of seeing her a handful of times a year. I had always been curious about her, and never quite knew what to make of our semi-flirtatious interactions. Her physical appearance was always very appealing to me: dark hair, green eyes, and a naturally athletic body. For a Long Island Jew, Jill wore an impressively minimal amount of makeup, carried a modest bag, and didn't find it necessary to straighten her hair every time she left the house. I found her refreshing.

Our encounters were intoxicating, partly because I only saw Jill at bars or cocktail parties. When we greeted each other, I found myself getting surprisingly nervous yet pleasantly excited. Provided a little social lubrication, I'd contain my slight jitters and start chatting up Jill with startling ease. We were always very engaged in each other's words. Jill was funny, and at times I'd find myself staring at her. I hoped to God my undivided attention didn't make her feel uncomfortable. I loved making her laugh. I remember thinking how well we clicked for two people who hardly see each other.

Naturally, this thought led me to wonder if any part of Jill was attracted to me. Having literally no grounds (besides my own intuition) for answering yes to that question, I would try to erase the idea from my mind. I'd find myself disappointed when it came time to say good-bye to her at the end of the night. Time would pass, and I'd consider at length whether she was sending signals to my fine-tuned gaydar, or if being with Jill was an unrealistic wish fueled by one-sided attraction.

And then Valentine's Day hit—every single person's day to reflect on their loneliness. As I never seemed to be involved with anyone during this fraud of a holiday, I made a habit of celebrating my independence in front of the television. But Karen insisted on a night out with the girls to show Hallmark who's boss. With all my shows lined up for the evening, I was hesitant to get out of my sweats or off my couch. That was, until Karen mentioned that the party was starting at Jill's apartment. Suddenly, the idea of going out became a lot more appealing.

I arrived at Jill's, gave her a quick and perhaps nervous kiss hello (on the cheek), and greeted the rest of the girls in the living room. I went to put the bottle of wine I'd brought in the refrigerator. As I closed the fridge door, a hand touched me on the shoulder, and I heard Jill ask, "Are you finding what you'd like?" Even after she removed her hand, the feeling of her touch stayed with me. I assured Jill of my nondiscriminating tastes in liquor as I grabbed myself a beer. It wasn't long until our usual flirtatious chatter began, but this time I felt something that wasn't there before.

Sitting on the couch next to her, something was drawing us together. I know it sounds hokey, but it truly felt as though it would be impossible to leave her side because of the intense energy flowing between us. It was, of course, totally possible that I was concocting this whole thing in the spirit of the holiday, but something told me I wasn't. We were sitting just a little too close, looking at each other a little too long, and "unintentionally" touching each other a little too much for this to be in my head.

The ladies soon got restless, so we all headed out to the bar. For all I cared, I could have stayed on that couch with Jill all night, absorbed in our own world. On the way to the bar, we each walked with a friend, but I could feel myself keeping track of her every move, as if not to lose her. I was excited to see that this energy between us existed outside the confines of her apartment.

As we entered the bar, we encountered a sea of people. Jill was right in back of me now, and I welcomed what would usually be the annoyance of people pushing into you, because in this case it forced us to be as close together as possible. I could feel her body next to mine, and was tempted to grab her hand as we made our way through the mass of people, but I decided against it so as not to potentially scare her. When we finally made it to the back of the bar, I realized that Jill and I had lost our friends in the crowd behind us.

Before I could even ask her what she wanted to drink, she shot her green eyes at mine and said, "I've really been wanting to tell you something."

I was surprised by her timing and her sense of urgency. I asked, "Oh, is something wrong?"

She looked down for a moment, with a smile reeking of embarrassment. As her eyes met mine again, she murmured softly, "I don't think there's anything wrong with it. . . ."

A little perplexed and extremely curious, I waited to hear what she had to say next. I was tempted to interrupt the brief, awkward silence, but at that moment the words came out of her mouth. "I've always been attracted to you, and I can't explain it to myself."

Wow. Even the intensity and energy of things between us that night would never have led me to think this was what she wanted to tell me. It was a statement that confirmed all that I had felt. Nothing was held back. Yet there was this confusion about it; she knew how she felt but didn't know how those feelings belonged to her. I stared at her for a moment, finding the words to describe how I felt.

They came to me. "I've felt something between us for a long time, but I never knew if you felt it too. I know it's probably confusing right now, but I'm happy you were comfortable enough to tell me how you felt."

As the somewhat tense expression on her face turned to a genuine smile, she remarked, "I'm glad I told you."

Now that our feelings were out in the open, the energy between us flowed with even more force than before. With renewed confidence in my detection skills, I took her hand and asked, "Wanna dance?" She gave a little nod and we headed to the middle of the floor, where we could avoid the gazes of our friends. Just like our conversations, the way we danced together felt natural and unforced. Being so close to each other at that moment felt right. We no longer had to be self-conscious about touching each other or getting too close. Our hands were allowed to explore without restraint. The heat between us was exhilarating. There was nothing I wanted to do more than kiss her. Every part of my body was telling me to do so, and the way she was touching me told me to go for it.

I slowly brushed the hair from her face and met her lips with mine. Again, I was surprised by how in sync we were; nothing felt forced or awkward. For a first-timer, she was amazing! I didn't want this feeling to end, but I knew that it was only a matter of time before the ladies came searching for us.

We found our friends and spent the rest of the night with them. Jill and I shot little smiles and glances at each other in recognition of our secret. The thought of going home together was not an option. I knew that taking things too far that night would ruin the experience.

As we said good-bye to each other that night, I wasn't sure what was going to happen with us in the future. And, although the night ended with ambiguity, that did not overshadow the meaning it had for both of us. As we departed, I felt a mixture of fulfillment and pride. I was thrilled that this attraction was indeed two-sided, and that I was her first experience with a woman.

I guess you could say I "converted" Jill. After that night, we dated for a year. Today, she is still a good friend—a good lesbian friend!

# stephanie

When most girls my age were braiding their dolls' hair, I was figuring out how to wear boxer shorts under my tights. I was extremely athletic, even as a child. At an early age, there was a blurred line in terms of where my sexuality really lay. But I always knew I liked boys. While I was kicking the crap out of them on the field, I was also figuring out how to get them to kiss me off the field. I wanted to be a boy, but at the same time I wanted boys to want me. Since childhood, not much has changed. Even though I'm married to a man, I still want attention from other men—and, I guess, women.

The first girl I ever kissed in high school was cute, and also very confused. I saw her as a charity case I was going to help. Her mom had come out of the closet while we were the closest of friends, and now she was trying to figure out if she had the same genes running through her body. So I helped her figure it out. I don't think she's been with a boy since.

The same thing happened in college. A very curious girl, Amber, came along, and I offered her my services. Maybe it was just that I liked being the ruler by which confused girls measured their sexuality. Regardless, Amber took it a little too far for my heterosexual taste. She tried to go as far as she could, and I stopped her dead in her tracks before it got uncomfortable. I don't blame her for trying to have sex with me. Amber is a lesbian, even though she didn't know at the time. I was naive, and thought she'd know my limits without my telling her. The bottom line is, we both learned something that night. Amber learned she was a lesbian. And I learned that I liked kissing girls—no more, no less.

It wasn't until I met my college boyfriend that I traded in my baggy cords for skinny black pants. He liked feminine women, so I went from Patagonia to Prada. Transforming my wardrobe wasn't the only thing he tried to change about me. I broke it off with him, graduated, and moved to New York, where I became a loose cannon—a kissing bandit, if you will.

And then I met Brooke. It's a strange story, but try to follow along. At the time, I was dating Doug. He was a very rich, recently divorced, middle-aged man with two kids and a bitchy ex-wife. Looking back, he was the kind of guy who needed arm candy to overcompensate for his limp dick and receding hairline. I was the perfect girl for him. He didn't want another wife, and I didn't want to be tied down. The only person Doug spoke to on his ex-wife's side of the family was her sister, Brooke.

From the moment he described her to me, I knew Brooke and I would be instant friends. And when Doug told me she swung both ways, I thought, *Even better*. I was twenty-four years old, and my insecurities were at an all-time high. How perfect would it be if I got Doug's ex-wife's sister to fall madly in love with me? Without knowing it, Brooke had a target on her back. Little did I know that I had one on mine, too.

Upon first meeting Brooke, I knew we were cut from the same cloth. Without even saying a word, we snuck into some dimly lit corner, leaving our friends and boyfriends behind. We'd only been introduced an hour before, but here we were, in a dark corner of some seen-and-be-seen bar, trying not at all to be seen.

Once we reached our little hideaway, it took all of four seconds for Brooke to shove her tongue down my throat. Brooke's kiss threw electric jolts up my spine. I was putty in her hands. She knew exactly what she wanted: me. And that felt pretty damn good. I wasn't sure what had brought us to that moment, or why we both knew we wanted each other. All I knew was that, at that moment, it seemed as though everyone else was put on this earth to make sure Brooke and I ended up together.

Before I could even take a moment to enjoy her company, it was over. Brooke was back on the dance floor making some belligerently drunk investment banker think she wanted him. I loved everything about her.

I slowly made my way back to Doug, and with pure confidence lied to him about how standing in the long bathroom line made me miss him. To be honest, I don't remember how the night ended. All I know is, the next morning, when I looked at my call-back list, Brooke's number had been added. Bingo!

In the next few weeks, I saw Brooke a handful of times. Each meeting was the same. We would see each other out at one of Doug's chi-chi "dinner parties"—you know, the kind with tiny portions of overpriced food that didn't compensate for the dozen or so specialty drinks served before the food even hit the table.

I had yet to call Brooke, but at each party, like clockwork, the same thing went down. We would sit next to each other and flirt incessantly. Doug always packed his parties with plenty of single girls. Whether it was my friends, Brooke's friends, or randoms he'd picked up along the way, all the fresh meat stroked Doug's ego enough for him to forget that I existed until it was time to go home.

Brooke had both boys and girls in her life. While she preferred women, she knew that there was a small sliver of her that still craved the male species. That heterosexual sliver made me feel safe. I didn't have to worry about a cat-and-mouse game. We were each other's prey, and what we had was crystal clear. We were two girls who didn't want to be tied down, who knew they had something special.

It had been over a week since I last saw Brooke. Doug was back on the wagon, and not too eager to go out or throw parties. It was time to dial that number. Brooke picked up on the first ring. Immediately, I found myself throwing on something black and sexy, lipstick, and high heels. I ran out the door. Luckily, we only lived a couple blocks from each other and we had the same scene and place in mind.

We met upstairs at a small Thai-fusion restaurant. The hostess sat us at a little table in the corner, and we felt at home. It didn't take long—two bottles of wine, to be exact—for us to be intertwined in each other's arms, thinking we were the only ones in the joint. When I was with Brooke, I always forgot how, exactly, we had gotten to know each other. While Doug's name did get brought up from time to time, it was more in the line of stories about what a dork we thought he was.

Brooke always made sure to remind me that Doug was out for one thing only: my body, not my heart. She urged me not to take it to the next level, because he would never follow. I heard what she was saying, but my mind was racing all the same. I had so many questions. Was this our first date, or our first "something"? Did she really think this was going somewhere? Am I lesbian and just don't know it? Or is it the thrill of being with a girl and knowing that every single guy in the room wants us? Each question rang in my head. The more I drank, the louder the questions got.

As the night came to a close, we stumbled home to Brooke's apartment. The moment I walked in, I sobered up fast. For the first time, I had all the control in a situation with another woman. I had decided to meet her, I had decided to go home with her, and now I had to decide whether or not to stay. The night didn't end quite like I'd expected, and I'm sure Brooke felt the same way. I stayed for one drink, kept my distance, and when the drink ended, so did the night.

I had once again taught myself the same lesson I'd learned a few years back. I got thrills from Brooke because Brooke was thrilled with me. I loved the danger and fearless behavior surrounding the rendezvous. Being with her was a natural high, the kind of high people pay a lot of money for. I wanted attention and she gave it to me. The thought of us turning men on turned me on more than just Brooke herself. Brooke wanted more from me, and I wasn't the girl to give it to her.

I walked home that night laughing at myself and the situation. With every passing reflection, I stared at myself and mouthed, "What are you doing?" Since that night with Brooke, I've ditched Doug and married an amazing man. I treasure my passionate memories of kissing girls, and when my husband gets on my nerves, I wished I could've enjoyed them even more.

# one more thing . . .

The truth of the matter is, there are more of them than us. Statistically speaking, there's no way around it: Gay romance is a long shot. Even the best odds have straight people outnumbering us by ten to one. Subtract the millions of us who are out of circulation thanks to the closet or long-term relationships, and the odds worsen. So what are we supposed to do when those hormones hit? Save ourselves for gay marriage?

Consider yourself lucky if even three or four of your last ten crushes have been members of our tribe, and don't fret too much over the occasional straight eye candy. It's a big world, girls, and it's full of scenery.

CHAPTER TEN:
# lesbe friends

My bisexual dilemma was that my gay friends thought I'm a lesbian in denial and my straight friends thoughtžžžž'm a lesbian in denial.

—Lacie Harmon

When it comes to functioning in this world, friends are as important as the air you breathe. They enrich your life in so many ways, and are the only ones who will tell you if that new sweater you bought really does make you look pregnant. Friends really are what get you through the day; they become your family and support system. Particularly as a lesbian, part of a minority, having other lesbian friends can be incredibly fulfilling. Relationships come and go, but friends are forever. Corny, we know, but it's the truth.

## My buddy—no, wait, my kid sister

Once you decide to play for the girls' team, having other lesbians on your side of the fence can really improve your batting average. You'll have someone to booze with when you take that first step into a lesbian bar. You have someone to ask insanely silly questions of, and you have someone to mentor you through trying times. Lesbian friends are your invitation to a level of acceptance you may not have been able to attain yourself. If that's not reason enough, our tribe tends to be made up of supercool, witty, confident, smart girls!

## Your Golden Girls

Making those friends creates a community within a larger community. Once you have a crew of at least three or four, you'll feel like you have your own little sapphic family. Being a lesbian can seem difficult at times, and sometimes family and straight friends make it even harder. Therefore, arming yourself with those lesbian friends can be a crucial move to make. They know how you feel, how to deal, are there for you to talk to, and make you feel safe. How much fun to trade war stories (aka coming-out stories), talk about each other's crushes on female celebrities, and your disdain for the lack of lesbian films available!

## Coupling up might cause the great divide

You certainly don't need to be as hot as the cast of *The L Word* (what group of lesbos is?), but at least you'll have friends to watch it with! But be forewarned: When two of your friends start dating, things can get complicated. These things happen, and unless that couple stays together forever, your group could fall faster than the Roman Empire. Hopefully, the couple in your group will be sensitive to this, and not ask people to take sides. Better yet, they'll try to remain friendly after the break. If that can't happen, attempt to hang with them separately. Just try not to take sides; you don't want to make anyone feel uncomfortable or hurt during an already painful time.

## What do you call a group of lesbians? Ex-girlfriends (insert laughter here)

Sadly, this joke is true. It seems there just aren't enough lesbians to go around! You might feel like your group or the lesbian community you know and love is just a bit incestuous. Well, that's mainly because it is. Your new friend might be your ex's ex, or she may have made out with your ex-ex-girlfriend one night. Don't be surprised by how many people you will become connected to as you make new friends. It's a reality, so try not to be too sensitive to having shared your loves.

It cannot be emphasized enough: Friends are what keep you sane, happy, and in good company. Life is short, and it seems the best way to ensure a happy existence is to surround yourself with good people.

# lauren levin

· · · · · · · · · · · · · · · · · · · · · · · · · · · · · · · · · · · · · · · · · · · · · · ·

Finding a solid group of lesbian friends is at least as important as finding a quality girlfriend. Many girls, as they rush to find love after coming out, overlook this.

I'm just as guilty of falling prey to my raging libido as the next girl. I always had a solid group of girlfriends. After coming out, I was more concerned with sexual relationships than platonic ones. I wanted *a* girlfriend, not more *girlfriends*. Truth be told, I always had enough friends to have at least one slightly ticked off at me at any given time. I had a hard time saying no to my friends, and often double-booked my weekends. But I'm learning to just say no instead of canceling plans.

I always had an abundance of girlfriends, but once I moved to the city, it was a group of great guy-friends I missed having. I had my requisite gay boyfriend, Daryl, but he didn't count. Daryl was as up on any of the latest fashion trends and *Us Weekly* gossip as any of my girlfriends.

We used to go out gay nearly every week. He'd tag along to the girl parties I frequented, and I'd join him for nights out with the boys. But, when Daryl recently left New York to get his Ph.D. in Art History at Yale, there was suddenly a whole lot more room on my couch, and a hole in my social calendar.

Still, I had Kat and Alex. My best friends, my staples in New York. But getting the three of us together at one time was nearly impossible. Kat holds two jobs, is a full-time grad student, and lives forty minutes away in Brooklyn. And between Alex's power job and dating schedule, it was harder to get into her week than it was to get a table at Nobu on a Friday night. It's a life only the most powerful PDA could keep straight.

My days were filled with writing, therapy, and softball games. I was also in the midst of a long-distance relationship with my girlfriend. Needless to say, I had a lot of free time and lonely nights on my hands. I realized there was a void in my life I needed to fill (and it wasn't just to get a real job).

Throughout all of this, I had Blitzer. The woman I met and quickly befriended during my most tumultuous year. She was there through my own self-realization, my coming out, and God knows how much dating drama.

Blitz was my first lesbian friend in the city, and, for a long time, my only one. She was the one who calmed my nerves before I flew to Minnesota to meet my girlfriend. It was her I gushed to when I came home. After I came out of the closet, Blitzer opened up my eyes to a whole new scene. She already had her group of lesbian friends established. Quickly, Blitz's friends became mine, too. It was then that I realized I didn't only like *The L Word* for its superfluous lesbian sex scenes; I liked it because it portrayed a group of fantastic lesbian friends. Exactly what I'd always wanted.

When Blitz went out of town the weekend of my first Gay Pride, I was sad. She'd been such a big part of my new gay lifestyle, I couldn't imagine standing on the sidelines of the parade without her. With or without her, she assured me, I'd have a great time. Soon enough, her friends were including me in all their festivities. Attending rooftop parties, gay-bar soirees, and walking the Dyke March with these girls proved to be a fun-filled weekend. Of course, I missed Lauren, but having to make new friends and build my own connections with hers were invaluable steps in creating my own lesbian community.

In fact, I had so much fun that weekend, I never wanted Gay Pride to end. So, in my world, it didn't. After Pride, doing the straight thing felt incredibly boring. Nearly all my adult life, I'd been going out with my straight friends. I felt better and more comfortable around my own kind. If you weren't a girl or a gay man, I didn't want to hang out with you. My longing for straight guy-friends soon faded.

In the next few months, we became a tight crew of six twenty-something femme lesbians. It goes without saying that frequenting gay bars is a lot more fun when you go with a group of girlfriends. Sure, there are couples in our group, and sometimes friends hook up with friends; but we never let sex get in our way of having a gay ole time.

Our friends have just as much fun crowding around a Scrabble board and a bottle of wine, as we do crowding a gay bar and checking out chicks. It's not all that different than hanging out with Kat or Alex. Like my straight girlfriends, my gay girls talk about overpriced haircuts, great sample sales, and why Nick and Jessica broke up. But, unlike my straight girls, my gay girls joke about strap-ons, shared flings, and the advantages of being a top or a bottom. We debate who's hotter, Angelina Jolie or Scarlett Johannson, to death. We even started a Monday-night bowling league—The Lesbowl, as we like to call it. Personally, I joined for the camaraderie and cute T-shirts we designed more than for the love of the sport. But, you get the picture.

We can dish about anything and everything, no holds barred. We fully understand each other's dating and relationship challenges. Lesbians share a special sapphic bond others don't. These friends have taught me more about being gay than I could've ever learned alone.

No one else sympathizes with passionate friendships, the torture of sorority rush, or the process of coming out quite like your fellow lesbian. Your friends can be your role models. You can look up to them and hope to one day follow in their footsteps. With my gay girls, I'm never the odd one out, I never feel alone, and I'm always having fun!

# lauren blitzer

I've got to give it to my amazing friends—they're the reason my life has become so rich. For two years I let myself get too involved in someone else's life, without maintaining my own. When my girlfriend and I broke up, I was alone, so incredibly alone. I felt like I knew only one person, and she was done with me.

It didn't take long for me to rebuild the friendships I'd neglected and start making new ones. Thankfully, my lesbian friends were sympathetic to my situation. They, too, had encountered relationships where they'd lost themselves. It was at that low point in my life that I realized how important surrounding myself with amazing people was. Never again would I put all my eggs in one basket. NEVER.

My friends lifted me up, made me feel good, and showed me how worthwhile I truly am. Gathering at a friend's apartment on a rainy Saturday night for some wine, music, laughter, and *Family Guy* is simply amazing. Being able to gossip with them about girls makes it all the better!

Don't get me wrong: I love my straight friends. I live with two of my best friends, Emily and Crystal. They are among my oldest and most important friends. They are my core, the people who sometimes know me better than I know myself. When it comes to my gay friends, though, there is an added level of comfort and security that "the sisterhood" brings along. Homo or hetero, we've all loved and been heartbroken. But, when you're with a friend who has been in that same female dynamic, it's a comfort you can't necessarily attain with anyone else.

As a newly single lesbian in the city, I started going out a lot. I made more connections than AT&T. I was going out almost every night, but not in a reckless way. Meeting new dating prospects, hanging with old friends, and getting to know new ones was what made me feel whole again. It was the most incredible feeling, and it taught me a very important lesson: Never lose yourself to anyone. I haven't felt alone or empty since.

Recently, I got a taste of how important my lesbo friends really are. I was getting ready to go out with my two straight friends to a bar on the Lower East Side. I was looking forward to a low-key night. It was pouring rain; therefore, I was not dressed to impress. I'd been at this bar for about an hour and a half when I received a text message from my friend Jules. It said: "Get your ass over to Cubby Hole, 'Close to Me' is on." I looked at my phone and smiled. Of course, Jules knew my favorite Cure song. I finished my drink, said my good-byes, and jumped in a cab to my favorite lesbian bar. When I walked into the Cubby, I heard a rush of my seven favorite lesbians say, "Fiiinallly!" "Where have you been?" And "Blitzer's here!!!" They had my vodka-soda waiting for me, and I joined them on the dance floor. I felt so welcome, so good.

I leaned against the bar, looked at my girls, and couldn't help but think how special this group was to me. I had wonderful friends, wonderful lesbian friends, who didn't want the night to end without me there. They made me feel as though I was on top of the world. To share this appreciation and admiration for your friends makes you realize how lucky you truly are. These girls will be with me through the good times and the bad. They'll either love or hate my girlfriends as they come and go. But no matter what, they'll be the shoulders I lean on when I can't seem to hold myself up. Your friends end up being the loves of your life. They open your mind, heart, and soul. They make you better people. At the end of the day, no matter what the rest of your life looks like, when in the company of friends, you're never alone.

# carlyn

The first time I knew I was attracted to another girl was at lacrosse camp after eighth grade. One of the counselors was so funny, so good at lacrosse, and so physically appealing that, not only did I want to *be* her, I wanted to be *with* her. I was thirteen. She was probably twenty-three. I didn't think I was a lesbian; I just thought the way I felt about this woman was different for some reason. It was okay—not because I had accepted being gay, but because my best friend at the camp felt the same way. The two of us would stay up late at night talking about our counselor. We both agreed it wasn't just admiration we felt for her, but that we wanted to rip her clothes off and try all those things we guessed that lesbians did in bed—which, at that point, we thought involved using your feet a lot. I think it was something my friend's brother told her.

It was in college, five years later, that I realized I was gay (thank goodness, because feet and vaginas really don't commingle the way we'd envisioned). After three weeks at Amherst, my realization occurred one night, when I attended a party with a bunch of lesbians. Amongst ten other topless women, I took off my shirt and began to dance. Something just clicked; I knew I was a big homo.

I came out to my best friend later that afternoon. My friend's reaction blew me away. She came out to me, too. The catalyst was not that we were attracted to each other. We'd been friends for six years, and never shared so much as a passionate kiss (a couple of drunk platonic showers together, sure, but never a real kiss). We were lucky in college. Our freshman year, there were three senior lesbians who took us under their wings and helped us along. They took us to lesbian bars in Boston, and they even managed to take us to bed once or twice. By the end of our first field hockey season, we thanked the Lord we'd found lesbian friends.

As we progressed through college, we went on double dates with each other and snuck into parties at Smith. We wrote our own songs about "not being born with a roadmap," which at the time we thought were deep and insightful. We were literally celebrating our realized selves together, and we were having a great time doing it. As we got older, the lesbian contingent of our tiny school grew. There were a bunch of us who hung out and talked about girls and punani pies together. It was awesome.

There were jocks, artsy chicks, and girls who were kind-of-sort-of gay-at-the-time in our group of friends. We were our own support group and social network. We'd eat dinner together in Valentine Hall, lingering over stories about how hot Angelina is and who we'd rather hook up with, Drew Barrymore or Clea Duvall. It wasn't because we were sex-crazed; it was because we had never had friendships like this before. Many of us needed to release all these thoughts, and it was therapeutic to have such a close community of lesbian ears listening. We even founded an annual lesbian party at Amherst called Dykes and Dates. To this day, the party is huge.

Years after graduation, we're still a close-knit bunch. Last spring, a few of us drove back to Amherst for a young-gay-alumni panel discussion. We talked about the different cities we lived in, our jobs, and gave insight into the transition from college to the real world.

I was working at an investment bank and having a hard time with the culture. The Old Boys in Gucci loafers atmosphere wasn't that fantastic for a young lesbian. The coworkers around me said "fag" at least eight times a day. I spoke to the panel about feeling uncomfortable and how I hoped to change my work environment. The support I got from the other alumni was amazing. Two days later, I started coming out to more of my colleagues. It's not an issue anymore, and I am better at my job because I'm out. If not for the support and encouragement of my lesbian friends, I wouldn't have had the confidence to come out in the workplace.

Without our network, I might still have been learning to accept myself for who I am. At most stages along the way, I've been lucky to have friends who were dealing with similar issues. As a gay woman, these types of friendships have given me confidence. Besides the sex, my lesbian friends are the reason I love being gay.

People say ten percent of the population is gay, but if that's true, then at least six percent of the population is in the closet. I am so glad I'm no longer one of them. Since coming out, I've woven my most intimate, honest relationships with other lesbians. They are out there, and if you're gay, I suggest that you go find them. Or at least be yourself, and they will find you!

# kathy
....................................................

I can't relate to straight people. Call me an uptight, right-wing
lesbian, if you will, but hear me out. For twenty very odd
years, I've gone out to straight bars. I've flirted with men, chatted up women, and led a life that satisfied everyone but me.
And now that I am out, and surrounded by a great network of
lesbian friends, I don't really want to hang out with anyone
else. So why the hell do I need to bullshit some straight guy
(who probably knows I'm gay) so he can fantasize about me
sleeping with a chick? Lord knows, I fantasize enough about
that myself!

   Growing up, Omaha, Nebraska wasn't exactly gay-friendly.
I knew just one other gay person, George. George worked at
the local bookstore and wore tight cutoff jean shorts and bright
tank tops, even in the middle of winter. After school, I would
walk past the store and watch him skip around, greeting everyone with a limp wrist and a huge, toothless smile. I longed to
go in there and talk to him. I was curious about his lifestyle
and desperate to be in the vicinity of someone who shared my
same sexual ambitions. When I finally got the guts to go in one
day, he looked at me as I bopped around to the sound of the
wind chimes hanging by the door. With attitude he said,
"Honey, I love your style. . . . Say . . . where did you get that
purse?" I froze and ran out, afraid people would associate his
gayness with my own.

   Living a secret lesbian lifestyle in Nebraska was too much
work. Among the negative gay stereotypes of Middle America,
I felt alone. I always had to watch my back, fearful that I would
be found out, yet anxious to experiment. In high school, I frequented two websites, one intended for lesbian lifestyles, and

the other, the home page of New York University. Whenever my parents walked in the computer room, I'd instantly maximize the one on NYU.

If I wanted any girl-on-girl action, I knew I had to move to New York. It was an innate feeling, something inside of me from the day I came out of my mother's own vagina. Before making the move to New York, I vocalized my sexual desires. Surprisingly, my family and friends were supportive. I was fortunate enough to be set up with a friend of a friend, Logan, a lesbian living in New York. I was relieved to find that being "set up" in the lesbian world does not necessarily mean a date with romantic intentions. Logan was all about showing me the gay scene and introducing me to her lesbian friends. We could just be friends and see what happened from there.

I'd met the right girl. Logan was the queen of NYC lesbian nightlife; she might as well have greeted me at LaGuardia Airport with rainbow flags. My first weekend in New York, she took me to Cherry Grove on Fire Island, a gay Disneyland. I was like a kid in a candy store. My first lesbian sexual experience ended up including five encounters in just one weekend! That's right, my little ole Nebraska ass drew the attention of five separate women, and I was sure to kiss them all.

All it took was a couple months in New York for me to be thankful I grew up in Nebraska. As a secluded closeted girl, I came to the Big Apple open-minded, without much of a guard up. I listened more than I talked, fascinated by all these women who embraced their same-sexuality. I was a pig in shit that first weekend, thinking that if New York City were anything like Fire Island, I was set for life. The first thing I wanted to do was get prophylactics, as this Midwest mama was about to have her favorite wet dream come true: having a lot of sex with women.

I was like a lioness thrown from her cage, going out every

night and experiencing the fabulous gay lifestyle. My fake ID allowed me access to gay bars, and a lot of hot pussy! Not only from bars, but from gay organizations on campus, I developed a wonderful crew of lesbian friends. These friendships were better than sex. If I happened to be attracted to one of my friends, it was the best of both worlds!

In general, women cuddle and hug more than men. I mean, come on. If you are a girl, I'll bet there is a ninety-nine percent chance that right now you are thinking back to the time you and your best friend were cuddling in your single bed, watching *Oprah*, when your friend lightly brushed her hand near your boob to get the remote and it turned you on. If you say you've never had a similar experience, then I'm sure you'll also tell me you've never masturbated, right? Prudes. In any case, nothing is better than sitting around in a room of gay girls watching the premiere of *The L Word*. Or getting tipsy before the bar, drawing vagina diagrams for your friend's new girlfriend, showing her tips on how to go down.

I was always so insecure about being attracted to women. Being surrounded by other females just like me was the single most important feat in achieving my own positive lesbian identity.

## one more thing . . .

It's important to have someone to go to when you are in distress or in need of chick advice. Not to say that your straight friends or gay boyfriends can't help you out, but being part of a community makes you feel less alone.

CHAPTER ELEVEN:

# your future as a gay woman

Soldiers who are not afraid of guns, bombs, capture, torture or death say they are afraid of homosexuals. Clearly we should not be used as soldiers; we should be used as weapons.
—Letter to the editor, *The Advocate*

I t may take years of therapy and introspection for you to realize that Prince Charming really is a Cinderella after all. For many gay women, learning to accept that, underneath all that shining armor, their knight is really a woman, is an integral step to overcome. Just remember, thousands of women have done just that. They've come to a point where being gay feels like just another part of who they are. Like any straight woman, a gay woman can have whatever it is she's always dreamed of having.

The media hardly depicts all the different ways to fall in love and start a family. Nowadays, it is one hundred percent possible to begin a family with the woman of your dreams, your best friend, your soul mate. Meeting this woman is undeniably the hardest part. Once you find her, hold on tight. An endless love like the one

Lionel Ritchie sings about is a rare and beautiful thing.

As crazy as it is, you can be fired from your job because you are gay or lesbian and it is perfectly legal in most states. That's right: You can't be discriminated against in employment because of your race, sex, religion, marital status, country of origin, or disability, but you can be for your sexual orientation or gender identity. Sadly, you can be kicked out of your housing because you are gay, and that, too, is also legal in most states. Not that this type of thing happens all the time; it's just scary to think that it can. Gays and lesbians cannot even adopt children in Florida, or serve openly in the U. S. military.

Hopefully, one day soon, gay marriage will be legalized. It really isn't too far away. People act like this institution is so incredibly delicate and that opening up marriage to same-sex couples would damage it. Ha! That is so untrue. The current divorce rate among heterosexual couples is growing every year. Giving gays the same rights and tax breaks as straight couples is not only practical, it's undisputedly unconstitutional to do otherwise. In the meantime, don't give up hope! There are a number of things you can do to further the cause.

If you don't live in Canada, Massachusetts, or one of many countries in Europe, you cannot legally marry your girlfriend. The simple fact is, gays and lesbians do not have the same rights as everybody else. You are far from alone in wanting to have the same rights that everyone else has. But gays and lesbians don't have equal rights. Even if you are legally married in Massachusetts, it will not be recognized in Alabama, or in any other state for that matter.

## Can you tell me the one about you meeting mommy again, mommy?

Unfortunately, when kids are growing up, there are no gay fairy tales for them to read. Aside from the occasional *Heather Has Two Mommies* title, you are led to believe there is one narrow path to starting a family. That you must meet Prince Charming, marry him, and carry his children. We'll be the first ones to tell you, from first-hand experience, this is not the case.

## Knowledge is power

The first thing you can do is talk about it. If you picked up this book and didn't already know that gays and lesbians are entitled to these rights, do you think your straight friends and family members do? Tell them. Point out to them how the very basic things they take for granted are denied to you.

## Fight for your rights, be active

Find a local group to get involved with. Since many of the gains for gays and lesbians will take place on the local and state levels, find out what groups in your area are working for gay and lesbian rights. Write to your state representatives and ask them what they are doing for gay and lesbian rights. You can be assured, they are hearing from people who oppose gay rights!

## Patience is a virtue

Just remember, social change takes time and effort. Think of the fight for women to get the right to vote. Being able to vote may seem like a no-brainer now, but it was only eighty-five years ago that the Nineteenth Amendment was passed.

## All you need is love

About those kids you've always dreamed of having: Research has proven that children raised in same-sex households are normal, well-adjusted, and no more apt to become gay than children raised in heterosexual households. We believe growing up in a household surrounded by love is the most natural and healthy way to grow up.

## Be like Angelina

In order to have children, there are many different routes two women can follow. Firstly, there is always adoption. In many states, it is no harder for two loving women to adopt children than it is for a man and a woman. It blows our minds that some people would rather a child grow up in an orphanage than in a loving homosexual household.

## Who's your daddy?

If you and your partner are more interested in giving birth to a child than in adoption, there are always sperm banks. Artificial insemination is rapidly growing in popularity. Interestingly enough, if it's a son you've always dreamed of having, it's more likely for a woman to have a boy than a girl through artificial insemination. In that scenario, it's just more likely for sperm with male chromosomes to survive.

As women in our early twenties, marriage, family, and settling down are things we look forward to. We are in no rush, but we're so fortunate to have gay friends with a wife and kids who have gone through so much to be recognized and respected. We hope some day the world will recognize that love is universal and should be respected, regardless of whether it is same-sex or not. The future is the great unknown and that's what makes life so exciting!

# christine
• • • • • • • • • • • • • • • • • • • • • • • • • • • • • • • • • • • • • • • • • • •

It was Fall 2002. My girlfriend, Selma, and I had been living in New York City together for over two years. We met while I was still in college. It's funny, because I was completely "straight" until I met her. Selma had just graduated from Skidmore and I had one more year left to go. We were completely in love; we were each other's first loves. She grew up all over the world, so NYC seemed like a logical compromise when it came time for me to graduate.

When I moved to Manhattan, I played in a women's basketball league over at Chelsea Piers. One night during a game, an inexperienced player undercut me and I blew out my knee. Disabled, I called Selma to help me get home. She came to get me, and greeted me with great concern and compassion. I say this because it was the time I remember being a priority in Selma's life.

Unfortunately, I had torn my ACL, which meant I needed knee surgery. Doctor's orders, I was to be on crutches for about two to three weeks and go through intense physical therapy. Around this time, Selma decided she wanted to change careers and get into journalism, to become an international correspondent. I was extremely supportive when she quit her job and financially and emotionally supported her during this time. I wanted her to be successful. But her drive for success was consuming her. All of her priorities, her friends, and her interests were changing.

She got her big break, and had to go to Baghdad, Iraq. She left at the end of March 2003, right when my rehab began. She was supposed to be gone for about two to three weeks, which turned into six months. President Bush gave Sadaam Hussein forty-eight hours to leave the country or we would invade. That moment changed everything.

I was still living in our apartment on Christopher Street, trying to stay positive. Plus, I think I was really scared to be alone and "gay." I knew she loved me very much, but I also knew she was willing to do almost anything to further her career. Needless to say, after a lot of drama, betrayal while she was away, and heartache, it was time for things to finally end.

Her decisions will have an effect on me for the rest of my life. It took me a very long time to pull myself together after we broke up, as I unfortunately had lost my identity while maintaining the relationship. But I cut myself a little slack, as Selma was my first love and first heartbreak.

With the help and support of great friends and family, I came out of my post-breakup depression. I don't want to oversimplify the process, but after many months it was time to move on. I had come to realize she was not the woman for me anymore.

I found myself alone in New York City for the first time. I must say, being single in Manhattan seemed like it might actually be fun. My problem was, I'd never been "out" and single in this city.

One year had passed, and I'd only really dated one person since the breakup. Rebounds are supposed to end with your confidence soaring, but that wasn't the case for me. So there I was, ego wounded one more time; but I managed to survive, like most girls do. I dragged my ass back out into the scene and tried not to get discouraged.

It was really hard, because I think I am way too picky. I still hadn't run into anyone who gave me that "tummy feeling," so to speak. I mean, there was this one girl who gave me that feeling, but I hadn't seen her out since I first moved to New York. I was in a relationship back then, but had gone out with my straight college friends to the local girl bar. It was during a snowstorm, we'd been drinking all night, and I had that whole T-shirt-sweatshirt-ponytail look going on.

Suddenly, it felt like the music stopped, and this woman walked in. I mean, I had never seen anyone like her before. She was really exotic-looking, with a unique sense of style, somewhat of an attitude, and piercing dark eyes. I think I just stopped breathing for a moment. Anyway, it must have been incredibly obvious that I was staring with my jaw hanging open, because she turned and said, "Do you want to dance or something?" I didn't say a word; I think I just nodded. I swear, I'm not usually this awkward; but in my own defense, I was only twenty-one and just starting to date women. I still considered myself bisexual, and had never really gone to gay bars before. So, we danced, we talked a little bit, and I was enjoying myself. Then the song ended, her friends called her over, and she disappeared into the night. I know it doesn't sound like much, but for some reason I never forgot that night.

I never thought I would see her again. And then, randomly, I saw her at a New York Liberty game later that year. At that point, I was seriously involved with another woman, so I didn't approach the exotic beauty. I saw her six months later on the street during Gay Pride. We only made eye contact and I assumed she didn't make any connection to "the night we danced." Thankfully, I'd grown into myself more since our first encounter.

One night, a group of us all went barhopping in the Village. We ended up at a girl bar, and most of my friends were wrapping up their nights when guess who walks into the bar? The "tummy" girl! So, I watched her and her friends for a little while. They were dancing and having a great time. In fact, it felt as though they were the focal point on the dance floor. I started to convince myself that I should go over there and talk to her. Even though I knew there was little chance she'd remember our little dance together, over three years ago.

So, finally, I approached her and got the nerve to say something. "I know you aren't going to remember this, but (repeat the story from above), and I just want to thank you for being so nice to me when I was still trying to figure everything out."

She said, "Actually, I do remember. I mean, I didn't till you reminded me of the story, but we were right over there in the corner by the bathroom. You know, it isn't that often that a little white blond girl stares at me like that." We laughed. Unfortunately, she was dating someone at the time. Her girl was easily jealous and didn't like us speaking to each other. Turns out, Tummy Girl is one of the largest lesbian party promoters in New York, so she told me to check out one of her parties or e-mail her at her website.

A few more months rolled by, and I never quite made it to one of her parties. I did e-mail her, casually asking if she wanted to hang out sometime. But, after her initial response of, "Sure, that would be great," I never heard from her again.

Still disillusioned with being single again in New York, I ventured out one evening to GO NYC magazine's annual party. I ran into her and said hello, but she still just didn't seem interested, so I let it go. About half an hour later, I felt someone staring at me. I looked, and there she was, staring at me. It was confusing but great, because I still wanted to go out with her at least once and see if I liked her. Anyway, we never really spoke that night, because she was with a date. Angelique was quite popular with the ladies.

When I checked my e-mail later the next week, I had a message from Angelique asking me out! We finally made it out and we had a great time. Right away, she told me she wasn't looking to get involved in anything serious, and I agreed.

Angelique and I took things slow for multiple reasons. One, she'd been a serial dater for the last several years. That, in and of itself, intimidated me. She'd done what most gay women are incapable of doing: dating. But we didn't sleep together until we'd been hanging out for at least a month or two. It was great when we finally did, but if I go into too much detail about our bedroom talk, it alone would take up a whole chapter.

I was being careful, since I knew it was likely she was seeing other women. We were only dating and not exclusive. But, I must say, I could tell she liked me. Soon enough, we had the I-don't-want-to-see-other-people conversation. We spent the summer on Fire Island, and had·the time of our lives. I fell in love with her, and it was amazing. Over the next eight months, we became very serious and spent a lot of time together.

Imagining your future with someone can be tricky. I think the best way to get comfortable seeing a future with a woman is to approach a relationship without the future in mind. Like in any relationship, you want there to be common ground, with an added dose of excitement and intrigue. You almost need to admire your partner. There's got to be some sort of awe factor about her. Whether it's her career, or how open she is with her emotions, it's got to be something. Also, you need to have felt like you have lived, and done the single thing for a while, or had relationships. You don't want to commit to someone and still feel like you have a longing to play the lesbian softball field. Some people are not ready, nor do they want the pressure or responsibility of a long-term arrangement. It isn't for everyone. But, when you meet someone who just blows your mind, these rationales disappear.

Other then the "tummy" factor (and the fact that she's a TOTAL hottie), there are almost too many reasons to explain why I want to spend the rest of my life with Angelique. I love that she is a Renaissance woman. I love how strong a person she is. She comes from an extremely underprivileged background, and has become one of the most successful power lesbians in NYC. She is a full-time teacher, a head volleyball coach at a high school in New Jersey, one of the owners of the restaurant Orbit in East Harlem, an owner of the biggest lesbian promotion company in New York, AND she owns her own home. Angelique is a decent artist, an excellent carpenter, and a phenomenal break dancer. To be honest, there isn't anything she can't do. Honestly, there really isn't. . . .

I admire her work ethic, business savvy, goofy sense of humor, and tremendous heart. She's the type of girl who can gather fifty gay boys (in just ten minutes) for a game of dodge-ball on a beach in Fire Island!

Family is very important to us. We both want kids someday, but, as it stands now, we already have two little ones (Lady, our American pit-bull terrier, and Paris, an all-white cat Angelique found in a Dumpster in Spanish Harlem four years ago.) Right now, that is really all I can handle.

A year into our relationship, we decided to take a vacation together, before my job started to get crazy and her school year began. We went on a cruise to the Bahamas. So, for seven days we were alone, enjoying each other's company. On the second day of the cruise we made plans to go to the spa. I am a massage girl, and Angelique wanted a facial. Apparently, her appointment got moved, so we weren't going at the same time. I was a little bummed, but no big deal; it was just for a few hours. I finished my massage and headed back to our room on the cruise ship. I opened the door and saw that the curtain by the bed was pulled shut. There was music playing as well. Angelique had turned our room into a romantic little restaurant! She laid an outfit out on the bed for me, and demanded I shower and get ready within fifteen minutes. I hopped in the shower and got ready.

Somehow, Ang had made friends with the cruise staff, and they were in our room serving us. As we ate our dinner by candlelight, Angelique played with the centerpiece in the middle of the table. We started talking about the future. She asked if I saw myself with her in the future. I told her that I did, and hoped that's where this was going. She then pulled a flower out of the vase and this beautiful diamond ring popped up. Angelique then smiled at me and said, "Well, then—will you?"

Our wedding date is set for September 2006!

# heidi

• • • • • • • • • • • • • • • • • • • • • • • • • • • • • • • • • • • • • • •

I still have conflicting notions about "coming out," in the popular sense of the term. It's somewhat ironic, considering I'm
writing this on National Coming Out Day. I've been accused
of being in denial, but I don't feel the need to conform to the
labels that our society has created. I want to be myself, love
whom I want to love, and spend the rest of my life with
whomever I chose (male, female, trans, or other). If people
find the need to label me as a lesbian, then, sure, I'll accept it.
But I don't think it's denial that keeps me from labeling myself;
I just refuse to restrict my sexuality to such narrow terms.

The gist of my story is that I was not "out" in college, and certainly not in high school. I was too concerned with the stereotype that persisted of women ice hockey players being lesbians.
And, as a goalie, I wanted to do my best not to perpetuate that
stereotype, especially since I grew up in a small, white, upper-
middle-class, conservative suburb of Minnesota. Even though I
knew I was attracted to people of both sexes, I would never have
acted on my desires back then. I'd have been shocked to know
that I would date women in college and gradually announce
my relationships to my friends and family.

I was drawn to the women at Amherst College who identified as lesbians, bisexual, or just "not straight." Fortunately for
me, they were affiliated with my group of friends in some way
or another, be it through athletics, extracurriculars, classes, et
cetera. Because of this, I could hang out with them without
worrying that anyone would suspect I wasn't so straight myself.
Increasingly, I spent more time with these girls, and, wow, was
it exciting. The confusion that persisted throughout my college
experience was marked by novel sexual experiences, secretive
sexual partners, and the formation of new friendships. Most

importantly, all of this led to an increased self-awareness.

Post–graduation and self-discovery, I've become active in promoting LGBT initiatives and equal rights. Recently, I returned to Amherst to speak on the Pride Alumni Panel, and have formed LGBT networks with Amherst alum. My gradual "coming out" (in the sense of a personal revelation) has led me to commit my life to fight for equality. Specifically, I want to help acquire equal rights for LGBT people. I'm only applying to law schools that have LGBT organizations, LGBT-friendly professors, "out" professors, and courses focusing on LGBT issues. Not only do I want to spend my life fighting for legal equality, I want to ensure overall respect for people, regardless of their sexual orientation. It's not only important to be "out," but to be informed. For this reason, I have "come out" to my colleagues at work. It was much easier then I'd expected, and I haven't been treated any differently. From time to time, my coworkers even ask about my girlfriend, which has made my life much easier and happier. I've even opened the mind of one very conservative and religious colleague.

I have a pretty idealistic view of people in general. Most are kindhearted and are willing to be accepting—unless, of course, they are blinded by this bureaucratic, evangelical, and discriminatory administration. It's a fact of life: People tend to be afraid of change. Although homosexuality has been around since the beginning of time, people fear the increasing visibility of relationships they believe are outside the norm (whatever that may be). I think it's about time to redefine the "norm."

## lauren and lissy

From the very beginning, we knew we wanted to spend the rest of our lives together. Not to say that we didn't, and still don't, go through rough patches. But, when you find her, you just know it. And even though we've established our love, recognizing it has been a struggle. Regardless, we turned away from the critics, gathered up our families, and got married.

We met about six years ago. We'd both gone through our fair share of relationships and, like they say, when you're not looking for love, you find it. We were going to meet a group of mutual friends. For one reason or another, we hadn't been introduced. We flirted throughout the evening and ended up at a friend's house. The drinks were done flowing. Everyone was asleep in the living room. Lissy lay on an oversize chair, big enough for two bodies, sardine-style. I put myself on the floor, even though I was dying to be close to her. Finally, she awkwardly invited me up. We both were testing the waters. Her body was radiating heat but rigid with fear. I later teased her and called her "rigor mortis girl." I put my hand on her heart and told her I was nervous too . . . and I was. Our bodies melted into each other, and we hadn't even kissed yet. We slept zipped together for a few hours. It felt exciting, terrifying, and completely new. Strangely, it felt like home. In the morning, we kissed. A door opened for me that morning. I walked through and never looked back. I had found the one.

Things moved quickly. Passion often takes its own route. We moved in after eight months, despite snickers from our friends. It was easy; with her, life just flowed. Our relationship was perfect. We had a very natural, open line of communication. It's what makes our relationship what it is today. We also had an unbelievable connection, right from the start. We clicked very easily. We never hesitated to bring our issues to the table, and our arguments were healthy and always resolved.

After three years, we decided to take the big plunge. Marriage was in our cards, and although we knew that it wouldn't be legally recognized, we didn't care. Our friends and family were there, and that's all that mattered. This was about our love and celebrating our lifetime commitment to each other. It was going to be the happiest day of our lives.

Unfortunately, I experienced a devastating loss right before our wedding. My mother's tragic passing made the day seem bittersweet. As hard as it was not having my mom there to share this day with us, she was there in spirit. As we both stood in white dresses, under a tent amongst our loved ones, I couldn't help but shed a tear. I was overwhelmed by all the love and support in our vicinity. Our fathers made touching speeches. They praised our union, and the fact that we had found what people spend their lives searching for: true love.

Most people see our rings and assume that we have husbands at home. But you just get used to telling people that there is no man; instead, there is a beautiful wife waiting at home for you. Most are taken aback at the response, as we both have long dark hair and are extremely feminine. By now, we are immune to the shock that comes along with being part of a beautiful lesbian couple. But most people are not, and that's okay. Give them a day or two to get used to it!

What we haven't gotten used to is the difficulty that comes along with a nonlegal, nonrecognized union. Lissy and I recently went to Italy for a wedding. We treated the trip like a vacation, extending our visit a good two weeks to take in the Italian countryside. After soaking in the Tuscan sun, we prepared for our long flight home. After the ninth hour onboard the Boeing 767, the flight attendant came around with immigration papers. Being that Lissy and I are married, I filled out one form for both of us, not even thinking twice about it.

Jet-lagged and tired, we waited on the long immigration line. I held the papers in my hand as we were approached the head of the line. We gave the man our passports and the form.

He looked at Lissy and asked for her papers. She explained that we were together. We'd had a commitment ceremony and, therefore, were a couple. Lissy pointed to the man and woman the officer had cleared a mere three minutes ago. He looked at us blankly. The man just didn't get it. We stood there, firm in our belief that we should be able to pass through on one piece of paper. He argued that there was nothing legal about what we had committed to. A frustrating hour passed, and the right-wing jackass on a power trip wouldn't budge. Aside from being extremely irritating, the worst part was that he was right.

Our marriage is not legal. Not because we haven't gone through the motions and made the commitment, but because this country and our liberal state of New York refuses to recognize our love. What an unfortunate way to end such an amazing vacation.

That was our first taste of how unfair and unjust the system is. For the first time, we felt like outsiders. I envied the ease and security the couple who went before us had. It doesn't matter how in love you are, or how committed you vow to be; if the government doesn't legitimize your union, you cease to exist as one. My wife is the biggest part of me, but our nation's ignorance turns a blind eye to our love. No matter how innately we fit together, strangers will try to tear us apart. With time, we hope this discrepancy will change, and small things like leaving the country won't seem like such a battle.

Our life together is so incredibly rich and amazing. Aside from the obstacles we face, Lissy and I will continue to build our relationship and a family. In fact, just the other week we had out first appointment at the fertility clinic. At thirty-five, I am ready to take that next step and start a family.

We've decided to leave our cramped apartment in Chelsea for a spacious brownstone in Brooklyn Heights. Chelsea may be the epicenter of an active gay nightlife, but it's not where we want to raise our children. Brooklyn is more affordable, and just as liberal.

For a lesbian couple, so many factors come into play when deciding to have kids. Do we use an anonymous donor, or someone we know? Which of us will carry the baby? Is it legally complicating? Will we get stared at on the street as we stroll together, hand in hand, with our child?

These are all questions we will answer along the way. With the help of other lesbian mothers, we are on our way to making decisions on which direction to take. In all honestly, thinking about the multitude of available options is fun and exciting. Though, at times, I wish it could be simple. I wish I could just make love to Lissy and produce a child from one night of passion, a child that is genetically a product of us both. But that's just not the way it is.

Learning to accept your future as a lesbian is about understanding that not everything in life is fair. It's about looking at your wife and knowing that, no matter what hurdles you're forced to jump, your life without her is not complete.

## one more thing . . .

There is not one model for a straight or gay couple to follow. There are many different types of families, homosexual and heterosexual alike. What's important is that choosing to be comfortable with who you really are doesn't mean giving up the life you always wanted. Being gay and having children are not mutually exclusive. You can have a wonderful life filled with love and laughter by choosing to commit to spending the rest of your life with the woman of your dreams. So, don't worry if your Prince Charming really is a Cinderella after all. Just bend down and make sure the glass slipper fits!

Printed in the United States
By Bookmasters